# AMERICAN VIOLENCE
# AND PUBLIC POLICY

# AMERICAN VIOLENCE AND PUBLIC POLICY

An Update of the National Commission on
the Causes and Prevention of Violence

**EDITED BY LYNN A. CURTIS**

**Yale University Press**
New Haven and London

Designed by Nancy Ovedovitz and set in Times Roman type by
Brevis Press. Printed in the United States of America by Vail-
Ballou Press, Binghamton, New York.

**Library of Congress Cataloging in Publication Data**

Main entry under title:
American violence and public policy.
  Bibliography: p.
  Includes index.
  1. Violent crimes—Government policy—United States—
Addresses, essays, lectures. I. Curtis, Lynn A. II. United States.
National Commission on the Causes and Prevention of Violence.
HV6791.A72  1985     364.1     84–40194
ISBN 0–300–03231–5 (alk. paper)

The paper in this book meets the guidelines for permanence and
durability of the Committee on Production Guidelines for Book
Longevity of the Council on Library Resources.

10    9    8    7    6    5    4    3    2    1

*To those who would
reduce the underclass*

# CONTENTS

# FOREWORD

Much has been written about violence in our country, and many have been violated within our own shores. For a society that boasts of individual freedom, the dignity and safety of its citizens, law and order, and responsibility, the statistics on violent acts in the United States are appalling.

I write this foreword to *American Violence and Public Policy* as a concerned citizen who is sensitive to the societal imbalances that breed violence as well as to the awful plight of those who are victimized; as a former president of a major university whose aim is to expose its students to the experiences of history and the mandate for change each generation inherits; as the former chairman of the bipartisan National Commission on the Causes and Prevention of Violence; and most recently as chairman of the foundation that bears my name, whose purpose is to enable individual citizens in their own communities to do something about the causes of crime and thereby reduce its incidence and further improve the quality of life for all of us—especially the poor, whose options are so limited.

As Lynn Curtis points out in his introduction, two decades of practical experience and hard research have shown that improving neighborhood cohesion and mechanisms for citizen self-help, strengthening and expanding the basic family unit, and providing for employment opportunities are at the heart of what the Violence Commission called "social reconstruction."

Dealing with violence and its causes is an enormous task, but it is in the self-interest of all of us to make our country a safer and more equitable republic in which to live.

This book focuses on how policies and plans carefully determined by the Violence Commission and others can be translated into an immediate and effective action.

Milton E. Eisenhower
*Chairman Emeritus*
*The Eisenhower Foundation*

October, 1984

# ACKNOWLEDGMENTS

We are grateful to the Ford Foundation for the grant that made this book possible. Shepard Forman, program officer in charge of Ford's Human Rights and Governance Program, was as patient as he was supportive. Gladys Topkis, senior editor, and Charlotte Dihoff, production editor, at Yale University Press guided the manuscript through various stages with care and wisdom. There was a quiet grace about Pam Green's typing.

# Introduction

LYNN A. CURTIS

On June 10, 1968, a few days after the assassination of Senator Robert F. Kennedy, President Lyndon B. Johnson issued an executive order authorizing the establishment of a National Commission on the Causes and Prevention of Violence with Milton S. Eisenhower as chairman and A. Leon Higginbotham as vice-chairman. In 1969, the commission issued its final report, preceded by many volumes of staff task force reports.

The Violence Commission followed closely on the heels of two other presidential commissions that overlapped in scope and had similar philosophies. The 1966–67 President's Commission on Law Enforcement and the Administration of Justice, chaired by Nicholas deB. Katzenbach, addressed the criminal justice system and, to a lesser extent, prevention of crime outside of that system. The 1967–68 National Advisory Commission on Civil Disorders, chaired by Governor Otto Kerner and directed by David Ginsburg, assessed the urban riots of the late 1960s.

The Eisenhower Foundation was established in the early 1980s as a private-sector re-creation of the Violence Commission, with the same chairman and vice-chairman. Many of its board members had been commissioners or part of the staff on one of the three public bodies.

In a selective way, the foundation is carrying out some of the recommendations of the commissions, such as community and victim programs. We also believe that it is time to update the main policy conclusions of the Violence Commission, as well as consonant recommendations from the Kerner and Katzenbach commissions. The basic question we address is what federal policy should be for the remainder of the twentieth century.

Although the Violence Commission report examined collective and political violence, greater attention was directed to individual acts of violence, such as common crime in the street and violence in the home,[1] in part because the Kerner Commission report on collective violence had been issued only a year earlier. The present volume also addresses individual, collective, and political violence, paying most attention to individual crime though pointing to many common causes underlying individual and collective violence.

We have chosen to describe the incidence of violence over the past fifteen years and to provide a policy update of what can be done in response. Neil Alan Weiner and Marvin E. Wolfgang begin by assessing levels and trends of individual violence since the commission reports. Federal policy against crimes of violence—from social reform and the role of minorities to law enforcement and the role of firearms—is reviewed by Elliot Currie, James P. Comer, Paul J. Lavrakas, Alan R. Gordon and Norval Morris, and Franklin E. Zimring. Sandra Ball-Rokeach and James F. Short, Jr., explain why collective violence declined while individual violence rose over the 1970s and direct the attention of policymakers to what has become known as the underclass. Robert H. Kupperman, surveying some aspects of political violence, shows how assassinations have continued since the commission's report in the absence of adequate policy reforms. He argues that terrorism is emerging as a domestic threat requiring a new policy. In the Epilogue, building on the recommendations of the other authors, I remind the reader when law enforcement is and is not the most appropriate policy response to various forms of violence and advocate a new framework to reduce individual violence—a framework that would be based on a coordinated national neighborhood, family, and employment policy.

Whereas the Violence Commission reports were exhaustive, this volume is highly selective. We do not have the resources for a thousand-page study, nor is it really necessary. Most explanations have remained essentially the same since the Violence Commission reports were issued. Any good contemporary textbook will detail the accepted biological, psychological, psychiatric, cultural, social, economic, and political interpretations of violence.[2] By comparison, this book begins by recalling, in very brief form, the commission's explanations of violence and tracing their broad policy implications—past, present, and future. In deciding what to include, we have focused on phenomena that have emerged since the commission (such as the threat of domestic terrorism) and identified recommendations made by the commission that are being encouraged by practical experience (such as more community involvement). We have not pursued subjects, however meritorious, on which more precise scientific evidence may be required to settle ongoing controversies.[3] Above all, we have been selective in order to establish a firm sense of priority. What issues should decision makers, the citizenry, and the media keep uppermost in mind if for the rest of the century we are to have an informed public policy with the greatest potential for reducing violence?

The answers to this question by individual contributors, including myself, are recommendations *to* the board of the Eisenhower Foundation and to the nation; they are not an official policy statement *by* the board itself.

## LEVELS AND TRENDS

In the late 1960s, the Violence Commission concluded that the "United States was the clear leader among modern stable democratic nations in its rates of homicide, assault, rape, and robbery."[4] The Kerner Commission documented riots in twenty-three cities during 1967, and the assassinations of Robert Kennedy and Martin Luther King, Jr., continued a tradition of political violence.

Fifteen years later, after a careful review of the imperfect measures available, Weiner and Wolfgang conclude that there has been an increase in violent crimes like murder, assault, rape, and robbery. Minorities are disproportionately involved as both offenders and victims. Today, the chance of becoming a victim of violent crime is greater than the chance of "being affected by divorce," the risk of being in an automobile accident, or the probability of dying from cancer, according to the Justice Department.[5]

Just as important as the trend over time is that the level of crime in the United States remains astronomical when compared to that in other democratic nations. Currie points out that the United States, in respect to crime, increasingly resembles some underdeveloped countries in the Third World more than does any other advanced industrial society. The fact that our level of violence continues to be high is often lost in journalistic accounts of short-term changes and in statements by politicians, whatever their affiliation, of marginal increases or declines.

Regardless of actual crime rates, the level of *fear* of crime remains at least as high today as it was in the 1960s, according to Weiner and Wolfgang. In a recent national ABC poll, 86 percent of the persons sampled perceived that crime was going up.[6] Because they influence how we live and act, fear and perception are important measures of crime. Some age groups, such as senior citizens, even when they are victimized less frequently than other age groups, nonetheless remain extremely fearful of crime.[7]

Although violent crime rates have risen and fear continues at high levels, Ball-Rokeach and Short observe that disorders and street rioting have declined sharply in the past fifteen years. The most notable and publicized exceptions have been the Liberty City and Overtown riots in Miami during the early 1980s.

As for political violence, the 1982 assassination attempt on President Reagan and the two attempts on Gerald Ford during his presidency suggest that the threat remains. Kupperman shows that what has changed since the Violence Commission reports is the frequency of terrorism. Attacks against Americans usually take place abroad; the Iranian hostage crisis and the Beirut bombings are examples from the 1980s. In the United States, incidents have been scattered—air hijackings, the 1981 takeover of the B'nai B'rith headquarters in Washington, D.C., the real or imagined Libyan hit squad of 1982, and the bombing of the Capitol building in 1983—but Kupperman predicts more attacks by professional terrorists in the years to come.

## UNDERSTANDING INDIVIDUAL VIOLENCE

In its core statement, the Violence Commission concluded:

> To be a young, poor male; to be undereducated and without means of escape
> from an oppressive urban environment; to want what the society claims is avail-
> able (but mostly to others); to see around oneself illegitimate and often violent
> methods being used to achieve material success; and to observe others using
> these means with impunity—all this is to be burdened with an enormous set of
> influences that pull many toward crime and delinquency. To be also a Black,
> Mexican or Puerto Rican American and subject to discrimination adds consid-
> erably to the pull.[8]

Violent crime is so complex that neither this nor any other single explanation can account for all its forms and all the combinations of victims and
offenders. But here was the central observation of the Violence Commission, and it also lay behind the Kerner Commission's conclusion that we
consist of two societies, black and white, separate and unequal. Almost
fifty years ago, George Orwell wrote that "the restatement of the obvious
is the first duty of intelligent [citizens]."[9] Both commissions restated the
obvious—that the poverty of the disadvantaged and the nation's history of
racial oppression are deeply involved in our high rates of violence.

After the Violence Commission reports, however, it became fashionable
to deny the obvious and to search for other explanations. Consider some
examples.

One explanation for individual violence pointed out that the proportion
of youth in the population was extremely high. Because young males commit crime at a disproportionate rate, this demographic bulge meant more
crime. Policy intervention was not indicated, so the argument went, because
there was nothing one could do about demographic patterns short of birth-
control policies that would be unacceptable to most Americans. But recent
research by Northwestern University for the National Institute of Justice
has shown statistically that the demographic interpretation of high crime is
not as helpful as originally thought in understanding our high level of crime
or its increase since the 1960s.[10]

In addition, regardless of what the proportion of high-risk youth has been
in the overall population at any point in time since the late sixties, the
figures assembled by Weiner and Wolfgang show that, within this group,
rates for specific crimes have, with few exceptions, risen since the Violence
Commission made its report. The ultimate test of any national policy is
whether rates within the highest crime population decline over such a trend
period, longer than just a few years—and we have failed that test.

Some asserted that poverty and race could not have been responsible for
the increase in violent crime in the 1960s and 1970s because blacks had
made "great advances."[11] There were indeed some gains. Perhaps most

publicized was the increase in the number of blacks and other minorities in managerial and professional jobs. By the end of the 1970s, over 1.5 million blacks held such jobs—a doubling in one decade. As Ball-Rokeach and Short conclude, these changes appear to have been primarily the result of federal education, employment, and affirmative-action programs targeted at minorities. Yet the gains were limited, and economic deprivation continued or increased for those in the group most likely to commit crime—young, poor, inner-city, minority males. The National Urban League's estimates of unemployment among this group during the 1970s were in the 50 percent to 60 percent range, and the rate increased over many of the same years when crime was increasing.[12] Ball-Rokeach and Short observe that the ratio of black to white unemployment was 1.8 in 1970 and 2.2 in 1982 and that minority families significantly weakened in the 1970s—both absolutely and relative to white families.

As proof that poverty is not a cause of crime, some advanced the curious argument that we had a high crime rate in the United States even though our poorest people were materially better off than the poorest people in countries with lower crime rates. But there is no evidence that a poor black in Harlem compares himself to a poor black in Tanzania rather than to a rich white on Park Avenue. The logic of the "proof" followed the position of the government of South Africa, which argued that income and living conditions in Soweto, the all-black suburban ghetto compound outside of Johannesburg, were better than in black-ruled African states. Could the Soweto blacks whose violent-crime rates were so much higher than those of American cities have been thinking of conditions in other countries? Or might they have been comparing the privilege and luxury of Johannesburg to their own political disenfranchisement and to the reality that only 20 percent of their houses had electricity and only 15 percent had toilets?[13]

One response to those who said they had never seen a cause of crime is James Baldwin's observation that to be black in the United States "and be relatively conscious is to be in a rage almost all the time." The framers of the Constitution decreed that, for purposes of representation, a black slave would count as only three-fifths of a man. Two centuries later, the per capita income of blacks remains barely three-fifths that of whites.[14]

More than any other work since the Violence and Kerner commission reports, Charles E. Silberman's *Criminal Violence, Criminal Justice* (1978) reminded us of the obvious truth of relative poverty and race. In the present volume, the chapters by Comer and by Ball-Rokeach and Short provide updates and place the experience of blacks in the perspective of three hundred years of American history. Comer reminds us that "unlike Nazi concentration camp victims, . . . Afro-Americans did not bring a largely self-determined culture into an oppressive system [and] hold on to it as best possible." Rather, unlike other immigrant groups that were allowed to use family and kinship as a source of security and a basis for development, West African culture was "broken in the enslavement process and replaced by the powerlessness and degradation of the slave culture." After slavery and up to the present, the "master-slave relationship [was] the basis of symbolic and underlying conflict and violence—individual and collective, covert and overt—in black-white relationships." Acquisitive violence can thus be an attempt, however illusory or symbolic, to take back that which was denied. Assaultive behavior, even if it is predominantly inflicted by minorities on other minorities, can reflect an acceptance of violence in everyday life as an available means of expressing anger, frustration, and masculinity.

In sum, Comer and Ball-Rokeach and Short trace the emergence of a permanently poor underclass that has remained immune to the employment and educational gains made by some blacks during the 1970s. Such an underclass also represents a sizable portion of Hispanics.

The period since the Violence Commission reports were issued is not the first time in the history of American ethnic groups when it was necessary to dispute those who see no relation among crime, relative poverty, and discrimination. In the last part of the nineteenth century and the first part of the twentieth, many of the people most responsible for street crime were Irish-, German-, Italian-, and Polish-Americans. During each period, there were "experts" who were certain that reducing poverty would have little effect on crime because the poor, it was said, actually preferred their crime-ridden way of life. Yet each of these groups has moved out of crime as it moved into the middle class.[15] This volume reaffirms that upward mobility can do the same for the ethnic groups that are associated with crime today. But it warns the reader that the underclass has remained in spite of some progress by some minorities and reminds us that Gunnar Myrdal's *American Dilemma*[16] of race and inequality remains.

### WHAT HAPPENED TO THE FISCAL DIVIDEND?

Currie describes two broad policies recommended by the Violence Commission in response to these continuing realities. It joined the Kerner and Katzenbach commissions in calling both for a more equitable and efficient criminal justice system and for a range of economic, social, and civil rights reforms. To pursue reform, the Violence Commission proposed a "domestic Marshall Plan" for the cities to be financed from the "fiscal dividend" that would be realized from the money saved at the end of the Vietnam War.

This, of course, did not happen. Yet, even if it had, the envisioned economic and social reconstruction assumed a trickle-down process. Somehow, doing good at the top would result in less crime at the bottom. There was little sense of how to target specific reforms to specific groups in specific ways so as to reduce specific crimes and fears. Little attention was paid to implementation—to exactly how crime and fear reduction in the real world could be carried out by the public and private sectors.

In the 1970s, most agencies other than the Justice Department continued their employment, antipoverty, human-service, housing, and economic-development programs with, at best, some vague sense that their policies also might affect crime and urban disorder. Within these bureaucracies, some specific efforts related to crime prevention were made. For example, the Labor Department assessed some of its Comprehensive Employment and Training Act (CETA) programs in terms of their impact on crime; Health and Human Services (HHS) dealt with drug abuse and youth programs; and Housing and Urban Development (HUD) and ACTION started community-based anticrime efforts. But these programs merely responded to piecemeal legislation or reflected enlightened administrators, some of whom were knowledgeable about the commission reports or were themselves former commissioners. The programs were not based on an overriding domestic or urban policy that consciously sought to reduce crime, fear, or group disorder.

## DETERRENCE, HARDWARE, AND THE LAW ENFORCEMENT ASSISTANCE ADMINISTRATION

When compared to a "domestic Marshall Plan," the Violence Commission's recommendations for improving the equity and efficiency of the criminal justice system were more manageable financially and more feasible politically. They were also more in line with the philosophy of many influential people that efforts at the federal level to reduce crime should be conducted by a new office in the Justice Department, not in the economic, social, or human rights agencies. The Katzenbach Commission called for such an office, and the Violence Commission concurred.

The Law Enforcement Assistance Administration (LEAA) was established in the late 1960s. One of its goals was to increase police apprehension rates. Only half of all crime was reported to police; arrests were made in fewer than twenty of every one hundred reported burglaries, larcenies, and auto thefts, and the apprehension rate for robbery was only a few percentage points higher.[17]

In its early days, LEAA distributed many grants for police hardware and command-and-control systems. The San Diego police acquired a submarine to patrol the waterfront, and Mobile, Alabama, received tanks for crowd control.[18] (The word around Washington was that at least landlocked Mobile didn't get the submarine.) The submarines and tanks reflected in part LEAA administrative priorities and in part a legislative mandate, which,

Gordon and Morris show, had the effect initially of shutting out people-intensive programs, such as neighborhood-based crime prevention. In Currie's view, in our crime-control policy as in our policy in Southeast Asia, we sought to resolve problems that were social and communal in nature through high technology and big money.

Ball-Rokeach and Short suggest that high-tech command-and-control did in fact "gulag" the ghetto. That is, the hardware may have instilled enough fear among minorities in the 1970s to discourage the kind of group rioting and civil disorder that was prevalent in the late 1960s. It also has been suggested that the decline in riots reflected a decline in expectations and hope. The Violence Commission explained the civil disorders of the 1960s in terms of a confrontation between declining resources and the rising expectations that were due to civil rights and Great Society programs. In the 1970s, resources continued to decline, but so did expectations—enough perhaps to stop more public forms of protest, like rioting.

Street crime is, in many ways, a form of slow rioting. The criminal on a dark street is less vulnerable to police hardware and command-and-control tactics than is a group of looters. It is possible that some crime, like street muggings, became the safer, more private expression of protest in the 1970s.

For whatever reasons, police apprehension rates did not improve. Crime rates did not go down. As Gordon and Morris explain, all that went down was LEAA. It was a victim of the expectations raised by the war on crime of the early 1970s and the budget cutting of the late 1970s and early 1980s.

LEAA did have some notable successes—particularly in improving planning and coordination among local criminal justice agencies. But its legacy has been further obscured by the agency's failure to evaluate systematically what worked and what didn't among individual programs, according to Gordon and Morris.

Parallel to the effort to improve police apprehension rates was an attempt, evolving partly out of the Katzenbach and Violence commission recommendations, to provide swifter, surer punishment. Through grants, LEAA tried to improve court efficiency, and its recommendations often were carried out locally. Sentencing did become more severe for those apprehended for predatory violence, and the rate of state prison incarceration doubled during the 1970s. Today, American incarceration rates are higher than those of any other industrialized country except, notably, South Africa and the Soviet Union. This is especially true in the case of black males, who, Ball-Rokeach and Short tell us, account for about 50 percent of the prison population. One result is that prison is one of the few U.S. institutions dominated by blacks—or, in some regions, Hispanics.

In spite of the high incarceration rate, however, our extraordinarily high levels of violent crime have persisted since the 1960s. As Currie concludes on the basis of this practical experience as well as of prestigious academic studies, the theory of deterrence has not been borne out. That is, there is little useful evidence that raising the costs of crime by inflicting more punishment (or speedier or more severe or more certain punishment) results in less crime.

In part because of the shortcomings of the theory of deterrence, the notion of selective incapacitation—a rather surgical-sounding phrase to nonspecialists—has come into vogue. Selective incapacitation seeks early identification of the relatively few repeaters who are associated with so much violent crime and the continued incarceration of this group for periods of time that are still being debated. When applied with considered judgment rather than wholesale abandon, incapacitation has a role. But Currie and I warn that it also has many limitations. Offenders, for example, could be unjustly sentenced to prison on the basis of a false prediction of criminality. More importantly, the same evidence that is used to support selective incapacitation more convincingly supports community-based programs, which cost much less. The philosophy conveniently avoids the underlying causes of crime, and the possibility exists that incapacitated repeaters will simply be replaced by others generated from an unchanged society, economy, and polity.

## LAW AND ORDER RECONSIDERED

In reconsidering law and order, then, the central message of this volume is conveyed by Lavrakas. Most policy observers still do not understand that the criminal justice system—police, courts, and prisons—merely reacts to crime and cannot do much to prevent it. We do need to continue improving the equity and efficiency of the system, as advocated by the Violence and Katzenbach commissions, because, among other reasons, victims require better treatment and society deserves more protection from those who have committed crime. But, although we must maintain present resources, we must learn from the 1970s that massive new investments in the justice system will not reduce our historically high levels of crime.

A realistic assessment of the criminal justice system is not inconsistent with a need for social control. Restriction of handguns, protection against assassination, and coordination against terrorism are proposed by some of the contributors to this volume as necessary controls.

The Violence Commission concluded that firearms facilitate rather than cause violence, but that in this way the widespread possession of handguns contributes substantially to violence in American society.[19] It recommended federal legislation to encourage state licensing of handguns, a proposal that later was resoundingly defeated in Congress. Zimring, on the basis of public opinion polls, predicts a national legislated policy of handgun restriction rather than restrictive licensing. But the future of this volatile issue, suggests Zimring, may be determined not by rates of crime and fear but by the beliefs and actions of key opinion groups—women, minorities, senior citizens—within which a clear consensus has not yet emerged.

There has long been consensus on the need to protect our leaders against political violence. The Violence Commission found that "presidential assassins typically have been white, male, and slightly built. Nearly all were loners and had difficulty making friends of either sex and especially in forming lasting normal relationships with women."[20] The commission recommended expansion of the functions of the Secret Service to protect any federal officeholder or candidate determined to be at risk, improved protection of state and local officeholders and candidates, restriction of handguns through licensing, improved weapons detection, and reduction of risky public appearances by the president. Some of these recommendations have been carried out to differing degrees. But the Violence Commission's recommendations have been insufficiently implemented. We need to move forward more comprehensively with all the law-enforcement and control technology at our disposal.

In his chapter, Kupperman foresees more attacks by professional terrorists within the United States. He predicts attacks on the infrastructures of our cities as well as direct threats to large numbers of people. Yet this nation, unlike others in the Western alliance, has no internal consensus on how to respond either to acts of supercriminal violence or to coercive political threats. The policy framework advocated by Kupperman for responding to a crisis begins with immediate isolation and containment of the incident in order to control its development. Thereafter, the need is for a policy of "damage control" to deal with the "political, social, economic, security, and military implications, including reassurance of local governments that basic commitments will be upheld (after, say, the breakdown of a city's water system)." Kupperman agrees that local officials need to be in charge of such responses because they are closest to the action. But he believes that White House leadership is necessary at an appropriate point, when an incident has become extremely serious and is of national or international importance. A small, predetermined presidential group is recommended. As we move toward a policy against domestic terrorism, it will be important to respond effectively, yet in a way that avoids government repression and a disruption of the democratic process. Such a balance seems to have been achieved by countries like Germany and Italy.

## NEIGHBORHOOD, FAMILY, AND EMPLOYMENT

Reliance on agencies of law enforcement and methods of control often concludes contemporary policy discussions, with an added qualifier that the criminal justice system nonetheless cannot do the job alone. This volume reaches the opposite conclusion. Speaking of individual and group violence, Comer warns that "we will never be able to mop the water off the floor unless we turn off the faucet that is causing the tub to overflow. And time is running out. Unlike decaying streets and bridges, the tear in the [human] fabric . . . somewhere down the line will be beyond repair."

The history of institutional denial of opportunity to minorities and the present existence of a black and Hispanic underclass mean that providing access to opportunity must remain a policy priority, as the reader will find in the education and civil rights recommendations of Comer and Ball-Rokeach and Short.

These recommendations, despite their importance, recall the diffuse social reforms of the Violence Commission. Yet there are other recommendations, around which Comer, Ball-Rokeach and Short, Currie, Lavrakas, and I tend to converge, that address the causes of individual (and group) violence and refrain from merely throwing money at the problem. We would replace the inexact trickle-down process of change with more carefully evaluated direct actions in specific geographic areas targeted at specific populations, crimes, and fears. These consensus recommendations, based on two decades of empirical research, scientific program evaluations, practical experience, and political feasibility, can be summarized by the words *neighborhood, family,* and *employment.*

During recent years, a good number of inner-city neighborhood nonprofit organizations have become sufficiently empowered to successfully use crime prevention as a means to the ultimate end of securing community regeneration, economic development, housing rehabilitation, and youth employment. In part, the development process has been made secure by reducing opportunities for crime, for example, through patrols, block watches, and escort services. But to avoid merely displacing violence elsewhere, the causes of crime also have been addressed. One way has been through replacing or supplementing weakened families with alternative, community-based extended families that, along with ethnic and cultural identification, help restore to children and teenagers the consistent discipline and self-respect created by strong natural families. Such extended-family influences also have helped channel illegal market activity by youngsters into more productive legal markets. Research and experience have demonstrated that both the support of an extended family and stable, quality, legal-market employment, not make-work, are needed by young, poor, inner-city males if the incidence of crime among them is to be reduced. Such employment needs to promise upward mobility and often can be targeted on developing the inner city. The strategy amounts to coordinating a federal labor policy for the structurally unemployed with federal neighborhood crime-prevention and national family policies.

Learning from the bureaucratic mistakes of the 1970s and applying a second-generation sense of how better to implement programs on a day-to-day basis, the public sector needs to facilitate the emergence of many more inner-city organizations capable of combining neighborhood, family, and employment in ways that simultaneously reduce crime and the underclass. Locally, minority organizations with residents who have a stake in their own turf need to lead rather than take a back seat to less qualified agencies, like the police. Although the following pages suggest it is the public sector that has the resources and outlook to significantly reduce crime and the underclass, partnerships with the private sector must be strongly encouraged.

Today, 75 percent of the population believes that we are making no headway in reducing violence and crime.[21] A framework of neighborhood, family, and employment promises a new departure that avoids the limitations of deterrence, the shortcomings of incapacitation, and the naiveté of past social reform. It also is politically feasible, offering, as these pages show, some common ground among those who would "mobilize youth" or create "community action" and those who want people to "pull themselves up by their bootstraps." Political feasibility cannot be underestimated in a real world of conventional wisdoms. If Orwell was right, so was Barbara Tuchman: "To halt the momentum of an accepted idea, to reexamine assumptions, is a disturbing process and requires more courage than governments can generally summon."[22]

## NOTES

1. The Violence Commission was concerned particularly with murder, assault, sexual attack, robbery, street mugging, larceny, burglary, and car theft. The findings on collective violence paid special attention to the inner-city street riots of the 1960s and the college protests over the Vietnam War. Political violence was discussed mostly in terms of assassination. Some attention was paid to terrorism, which was just emerging as a domestic issue in the late 1960s.
2. See, for example, John Conklin, *Criminology* (New York: Macmillan, 1981).
3. One example of our selectivity is the decision not to include a chapter on television and violent behavior. The Violence Commission concluded that television violence is not a cause per se, but that it can encourage real-world violent behavior. In particular, the commission's final report said that television violence can be a "particularly potent force" in inner-city areas, where violent life-styles may already be followed by some individuals, where low-income youngsters spend long hours watching television, and where children give high credence to what they watch. Still, it was difficult to measure the exact effects (National Commission on the Causes and Prevention of Violence, *To Establish Justice, To Insure Domestic Tranquility, Final Report* [Washington, D.C.: U.S. Government Printing Office, 1969], p. 199). Little evidence has been presented since the commission's report to alter these conclusions or significantly to improve measurement of the exact impact. See, for example, Melvin DeFleur and Sandra Ball-Rokeach, *Theories of Mass Communication* (New York: Longman, 1982).

   The commission also concluded that, although handguns per se are not a cause of violence, they are a direct facilitator. Studies were cited which demonstrated that most persons who commit homicide are not predetermined killers but act in a moment of rage or passion without intent to kill. No concrete evidence was found to prove or disprove the thesis that, lacking a gun, an enraged person would resort to a knife or some other weapon. But there was evidence that the fatality rate of firearm attacks was four times greater than the fatality rate of knife attacks (knives being the next most frequent and lethal weapon used in homicide). Thus, the commission concluded that, even if the number of violent attacks did not go down, the number of fatalities resulting from violent attacks would be substantially reduced if the attackers did not have handguns (National Commission on the Causes and Prevention of Violence, ibid., p. 174). These conclusions remain valid today.

Because of the better measures, the Violence Commission felt more comfortable in pointing to a direct relationship between handguns and violence than between television programs and violence. Available evidence still does not contradict this position. Given our need to be selective, therefore, we felt comfortable in including a chapter on firearms but not giving similar attention to television violence in a volume designed to highlight priorities on today's policy agenda. When more definitive measures on the impact of television violence become available, we may well need to elevate the relative priority of policy on media violence.

4. National Commission on the Causes and Prevention of Violence, ibid., p. xv.
5. Leslie Maitland Werner, "Risk of Crime Said to Exceed That of Divorce," *New York Times,* December 11, 1983, p. 41.
6. ABC poll reported on "Nightline," March 3, 1983.
7. Lynn A. Curtis and Imre R. Kohn, "Policy Responses to Problems Faced by Elderly in Public Housing," in Jordan Kosberg, *Abuse and Maltreatment of the Elderly* (Littleton, Mass.: John Wright-PSG, 1983).
8. National Commission on the Causes and Prevention of Violence, p. 35.
9. George Orwell, quoted in Charles E. Silberman, *Criminal Violence, Criminal Justice* (New York: Random House, 1978), p. 446.
10. Herbert Jacob and Robert L. Lindberry, *Governmental Responses to Crime: Executive Summary* (Washington, D.C.: National Institute of Justice, June 1982).
11. For a review and critique of these assertions, see Lynn A. Curtis, "The New Criminology," *Society,* March–April 1977, p. 8.
12. National Urban League, *State of Black America, 1984* (New York: National Urban League, 1984).
13. Curtis, "The New Criminology."
14. Silberman, *Criminal Violence,* pp. 118, 163.
15. Ibid., p. 164.
16. Gunnar Myrdal, *An American Dilemma* (New York: Harper & Row, 1944).
17. Lynn A. Curtis, *Criminal Violence* (Lexington, Mass.: Lexington Books, 1974).
18. Ibid.
19. See note 3 above.
20. National Commission on the Causes and Prevention of Violence, p. 124.
21. Kenneth R. Feinberg, ed., *Violent Crime in America* (Washington, D.C.: National Policy Exchange, 1983), p. i.
22. Barbara W. Tuchman, *Stillwell and the American Experience in China, 1911–1945* (New York: Macmillan, 1981).

# PART I

## INDIVIDUAL VIOLENCE

# 1

# The Extent and Character of Violent Crime in America, 1969 to 1982

NEIL ALAN WEINER AND
MARVIN E. WOLFGANG

In recognition of the "urgency of the Nation's crime problem and the depth of ignorance about it," President Johnson signed Executive Order 11,236 on July 23, 1965, which established the President's Commission on Law Enforcement and Administration of Justice (the Katzenbach Commission).[1] The in-depth report drafted in 1967 by the commission, *The Challenge of Crime in a Free Society,* investigated many complex aspects of crime in America: those who commit crimes, those who are victims of crimes, and those institutions formally entrusted with the responsibility of responding to criminals and their victims. The Katzenbach Commission observed that "the existence of crime, the talk about crime, the reports of crime, and the fear of crime have eroded the basic quality of life of many Americans."[2] Apprehension about crime, most often manifested as fear of physical and emotional harm, forced Americans in increasing numbers to alter their life-styles—to stay off the streets at night, to change their patterns of movement when on the streets, to avoid contact with strangers, and to consider moving to other, safer neighborhoods. Of the basic quality of life that Americans presumed to be secure, perhaps the most eroded facet was their "domestic tranquility"—their sense of personal safety and inviolability within their homes and neighborhoods.

This review was supported in part by the National Institute of Justice, U.S. Department of Justice, the Center for the Study of Crime Correlates and Criminal Behavior, grant no. 81–IJ–CX–0086, which established the Center for the Interdisciplinary Study of Criminal Violence at the Center for Studies in Criminology and Criminal Law at the Wharton School, The University of Pennsylvania. The authors would like to thank Deborah Denno and Jocelyn Young for their comments on an earlier draft of this report. Our appreciation also to Selma Pastor, Shannon Griffiths, and Ivonka Piper for their technical assistance.

During the period in which the Katzenbach Commission was framing its deliberations, America found itself in the midst of increasing collective unrest—both on the home front, in the form of collective protest and violence surrounding the civil rights movement, and abroad, in the form of escalating military intervention in Vietnam, a foreign policy course that precipitated campus protests and disorder and violence at home. Now wed to the challenge of crime—more specifically, violent crime—in a free society was the challenge of collective protests and violence marching across America in the wake of the civil rights and antiwar movements.

The convergence of these historical threads in conjunction with increasing acknowledgment of the grievous effects of violent crime on the social fabric of the nation impelled President Johnson to sign Executive Order 11,412 on June 10, 1968, creating the National Commission on the Causes and Prevention of Violence (the Violence Commission). One of the substantive foci of this commission was to present for the first time in a systematic and comprehensive manner the current state of knowledge about criminal violence in the United States.

The Violence Commission summed up its findings about violence in America with the following sobering appraisal:

> Violence in the United States has risen to alarmingly high levels. Whether one considers assassination, group violence, or individual acts of violence, the decade of the 1960s was considerably more violent than the several decades preceding it and ranks among the most violent in our history. The United States is the clear leader among modern, stable democratic nations in its rates of homicide, assault, rape, and robbery, and it is at least among the highest in incidence of group violence and assassination. . . . In our judgment, the time is upon us for a reordering of national priorities and for a greater investment of resources in the fulfillment of two basic purposes of our Constitution—to "establish justice" and to "insure domestic tranquility."[3]

How has America met the challenge of violent crime since 1969, when the Violence Commission presented its findings? Apparently not very well. Attorney General William French Smith recently observed, in language reminiscent of that used by the Violence Commission, that "the alarming and continuous increase in the commission of violent crimes raises a serious question whether the federal government is doing enough to insure domestic tranquility."[4] As is true of every rhetorical question, to ask this question is to answer it—in this case, in the negative. The failure of the federal government to contain violent crime as well as the public's fear of it has recently catapulted violent crime into a national "first priority."[5] In response to criminal violence, Attorney General Smith appointed a Task Force on Violent Crime in April 1981, "to make specific recommendations . . . on ways in which the federal government could do more to combat violent crime."[6]

Clearly, the appointment of the Violence Commission in 1969 and of the

Task Force on Violent Crime more than a decade later attests to the long-standing and continuing concern regarding violent crime in the nation. Implementing policy may be defined as rationally carrying out the implications of compelling research evidence. This perspective demands that a coordinated response to violent crime in the nation be informed by the best available facts about its extent and character. In the pages that follow, we provide information at the national level that might be used to translate public concern into a broad-based national policy. Toward this end, we will integrate data that have been in the public domain but have not been presented as part of a systematic overview of violent crime in America.

In this report we will examine public apprehension about violent crime, discuss the parameters of the problem as it was found at the end of the 1960s, trace the patterns in violent crime since that time, and situate the challenge of violent crime in America within an international context.

## PUBLIC ATTITUDES TOWARD VIOLENT CRIME

Both before and since 1969, a large segment of the American public has voiced concern over the problem of violent crime, thus lending considerable support to Attorney General Smith's conclusion that the federal government has been relatively ineffective in checking this problem. One of the earliest national surveys of attitudes toward crime, conducted for the Katzenbach Commission in 1966, revealed that nearly a quarter of the American people believed that the likelihood of personal attack or robbery existed in their neighborhoods, with nonwhites in particular expressing concern about this prospect.[7] The same survey found that one-third of the respondents felt moderately or very unsafe walking alone in their neighborhoods at night. Females were more apprehensive in this regard than males, and nonwhites were more apprehensive than whites.[8]

The public malaise revealed in the 1966 survey did not abate during the 1970s, for several city surveys uncovered continuing high levels of concern.[9] Between 60 and 80 percent of the inhabitants aged 16 and older in six of America's major cities (Boston, Houston, Miami, Minneapolis, San Francisco, and Washington, D.C.) reported in 1974 that they believed crime to be on the increase; almost no one believed that it had decreased (table 1).[10] Respondents in these cities also voiced concern about crime in their immediate areas and their chances of being attacked or robbed. Between 25 and 40 percent of those surveyed believed crime to be rising in their neighborhoods, and between 40 and 60 percent felt that the chances of their being attacked or robbed had also risen. Once again, very few respondents believed that crime was decreasing close to their residences or that the chances of suffering an attack or robbery had diminished. Persons who had been victimized by rape, personal robbery, assault, or personal attack during the twelve months prior to the survey believed more often than those who had not been victimized that neighborhood crime and the likelihood of being attacked or robbed had increased.[11] Apprehension about crime in one's neighborhood, exacerbated by the more specific fear of personal attacks, can translate into disruptions of personal routines. That these disruptions occurred to a substantial degree is confirmed by between one-third and more than two-fifths of those questioned in these surveys.[12]

Concern over increasing crime has persisted from the late 1960s to the present. The Harris and Gallup polls conducted during this period indicate a relatively high proportion of people who believed that crime had increased, ranging from a low of 46 percent in both 1969 and 1978 to a high of 70 percent in 1975 (table 2).[13] During this same period, between one-third and one-half of the American public remained fearful of walking alone at night in areas close to their homes (table 3).

By all accounts, perceptions that crime in general and violent crime in particular is a major problem continue to be a manifest part of the American scene. These clear statements of discontent most certainly have fueled the recent decision by the federal government to make violent crime a national "first priority." We shall see that these perceptions have a basis in fact.

## THE EXTENT AND CHARACTER OF VIOLENT
## CRIME: SOME PRELIMINARY CONSIDERATIONS

This overview of violent crime in the United States during the last decade and a half will be developed from two complementary data sources: the *Uniform Crime Reports* (*UCR*), prepared annually by the Federal Bureau of Investigation (FBI), and the "National Crime Survey" (NCS), prepared annually for the Bureau of Justice Statistics by the U.S. Bureau of the Census. The *UCR* information is based on records collected and maintained each year by approximately fourteen thousand local and state law-enforcement agencies about offenses established by these agencies as having occurred and about persons arrested for these offenses. These data are submitted to the FBI either directly or through state *UCR* programs according to standardized reporting procedures to enhance comparability of data across jurisdictions.

The reliability of *UCR* data has been the subject of continuing discussion; *UCR* statistics remain, however, the only source of official information compiled at the national level over time (since 1930).[14] When proper caution is exercised in interpreting them, they can provide considerable insight into the volume and character of crime in the nation, particularly serious violent crime.

The *UCR* presents an official statistical picture of criminal violence. NCS data, on the other hand, comprise information about crime that is obtained by structured interviews with the victims of crime.[15] The NCS is largely based on the seminal study of criminal victimization in the United States conducted in 1966 for the Law Enforcement Commission by the National Opinion Research Center.[16] Since 1973, when the NCS was initiated, data have been collected annually. To ensure that comprehensive information is obtained about criminal victimization in the United States, a national sample of households and commercial establishments was selected. Persons aged 12 and over in the sample have been interviewed twice yearly about their victimization experiences, including questions about the type, frequency, and effects of crime as well as about the characteristics of the offender(s) and of the victim(s).

The NCS was developed to correct some of the problems associated with the *UCR*—for example, the fact that the *UCR* represents an undercount of crime in the United States. Contributing to the undercount are victims who fail to report crime, law-enforcement agencies that do not record some of the crimes that are reported to them, and the failure of some local jurisdictions to submit reports to the FBI. Although the NCS corrects some of these problems, it is not without its own weaknesses: for example, its accuracy depends on the victim's ability to recall victimizations that have occurred, to identify accurately when they occurred, and to characterize them according to their proper statutory definition.[17] Despite these and other limitations of the *UCR* and the NCS, when these two sources of information about violent crime are used jointly, a measured and useful profile of criminal violence in America can be prepared.

When we refer to criminal violence in the following discussion, we mean legally proscribed behaviors that involve the use or threatened use of force by one party against another to secure some end against the will of the other party. Although many legal infractions fall within this definition, we restrict our investigation to the four offenses that the *UCR* defines as the most serious violent crimes: murder and nonnegligent manslaughter (what we also term criminal homicide), forcible rape, robbery, and aggravated assault.[18] The gravity of these offenses and their prominence in the public imagery of criminal violence warrant a detailed and independent examination.

## VIOLENT CRIME IN AMERICA: 1969 TO 1982

The four serious violent crimes considered here—criminal homicide, forcible rape, robbery, and aggravated assault—together with the serious property crimes—burglary, larceny-theft, and motor-vehicle theft—constitute what the *UCR* designates as "index crimes." The term *index* implies that because these crimes are serious, they are most likely to be reported to and recorded by law-enforcement agencies and therefore can serve as a valid barometer of changing patterns and trends in crime.

In its discussion of the levels and trends of criminal violence, the Violence Commission made two important observations: (1) the rates of serious violent crimes were substantially below those of serious property crimes, and (2) the rates of serious violent and property crimes were on the increase.[19]

The discrepancy between the rates of violent index crimes and property index crimes is so great that the combined violent crime rate has almost always been lower than the rate of each of the three property index crimes.[20] In any discussion of crime, however, a distinction should be drawn between seriousness defined in terms of the incidence of events and seriousness defined in terms of the gravity of their consequences. Violent index crimes, although dwarfed in incidence by property index crimes, are the more grievous offenses because of the potential physical and emotional harm to the victims.

The Violence Commission reported that the rates of both serious violent crimes and serious property crimes were rising in a parallel and dramatic fashion.[21] The commission concluded that the rates of violent crimes in the 1960s compared "unfavorably, even alarmingly, with those of the 1950s" and that there was good reason to believe, even on the basis of "fragmentary information," that these rates were higher than at any other time in this century, except perhaps for the earliest decades.[22] Drawing upon *UCR* data, the commission showed that the national rates of criminal homicide, forcible rape, and most notably, robbery and aggravated assault had been on the upswing.[23] Between 1958 and 1968 the national rate of criminal homicide had jumped from 4.6 to 6.8 per 100,000 population, that of forcible rape from 9.3 to 15.5, that of robbery from 54.9 to 131.0, and that of aggravated assault from 78.8 to 141.3. The combined violent crime rate had jumped from 147.6 to 294.6 in a matter of just ten years.[24] In percentage terms, the increase was 48 percent for criminal homicide, 67 percent for forcible rape, 139 percent for robbery, and 79 percent for aggravated assault, for an increase in the combined violent crime rate of nearly 100 percent.[25]

*UCR* data for 1969 to 1982 indicate that throughout this period violent index crimes constituted a modest (approximately 10 percent) but stable portion of all index crimes (table 4).[26] NCS statistics present a strikingly similar picture.[27] When victimizations against the person are grouped with criminal incidents committed against households, a composite category is created that is roughly the same as the *UCR* index offenses. (The most notable difference is that the NCS does not include criminal homicide.) For the years 1973 to 1980 major violent crimes against the person (forcible rape, robbery, and aggravated assault) constituted between 7.8 and 8.8 percent of all crimes (table 5).

The relatively low representation of serious violent crimes among all serious crimes can be examined in a different way by comparing the rates of violent index crimes to the rates of property index crimes. The rate discrepancies in the *UCR* noted by the Violence Commission persisted into the 1970s.[28] The rate of aggravated assault, which was generally highest among the violent offenses, was nevertheless still well below the rate of motor-vehicle theft, which had the lowest rate among the property offenses (table 6). Indeed, even when the violent index crimes are grouped together, their combined rate historically had been below that of motor-vehicle theft until 1975.

When the gravity of different types of offenses is considered, however, violent crime is probably the most salient of all crimes in the minds of Americans because of its potential for serious physical and emotional harm. We now focus on these particular offenses.

The rate increases in serious violent crimes documented by the Violence Commission have continued.[29] *UCR* data show that between 1969 and 1982 the rate of murder and nonnegligent manslaughter rose from 7.3 to 9.1 per 100,000 population; the rate of forcible rape climbed from 18.5 to 33.6; and the rates of robbery and aggravated assault jumped from 148.4 to 231.9 and from 154.5 to 280.8, respectively (table 6). These rates represent substantial percentage increases: 25 percent for criminal homicide, 82 percent for forcible rape, 56 percent for robbery, and 82 percent for aggravated assault. The combined violent crime rate, which is dominated by robbery and aggravated assault, soared from 328.7 to 555.3, an increase of 69 percent in fourteen years. Criminal homicide, forcible rape, and aggravated assault all reached their highest levels in 1981, and robbery did so one year later. Aggravated assault exhibited the highest rates, followed closely by robbery. If both the levels and the increases in violent crime reported in the *UCR* were cause for alarm in 1969, then these more recent data are cause for even greater alarm.

Since the 1980s began, the nation has witnessed declines in the official rates of every violent crime. The rates of criminal homicide, forcible rape, robbery, and aggravated assault were 10.2, 36.4, 243.5, and 290.6, respectively, in 1980, but had decreased to 9.1, 33.6, 231.9, and 280.8, respectively, in 1982 (table 6). Over a three-year period, then, the rates of criminal homicide, forcible rape, robbery, and aggravated assault dropped by 10.8 percent, 7.7 percent, 4.8 percent, and 3.4 percent, in order of mention. Whether this downswing represents the beginning of a long-term trend or only a short-term depression cannot yet be ascertained.

NCS statistics tell a somewhat different story. Forcible rape, personal robbery, and aggravated assault have not shown striking changes between 1973 and 1980. The rate (per 100,000 population aged 12 and over) of forcible rape was 100.0 in 1973 and 90.0 in 1980; the rate of personal robbery was 700.0 in 1973 and 650.0 in 1980; the rate of aggravated assault was 1,000.0 in 1973 and 920.0 in 1980; and the combined violent crime rate was 1,800.0 in 1973 and 1,660.0 in 1980 (table 7). These rate differences represent a decrease in forcible rape of 10 percent and decreases in personal robbery and aggravated assault of 7 and 8 percent, respectively. The combined violent crime rate fell by 8 percent over the eight-year period. In contrast to the *UCR,* which shows violent crime to have risen through the 1970s, reaching its highest levels in the first two years of the 1980s, the NCS shows no regular incline for forcible rape or aggravated assault, and for robbery it shows higher rates in the early 1970s.

For a fair comparison to be made between the *UCR* and the NCS, they should be examined for at least the years in which they overlap, 1973 to 1980. In this period, the *UCR* indicates an increase in forcible rape of 49 percent, whereas the NCS shows a decrease of 10 percent; the *UCR* shows that aggravated assault increased by 45 percent, but the NCS indicates only an 8 percent increase; the *UCR* shows that robbery increased by 33 percent, whereas the NCS indicates a 7 percent decrease (table 8).

These discrepancies between the two systems between 1973 and 1980 are just part of the picture, however. The annual rates show, according to the *UCR,* that forcible rape and aggravated assault increased consistently, whereas robbery first increased, then decreased, and subsequently increased again (table 8). The NCS, on the other hand, shows that forcible rape and aggravated assault remained fairly stable, whereas robbery was generally on the decline until the most recent years.

Turning from trend comparisons to magnitude comparisons, the NCS always registers substantially higher rates. Between 1973 and 1980, the NCS rates of forcible rape and robbery were 2.5 to 4 times higher than the corresponding *UCR* rates, and the rate of aggravated assault was 3.5 to 5 times higher (table 8). These figures should invite heightened concern over the levels of violent crime in America.

The divergences between the *UCR* and the NCS must certainly be examined more closely in the future if we are to formulate national policies to deal effectively with violent crime, for these are the only sources of national statistics collected over time. When the two sets of crime statistics are adjusted to produce greater comparability, the discrepancies lessen. For example, it has been shown recently that when *UCR* rates are based on the population aged 12 and over, when commercial robberies are excluded from *UCR* rates (as they are from NCS rates of personal robbery), and when the *UCR* is adjusted for persons who do not report violent crimes to law-enforcement agencies (information that is collected by the NCS), the two sets of data begin to look more alike in both magnitudes and trends and, by implication, in the rate changes they exhibit over time.[30]

Though much work remains to be done to bolster the reliability of these two important sources of criminal statistics, on balance we can conclude from them that violent crime has increased—but somewhat less than is indicated by the *UCR*—and that these rates are disturbingly high and would have to be viewed as such even without evidence of their increase.

When *UCR* violent offense rates are used to compute victimization probabilities (by dividing each offense rate into the population base of 100,000 used to calculate it), we find, as expected, that the probability of being victimized violently has increased between 1969 and 1981 (table 6).[31] The chances of being murdered were 1 in 13,699 in 1969 compared to 1 in 10,989 in 1982; the chances of being forcibly raped were 1 in 5,405 in 1969 compared to 1 in 2,976 in 1982; the chances of being robbed were 1 in 674 in 1969 compared to 1 in 431 in 1982; and the chances of being assaulted seriously were 1 in 647 in 1969 compared to 1 in 356 in 1982. These figures represent unsettling upturns of 34 percent for criminal homicide, 92 percent for forcible rape, 69 percent for robbery, and 82 percent for aggravated assault. (These are the percentage increases in the offense rates from which each of the victimization probabilities was computed.)

We can obtain a rough estimate of the number of persons responsible for acts of criminal violence in the nation by using a procedure outlined by the Violence Commission.[32] In 1969 there were approximately 1,972 seriously violent offenders for every 100,000 Americans; in 1981 this figure had climbed to 3,461. Viewed alternatively, approximately 1 in 50 Americans may have been involved in a violent crime in 1969 compared to 1 in 30 Americans in 1981, an increase of 76 percent. In terms of absolute numbers, more than 4 million people in 1969 and almost 8 million people in 1981 appear to have committed a criminally violent act, staggering numbers to say the least.

In the 1960s and persisting throughout the 1970s, disparities were observed in rates of violent crimes between city areas, areas adjacent to the city, and rural areas and between cities of different sizes.[33] *UCR* data indicate that cities continued to suffer higher rates of violent crime than rural areas by factors of about 1.5 for criminal homicide, 2–2.5 for both rape and aggravated assault, and 12–20 for robbery (table 9). This pattern is confirmed by the NCS data, which show that metropolitan areas (both central cities and the adjacent areas) have consistently higher rates of forcible rape, personal robbery, and aggravated assault than nonmetropolitan areas. When central-city metropolitan areas are compared with nonmetropolitan areas, the former registered forcible rape rates that were 1.5–3 times higher than the latter, aggravated assault rates that were about 2 times as high, and personal robbery rates that were 4–5 times higher (table 10). Cities exceeded both rural and nonmetropolitan areas to a much greater extent in robbery rates than was the case for any of the other serious violent crimes, indicating that robbery, more than these other crimes, is a city phenomenon.

Cities most plagued by violent crime are the larger ones (table 11). For example, cities with populations greater than 250,000 experienced substantially higher rates of violent crime than cities with populations of less than 10,000. Criminal homicide rates were about 6 times higher; forcible rape rates were between 4 and 6 times greater; robbery rates were between 15 and 25 times higher; and aggravated assault rates were about 2 to 3 times higher. Furthermore, as city size decreased from those with populations greater than 250,000 to those with less than 10,000, the rates of each type of violent crime also decreased consistently.

Data collected by the *UCR* indicate that all regions—the Northeast, North Central, South, and West—sustained rate increases between 1969 and 1982, a continuation of the upward trend noted by the Violence Commission (table 12).[34] The Northeast experienced the highest rate increases in robbery and aggravated assault and the second highest rate increases in criminal homicide and forcible rape, which together produced the highest overall rate increase among the four regions. During both the 1960s and the 1970s, the Northeast suffered some of the most dramatic upturns in the levels of violent crime in the nation.

The South continued to have the highest rates of criminal homicide (between 10.4 and 13.3 per 100,000 population), nearly 2 times greater than the rates of the Northeast and North Central regions. For the first half of the 1970s, the South also registered rates of criminal homicide that were nearly twice as high as those of the West, but rates in the West began to rise in the second half of the decade, and by the decade's end they were not far below those of the South. Although the South had the highest rates of aggravated assault throughout the 1960s, from 1973 on the West displayed the highest rates, ranging from 234.6 per 100,000 population in 1973 to 371.4 in 1980.

During the 1970s, the West displayed the highest rates of forcible rape, as it did during the 1960s. These rates, which ranged between 28.9 and 51.9 per 100,000 population, were approximately one and one-third to two times greater than those of the other regions. When robbery was considered, a clear shift in pattern obtained across the last two decades. Whereas the West and North Central regions had the highest robbery rates during the 1960s, the Northeast was so burdened during the 1970s, followed by the West. Between 1969 and 1982, the robbery rate in the Northeast shot upward from 188.6 to 348.5. Considering the total violent crime rate, from a closely clustered field in 1969 the West and the Northeast have emerged as the most beleaguered regions, mainly because of their relatively high rates of robbery and aggravated assault (table 12).

Work conducted for the Violence Commission showed that young male members of minority groups had been responsible for a disproportionately high share of the serious violent crimes during the 1960s.[35] *UCR* and NCS statistics for the 1970s indicate that these patterns have remained stable.[36] *UCR* data further indicate that the rates of violent crime among young males and among members of minority groups are increasing almost without exception.

During the past decade, males represented slightly less than half of the population of the United States;[37] yet according to *UCR* statistics they were responsible for a substantially higher proportion of the arrests for violent offenses: for more than eight out of every ten arrests for criminal homicide and aggravated assault, for virtually all the arrests for forcible rape, and for more than nine out of every ten arrests for robbery (table 13). NCS data show almost identical results, with male offenders accounting for more than 90 percent of forcible rapes and for 80 to 90 percent of the personal robberies and aggravated assaults.

Disparities between males and females in the commission of serious violent crime can be highlighted further by comparing their respective arrest rates. *UCR* data for the 1970s show that male rates far outstripped those of females for each type of violent crime: by a factor of between 5 and 6 for criminal homicide, by a factor of close to 7 for aggravated assault, and by a factor of between 13 and 16 for robbery (table 14). When the four violent crimes are combined, male arrest rates are about ten times greater than those of females.

During the past decade, both males and females sustained rate increases for robbery and aggravated assault—almost equal increases for aggravated assault but greater increases for females than for males for robbery (table 14). Male rates also increased for criminal homicide and forcible rape, but the female rate of criminal homicide displayed almost no change at all.

*UCR* data show that young adults (aged 18 to 24) and older juveniles (aged 15 to 17) have been responsible disproportionately for acts of criminal violence. Although young adults have constituted about 13 percent of the population of the United States, according to *UCR* statistics they have accounted generally for more than 30 percent of those arrested for criminal homicide and aggravated assault and for about 40 to 45 percent of those arrested for forcible rape and robbery (table 15). Older juveniles, who have constituted just under 6 percent of the population,[38] have accumulated approximately 10 to 15 percent of the arrests for forcible rape and between 20 and 25 percent of the arrests for robbery. This age group was also responsible for a disproportionately greater share of the arrests for criminal homicide (about 8 percent) and aggravated assault (about 11 percent); but clearly the magnitude of the disproportionality is less for these offenses than for forcible rape and robbery.

Striking results appear when arrest rates for the different age groups are computed from *UCR* data. Examination of the rates for violent index crimes combined indicates that young adults (aged 18 to 24) had the highest overall rates, followed fairly closely by older juveniles (aged 15 to 17) and then, far behind, by older adults (aged 25 and older) and, still further behind, by younger juveniles and children (below age 15) (table 16). Furthermore, young adults and older juveniles registered the highest rates regardless of the type of violent crime. When these two age groups were compared, young adults recorded higher arrest rates for three of the four violent offenses: criminal homicide by a factor of about two, forcible rape by a factor of about one and one-third, and aggravated assault by a factor of about one and one-quarter. Robbery, however, was committed more often by older juveniles, especially since the middle of the past decade, when their arrest rates began to exceed those of young adults by about one and one-third. Older juveniles also incurred a higher rate increase than young adults for robbery and fairly similar rate increases for criminal homicide and aggravated assault. Neither older juveniles nor young adults experienced much of a rate increase for forcible rape, however.

After World War II, the country entered a period of about a decade (1946 to 1956) in which the birthrate soared. The first of these large baby-boom cohorts entered its peak arrest ages (15 to 25) for violent crimes about 1963, the time at which the violent crime rate began to rise sharply in the nation. The last of these cohorts entered its peak arrest ages in the early 1970s and matured out of this high-risk period in about 1980. The high and increasing levels of violent crime witnessed in the 1960s and the 1970s are attributable in part to these birth cohorts. As the last of these cohorts has passed out of the high-risk ages, we might expect a decline in the level of violent crime during the latter part of the 1980s. The decline is likely to be modest, however, for those demographic groups that exhibit the highest arrest rates for violent crimes tend also to have the highest birthrates. As a result, even after the baby-boom cohorts have moved out of their high-risk ages, these age groups will nevertheless in forthcoming years still have a high proportion of persons most likely to engage in violent crimes.

Examination of *UCR* statistics on race indicates that although blacks have constituted approximately 12 percent of the nation's population,[39] they have accumulated 50 to 60 percent of the arrests for criminal homicide, about 50 percent of the arrests for forcible rape, close to 60 percent of the arrests for robbery, and between 40 and 50 percent of the arrests for aggravated assault (table 17). NCS data also show that blacks are responsible for a disproportionate amount of serious violent crime (tables 18–19).

Race-specific arrest rates computed from *UCR* figures show the size of these disparities in an alternative way. Relative to whites, blacks sustained criminal homicide rates that were between 7 and 13 times greater, forcible rape rates about 7 times higher, robbery rates 10 to 17 times higher, and aggravated assault rates between 4 and 7 times greater (table 20). Over the span of the decade, whites exhibited more pronounced increases in their arrest rates than did blacks for forcible rape, robbery, and aggravated assault. For criminal homicide, the white rate increased substantially, whereas the black rate decreased slightly.

That victims are very much like offenders in terms of social and demographic characteristics had been established by the Violence Commission;[40] that this has remained the case is confirmed by the NCS. Victimization rates were higher for males than for females (with the exception of forcible rape), for the young than for the old, for blacks than for whites, and for the poor than for the more affluent.

Males figured more prominently than females as victims of both robbery and aggravated assault, sustaining victimization rates that were more than 2 times as high for robbery and about 3 times as high for aggravated assault (table 21). Not surprisingly, females were much more likely to be forcibly raped than were males, by a factor of about 8.

Older juveniles (aged 16 to 19) and young adults (aged 20 to 24) have been found to be disproportionately the targets of violent crimes. NCS data firmly support the currency of this finding. Persons in these age groups experienced the highest and roughly comparable chances of being raped, which were approximately 2 times as high as those of other age groups. Older juveniles and young adults also suffered the highest and roughly comparable risks of being assaulted seriously. They were about twice as likely to be assaulted as their two closest rivals, the 12- to 15-year-olds and the 25- to 34-year-olds. Robbery victims also fell, for the most part, into the younger age brackets: 12- to 15-year-olds, 16- to 19-year-olds, and 20- to 24-year-olds all shared a similarly high risk of being robbed, which was 2 to 3 times higher than that of older age groups.

Victimization rates by race indicate that blacks have continued to sustain the highest risks. Focusing just on disparities between blacks and whites, NCS data show that blacks ran a risk of forcible rape that was one and one-half to two times greater, a risk of robbery two to three times higher, and a risk of aggravated assault more than one and one-third times higher, yielding an overall risk that was nearly twice as great (table 22).

Economically disadvantaged persons were most often victims of serious violent crimes. NCS data indicate that persons who belonged to families earning less than $3,000 annually bore the brunt of violent crime, for they were more than twice as likely as any other income group to be forcibly raped, more than one and one-half times more likely to be robbed, and more than one and one-third times more likely to be assaulted seriously. As annual family income increased, the ravages of violent crime generally decreased.

The NCS presents information for the years 1973 and 1979 that relates the victim and the offender by their respective races.[41] The only other personal characteristic for which similar information is presented is sex, but only for 1976. Forcible rape, robbery, and aggravated assault were predominantly intraracial; in general, more than seven out of every ten serious violent offenses committed against a black were committed by a black, and between three-fifths and four-fifths of the forcible rapes and assaults committed against whites were committed by whites. Robbery, however, was the exception to this pattern, as it has been historically: more than the other violent offenses, robbery was an interracial affair in which blacks were more likely to victimize whites. Although whites robbed other whites in substantial proportions, in more than half of the incidents involving a single offender and in more than one-third of the events involving multiple offenders, blacks also robbed whites in substantial numbers.

Looking at NCS data on the involvement of the sexes as victims and offenders in violent crimes, the overwhelming majority of these incidents were committed by males regardless of the sex of the victim: virtually all forcible rapes, more than four-fifths of the robberies, and more than two-thirds of the aggravated assaults. When females offended violently, they were most likely to engage in robbery and aggravated assault and were more likely to select a female victim than a male victim.[42]

NCS data show that when a violent crime erupts the victim is likely to be alone: in more than nine out of every ten forcible rapes and robberies and in more than eight out of every ten aggravated assaults. These data also show that a victim is most likely to be faced by a single offender in cases of forcible rape (about 80 percent of the incidents), is somewhat less likely to be so confronted in cases of aggravated assault (between 65 and 70 percent of the time), and is least likely to be confronted by a single offender in cases of robbery (50 percent of the incidents).

A significant part of the fear of violent crime is the fear of being victimized by a stranger. NCS data indicate that a majority of violent crimes have been committed historically by strangers: four-fifths of the robberies, two-thirds of the forcible rapes, and three-fifths of the aggravated assaults. Rates computed for these data tell the same story but in a different way: robberies were about six times more likely to be committed by a stranger than by someone who was known to the victim; forcible rapes were twice as likely to be carried out by a stranger; and aggravated assaults were about one and two-thirds times more likely to be performed by a stranger (table 23).

Much violent crime occurred outside the home and its immediate vicinity.

Approximately three-fifths of the robberies and two-fifths of both the forcible rapes and the aggravated assaults occurred in open public places, such as the street or a park (table 24). More intimate environments, the home and places nearby, were not immune from these events, however, for about one-third of the forcible rapes and about one-fifth of the robberies and aggravated assaults were committed there. Forcible rapes occurred about as often in the victim's home or close by as in an open public place. Robbery and aggravated assault, on the other hand, occurred more often in an open public place than in the home or nearby: robbery about three times more often and aggravated assault about twice as often. Robbery and aggravated assault have been violent street phenomena more than has forcible rape.

Central to the enigma of criminal violence is the outcome. In precisely how many incidents is the victim physically harmed? NCS data indicate that one of every three victims of personal robberies and assaults sustained an injury (table 25). Males and females were injured equally often. When age was examined, no clear pattern appeared, for the victims of both personal robberies and assaults had similar risks of injury across the age spectrum. Nor did the race of the victim bear strongly on the likelihood of injury. Interestingly, injuries were sustained more often by victims who knew their assailants in cases of personal robbery and assault than by victims who did not.

Americans have not behaved passively toward those who would victimize them violently: eight out of every ten victims of forcible rape, more than one out of every two robbery victims, and seven out of every ten victims of aggravated assault initiated some type of self-protective measure. Firearms and knives were used rarely for self-protection—in less than 4 percent of the personal robberies and aggravated assaults and almost never in cases of forcible rape. Victims of forcible rape most often attempted to get help or to frighten their attacker (about 30 percent of the time); somewhat less often, they used physical force or a weapon other than a firearm or knife or tried to threaten or to reason with their assailant (between 20 and 25 percent of the time). Robbery victims most often tried to use physical force or a weapon other than a firearm or knife (about 30 percent of the time); about equally often they tried to get help, to frighten the robber, to threaten or reason with the robber, or to use some other kind of nonviolent resistance like evasion (about 20 percent of the time). Use of physical force, a weapon other than a firearm or knife, or nonviolent resistance was the most favored tactic of persons subjected to serious assaults (between 25 and 30 percent of the time).

These findings complement research done during the Violence Commission, which showed that a sizable portion of violent crime, especially criminal homicide and aggravated assault, involved victims who were the first to use violence or some other provocation.[43]

In the past decade, considerable work has been done to determine whether a core group of offenders exists who repeatedly commit serious violent crimes and who, as a consequence, are responsible for the bulk of these acts. Efforts along this line have yielded the finding that the vast majority of violent crime is committed by a relatively few repetitively violent persons. Research conducted on two large birth cohorts born in Philadelphia in 1945 and 1958 indicates that chronic male offenders (those who compiled five or more police contacts) represented small segments of the offender populations: 18 percent of the offenders in the 1945 birth cohort and 23 percent in the 1958 cohort. These offenders accounted, however, for a disproportionately large share of the offenses: 52 percent in the 1945 birth cohort and 61 percent in the 1958 cohort.[44] More significant, the chronic offenders in each cohort were responsible for the major portion of serious violent offenses: 71 percent of the criminal homicides, 73 percent of the rapes, 82 percent of the robberies, and 69 percent of the aggravated assaults in the 1945 birth cohort; and 61 percent of the criminal homicides, 76 percent of the forcible rapes, 73 percent of the robberies, and 65 percent of the aggravated assaults in the 1958 birth cohort. Furthermore, offenders with five or more police contacts were most likely to injure their victims, for they compiled 58 percent of the injurious offenses in the 1945 birth cohort and 66 percent in the 1958 cohort.[45] A similar pattern of a high concentration of serious offenses among a small minority of offenders has been reported in other research.[46] Within already high-risk offender populations—urban, young, male, minority-group members—there is, then, a small group that is at even greater risk to do harm to others.

## INTERNATIONAL COMPARISONS

An accurate appraisal of the dimensions of criminal violence in America requires a comparative treatment at the international level. However, marshalling statistics that can be used reliably to establish patterns and trends in criminal violence for the United States and other members of the international community presents several difficulties. First, there is a history of poor record-keeping practices in countries outside Europe. Further difficulties are posed by national differences in legal definitions of crime, in customs concerning the reporting of crimes to and the recording of crimes by law-enforcement agencies, and in traditions in the administration of justice by law-enforcement and judicial institutions. To minimize these hindrances to cross-cultural analysis, we limit our discussion to nations that bear the greatest similarity to the United States in their history and institutions: the urban and industrial European nations and those non-European nations that share this cultural tradition.

The Violence Commission relied on data published by the United Nations in its analysis of criminal homicide and on data compiled by Canada, Denmark, England, and Wales for the UN investigation of forcible rape, robbery, and aggravated assault. These data clearly document that levels of violent crime in the United States were well above those of the comparison nations.[47] Statistics collected by the commission indicated that between 1955 and 1966 the rate of criminal homicide in the United States, which varied between about 4.5 and 6.0 per 100,000 population, was at least twice as high as the rates of the other nations: Australia, Austria, Belgium, Canada, Denmark, England, Finland, France, Germany, Italy, Norway, and Switzerland.[48] Furthermore, whereas the rate of criminal homicide in the United States showed a consistent incline over the twelve-year period, the rates of the other nations were either relatively stable or erratic, or they increased only modestly.

Similar disparities obtained when the rates of forcible rape, robbery, and aggravated assault were compared for the United States, Canada, Denmark, England, and Wales. U.S. rates in each of these categories exceeded those of each of the comparison countries by a factor of at least one and one-half.[49] As the Violence Commission pointed out, "For each major violent act, the reported American average rate [for the years 1963 to 1967] is greater than the reported average rate for the other three countries *combined.*"[50]

Cross-national patterns in homicide observed in 1969 continued throughout the 1970s. The United States still suffered a homicide rate at least three times higher than the rates sustained by European nations (table 26). Furthermore, for the early portion of the comparison period, 1970 to 1975, the United States experienced a much steeper incline in its homicide rate than did the other nations.

Data on robbery for the first half of the 1970s also conform to what we would expect, given the findings of the Violence Commission. Relative to European countries, the United States exhibited by far the highest mean robbery rate (191.2 per 100,000 population), exceeding its closest rival, Canada, by a factor of almost 3 (table 27).

Traditionally, then, America has experienced levels of criminal violence that either far exceed or are among the highest of nations most similar to it in culture and history. Unfortunately, this is as far as we can go in making international comparisons. Information is either unavailable, not of high quality, or not collected and published annually from other countries on the more detailed aspects of criminal violence discussed earlier in this report, such as age, sex, and race variations and the victim-offender relationship.

## SUMMARY: VIOLENT CRIME IN AMERICA

During the 1960s the United States suffered increases in the rates of all types of violent crime. On the basis of available historical information, the level of violent crime reached an all-time high in this decade. Regional trends mirrored that of the nation: the Northeast, North Central, South, and West all sustained rate increases in each category of violent crime, the sharpest increases being experienced by the Northeast and North Central areas. The South, however, had the highest rates of criminal homicide and aggravated assault; the West, the highest rates of forcible rape; and the West and North Central regions, the highest rates of robbery.

Official statistics indicate that the rate increases in violent crime sustained during the 1960s continued throughout the 1970s, both in the nation as a whole and in each of the four regions. Particularly disturbing were sharp rises in violent crime in the Northeast, a continuation of the trend begun in the 1960s. The South continued to experience the highest rates of criminal homicide, but the West began to draw closer to it by the decade's end. Whereas the South had the highest rates of aggravated assault when the Violence Commission reported its findings, the West dislodged it from this position in the 1970s. During each of the past two decades the West has had the highest levels of forcible rape. Robbery rates, which were highest in the West and North Central regions in the 1960s, were highest in the Northeast over the 1970s.

NCS data on national trends are somewhat at variance with the corresponding *UCR* statistics. A relative stability in the rates of forcible rape and aggravated assault was evidenced in the NCS data. Robbery showed a general decline, until recently. Preliminary efforts to reconcile differences between the *UCR* and the NCS, by making the two statistical sources more comparable, has not firmly established the greater validity of one over the other. However, on balance it would appear that violent crime has increased. But even if it were established that the level of violent crime has not risen, it is still unacceptably high. NCS information showed, for example, forcible rape and robbery rates to be three to four times higher than the corresponding *UCR* rates and the rate of aggravated assault to be nearly four times higher. Given these figures, rates of criminal violence need not be on the upswing for the nation to be legitimately concerned about their level.

Examination of the demographic characteristics of persons arrested for violent crimes has yielded a distinctive and consistent picture: violent crimes have been committed mostly by young male members of socially, economically, and politically disadvantaged minority groups. Data on offenders obtained from the victims of violent crime have been in agreement with this finding.

The victims of violent crimes were very much like their assailants in terms of demographic characteristics: they were most likely to be young, male, members of a minority group, poor, and urban.

Noteworthy patterns were found when the personal characteristics of violent offenders and their victims were considered together. These confrontations were predominantly intraracial, except for robbery, which often involved a minority-group member victimizing a majority-group member, and intrasexual, except for forcible rape. Data collected for the Violence Commission showed that both victims and offenders tended to be adults in cases of criminal homicide, aggravated assault, and armed robbery.

Victims of violent crimes were usually alone when the act occurred. The number of offenders who took part in violent crimes varied by the type of crime. Forcible rapes were most likely to be committed by a single offender, followed, in descending order, by aggravated assault and robbery. That strangers were involved in violent offenses in substantial numbers was borne out by victimization studies. Robberies in particular tended to be committed by persons unknown to the victim.

Fully one in three Americans subjected to a violent crime was injured during the course of the incident. Americans were not passive relative to their attackers, however. A sizable portion of the offenses, particularly criminal homicides and aggravated assaults, involved victims who were the first to use violence or some other form of provocation. Furthermore, victims often resisted during the course of offenses that they had not provoked, adopting techniques ranging from the use of firearms and knives (which occurred very infrequently) to threatening and trying to reason with their assailant.

Spatial analyses of violent crime have found that criminal homicides and forcible rapes occur more often at home than do aggravated assaults and robberies. These latter two offenses more often occur in open public places, especially robbery, which makes it the typical violent "street crime."

Studies done over the last decade have shown that a substantial portion of violent offenses are committed by a small cadre of offenders who commit these acts frequently.

In comparison with other nations that are most similar to the United States in their institutions and history, the United States either has the highest rates of serious violent crime or is among the nations with the highest rates.

## NOTES

1. U.S. President's Commission on Law Enforcement and Administration of Justice, *The Challenge of Crime in a Free Society* (Washington, D.C.: U.S. Government Printing Office, 1967), Foreword.
2. Ibid., p. v.
3. U.S. National Commission on the Causes and Prevention of Violence (hereafter, the Violence Commission), *To Establish Justice, To Insure Domestic Tranquility, Final Report* (Washington, D.C.: U.S. Government Printing Office, 1969), pp. xv, xxv.
4. William French Smith, "Violent Crime Task Force Created," *Justice Assistance News* 2: 3 (April 1981): 3.

5. "New Attorney General and Deputy Lack Crime Expertise," *Criminal Justice Newsletter* 12, no. 3 (February 2, 1981): 2.
6. U.S. Department of Justice, National Institute of Justice, *Attorney General's Task Force on Violent Crime: Final Report* (Washington, D.C.: U.S. Government Printing Office, 1981), p. v.
7. These figures were derived from Philip H. Ennis, *Criminal Victimization in the United States: A Report of a National Survey*; Field Surveys II of the President's Commission on Law Enforcement and Administration of Justice (Chicago: National Opinion Research Center, University of Chicago; for sale by the Superintendent of Documents, U.S. Government Printing Office, Washington, D.C., 1967), Table 45, p. 75.
8. Ibid., Table 42, p. 73.
9. U.S. Department of Justice, National Criminal Justice Information and Statistics Service, *Boston: Public Attitudes about Crime* (Washington, D.C.: U.S. Government Printing Office, 1979); *Houston: Public Attitudes about Crime* (Washington, D.C.: U.S. Government Printing Office, 1978); *Miami: Public Attitudes about Crime* (Washington, D.C.: U.S. Government Printing Office, 1979); *Minneapolis: Public Attitudes about Crime* (Washington, D.C.: U.S. Government Printing Office, 1978); *San Francisco: Public Attitudes about Crime* (Washington, D.C.: U.S. Government Printing Office, 1978); *Washington, D.C.: Public Attitudes about Crime* (Washington, D.C.: U.S. Government Printing Office, 1978).
10. Table 1 and all subsequent tables in this chapter will be found in the Appendix.
11. Ibid., *Boston: Public Attitudes about Crime,* Tables 2, 5, pp. 14, 16; *Houston: Public Attitudes about Crime,* Tables 2, 5, pp. 16, 18; *Miami: Public Attitudes about Crime,* Tables 2, 5, pp. 14, 16; *Minneapolis: Public Attitudes about Crime,* Tables 2, 5, pp. 16, 18; *San Francisco: Public Attitudes about Crime,* Tables 2, 5, pp. 16, 18; *Washington, D.C.: Public Attitudes about Crime,* Tables 2, 5, pp. 16, 18.
12. Ibid., *Boston: Public Attitudes about Crime,* Table 16, p. 24; *Houston: Public Attitudes about Crime,* Table 16, p. 26; *Miami: Public Attitudes about Crime,* Table 16, p. 26; *Minneapolis: Public Attitudes about Crime,* Table 16, p. 26; *San Francisco: Public Attitudes about Crime,* Table 16, p. 26; *Washington, D.C.: Public Attitudes about Crime,* Table 16, p. 26.
13. Louis Harris, *The Harris Survey,* May 9, 1977, p. 1; February 23, 1981, p. 2 (New York: The Chicago Tribune-New York News Syndicate); George H. Gallup, *The Gallup Poll* (Princeton, N.J.: The Gallup Poll, April 4, 1981), p. 3.
14. For additional discussion of the *UCR,* see Ronald Chilton, "Criminal Statistics in the United States," *Journal of Criminal Law and Criminology* 71 (1980): 56–67; John J. Kitsuse and Aaron V. Cicourel, "A Note on the Uses of Official Statistics," *Social Problems* 14 (1963): 131–39; Donald J. Newman, "The Effect of Accommodations in Justice Administration on Criminal Statistics," *Sociology and Social Research* 46 (1962): 144–55; D. J. Pittman and W. F. Handy, "Uniform Crime Reporting: Suggested Improvements," *Sociology and Social Research* 46 (1962): 135–43; Thorsten Sellin, "The Significance of Records of Crime," *Law Quarterly Review* 67 (1951): 489–504; Marvin E. Wolfgang, "Uniform Crime Reports: A Critical Appraisal," *University of Pennsylvania Law Review* 111 (1963): 708–38.
15. For a review of the NCS, see James Garofalo and Michael J. Hindelang, *An Introduction to the National Crime Survey* (Washington, D.C.: U.S. Government Printing Office, 1977).
16. Ennis, *Criminal Victimization in the United States.*
17. For further discussion of and suggested remedies for the limitations of the NCS, see Garofalo and Hindelang, *An Introduction to the National Crime Survey.*
18. These violent crimes are defined as follows by the U.S. Department of Justice, Federal Bureau of Investigation, *Uniform Crime Reports for the United States, 1982* (Washington, D.C.: U.S. Government Printing Office, 1983):

Murder and nonnegligent manslaughter . . . is the willful (nonnegligent) killing of one human being by another (p. 6).

Forcible rape is the carnal knowledge of a female forcibly and against her will . . . assaults or attempts to commit rape by force or threat of force are also included; however, statutory rape (without force) and other sex offenses are not included in this category (p. 13).

Robbery is the taking or attempting to take anything of value from the care, custody, or control of a person or persons by force or threat of force or violence and/or by putting the victim in fear (p. 16).

Aggravated assault is an unlawful attack by one person upon another for the purpose of inflicting severe or aggravated bodily injury. This type of assault is usually accompanied by the use of a weapon or by means likely to produce death or great bodily harm. Attempts are included since it is not necessary that an injury result when a gun, knife, or other weapon is used which could and probably would result in serious personal injury if the crime were successfully completed (p. 20).

19. Donald J. Mulvihill, Melvin M. Tumin, and Lynn A. Curtis, *Crimes of Violence,* a Staff Report Submitted to the National Commission on the Causes and Prevention of Violence (Washington, D.C.: U.S. Government Printing Office, 1969), 11: 53–56.
20. Ibid., p. 53.
21. Ibid.
22. Violence Commission, *To Establish Justice, To Insure Domestic Tranquility,* p. 19.
23. Mulvihill, Tumin, and Curtis, *Crimes of Violence,* 11: Tables 1, 2, pp. 54, 58; Figure 1, p. 55.
24. Ibid., Table 1, p. 54.
25. Ibid., Table 2, p. 58.
26. *UCR* data reviewed in the following discussion were obtained from U.S. Department of Justice, Federal Bureau of Investigation, *Uniform Crime Reports for the United States, 1969–82* (Washington, D.C.: U.S. Government Printing Office, 1970–83).
27. NCS data reviewed in the following discussion were obtained from U.S. Department of Justice, National Criminal Justice Information and Statistics Service, *Criminal Victimization in the United States, 1973–77* (Washington, D.C.: U.S. Government Printing Office, 1976, 1977, 1977, 1979, 1979); U.S. Department of Justice, Bureau of Justice Statistics, *Criminal Victimization in the United States, 1978–1980* (Washington, D.C.: U.S. Government Printing Office, 1980, 1981, 1982).
28. Mulvihill, Tumin, and Curtis, *Crimes of Violence,* 11: 53–59.
29. Ibid.
30. This was the conclusion reached by the Bureau of Justice Statistics in a memorandum from Benjamin H. Renshaw, acting director, Bureau of Justice Statistics, to Attorney General William French Smith, December 2, 1981.
31. For a brief statement about the procedure, see Mulvihill, Tumin, and Curtis, *Crimes of Violence,* 11: 56, 130, fn. 21.
32. Ibid., p. 56. The Violence Commission assumed that on the average two offenders participated in each violent index offense. Data collected subsequently by the NCS have shown that this figure is closer to one and one-half. Approximately 65 percent of the violent victimizations (including rapes, personal-sector robberies, and both aggravated and simple assaults) were committed by a single offender, 13 percent by two offenders, 7 percent by three offenders, and 8 percent by four or more offenders. (In about 7 percent of the cases, this information was either unknown or unavailable.) Therefore, for every 100 violent victimizations, approximately 150 offenders took part, which is 1.5 offenders per violent victimization. To preserve continuity with the Violence Commission, we use the figure of two offenders per victimization, which is not unreasonable given that the number used by the commission and the number derived from the NCS are not very

different. For information on the numbers of offenders per victimization, see U.S. Department of Justice, National Criminal Justice Information and Statistics Service, *Criminal Victimization in the United States, 1973,* Table 53, p. 95; *Criminal Victimization in the United States, 1974,* Table 53, p. 50; *Criminal Victimization in the United States, 1975,* Table 57, p. 52; *Criminal Victimization in the United States, 1976,* Table 59, p. 58; *Criminal Victimization in the United States, 1977,* Table 60, p. 52; U.S. Department of Justice, Bureau of Justice Statistics, *Criminal Victimization in the United States, 1978,* Table 61, p. 56; *Criminal Victimization in the United States, 1979,* Table 61, p. 60; *Criminal Victimization in the United States, 1980,* Table 61, p. 57.

To estimate the number of persons responsible for serious violent crimes, we multiply the average number of offenders per violent offense (which in the present case is two) by the rate of *UCR* violent index crimes for a particular year. This yields the number of violent index offenders per 100,000 population.

*UCR* statistics undercount the amount of violent crime: according to the NCS by at least a factor of 3 for rape, robbery, and aggravated assault (see table 8 in this report). To adjust for this, we multiply by 3 the product of the average number of offenders per offense and the combined *UCR* violent index crime rate for a particular year. (Here we differ from the Violence Commission, which adjusted for undercounting by multiplying by a factor of 2.) This computation yields the estimated number of violent index offenders per 100,000 population.

To illustrate: In 1969 and 1981 the combined violent index crime rates (per 100,000 population) were 328.7 and 576.9, respectively (table 6). First we multiply each rate by 2 (offenders per offense) and then we multiply each of these products by 3 (to adjust for undercounting), which produces estimates of 1,972.0 seriously violent offenders per 100,000 population in 1969 and 3,461.0 in 1981.

If we divide the estimated number of seriously violent offenders for these two years into the base population of 100,000, we obtain offender probabilities of approximately one chance in fifty of an American being a seriously violent offender in 1969 and nearly one chance in thirty in 1981.

To estimate the total number of Americans who might have participated in these violent offenses in the years 1969 and 1981, we take the estimated total population of the United States in each year (203,216,000 in 1969 and 229,307,000 in 1981), divide each by 100,000, and then multiply each result by the number of violent offenders per 100,000 population in that year. This procedure yields figures of 4,007,420 for 1969 and 7,936,315 for 1981. Population data were obtained from U.S. Bureau of the Census, Current Population Reports, *Estimates of the Population of the United States by Age, Race, and Sex, July 1, 1969* (Washington, D.C.: U.S. Government Printing Office, 1969), Table 2, p. 2; *Preliminary Estimates of the Population of the United States by Age, Sex, and Race: 1970 to 1981* (Washington, D.C.: U.S. Government Printing Office, 1982), Table 2, p. 26.

33. Mulvihill, Tumin, and Curtis, *Crimes of Violence,* 11: 62–69.

34. Ibid., pp. 69–80. The regional breakdowns by states are as follows: *Northeast:* Connecticut, Maine, Massachusetts, New Hampshire, New Jersey, New York, Pennsylvania, Rhode Island, Vermont; *North Central:* Illinois, Indiana, Iowa, Kansas, Michigan, Minnesota, Missouri, Nebraska, North Dakota, Ohio, South Dakota, Wisconsin; *South:* Alabama, Arkansas, Delaware, District of Columbia, Florida, Georgia, Kentucky, Louisiana, Maryland, Mississippi, North Carolina, Oklahoma, South Carolina, Tennessee, Texas, Virginia, West Virginia; *West:* Alaska, Arizona, California, Colorado, Hawaii, Idaho, Montana, Nevada, New Mexico, Oregon, Puerto Rico, Utah, Washington, Wyoming.

35. Ibid., pp. 80–96.

36. Prior to 1974, annual *UCR* arrest statistics presented by age, sex, and race were compiled

from state and local reporting agencies which submitted arrest information for the full year. However, since 1974, annual arrest statistics have been collected from reporting agencies which submit information for at least six months of the year. From 1974 onward, therefore, arrests are undercounted and, as a consequence, rates based on these figures will be somewhat low, but precisely how low cannot be determined from the published *UCR* data. Data reported for the years 1969 to 1973 are, therefore, not directly comparable to those reported for 1974 to 1981. Examination of the tables presented in this report that are based on these statistics does not show a marked discontinuity between statistics for these two time periods. Therefore, we cautiously proceed in our use of these data as part of a single analysis.

37. See U.S. Bureau of the Census, Current Population Reports, *Estimates of the Population of the United States,* Table 2, p. 2; *Preliminary Estimates of the Population of the United States,* Table 2, pp. 26–43.
38. U.S. Bureau of the Census, Current Population Reports, *Preliminary Estimates of the Population of the United States,* Table 2, pp. 26–43.
39. Ibid.; U.S. Bureau of the Census, Current Population Reports, *Estimates of the Population of the United States,* Table 2, p. 2.
40. Mulvihill, Tumin, and Curtis, *Crimes of Violence,* 11: 130–31, fn. 24, pp. 207–58.
41. NCS data on the race and sex of the offender are obtained from interviews with victims. Technically, therefore, offender characteristics are based on the victim's perception. Text discussion of this material should be understood in this light.
42. U.S. Department of Justice, National Criminal Justice Information and Statistics Service, *Criminal Victimization in the United States, 1976,* Tables 38, 43, pp. 46, 49.
43. Mulvihill, Tumin, and Curtis, *Crimes of Violence,* 11: 226.
44. Marvin E. Wolfgang and Paul E. Tracy, Jr., "The 1945 and the 1958 Birth Cohorts: A Comparison of the Prevalence, Incidence, and Severity of Delinquent Behavior," paper presented at the Conference on Public Danger, Dangerousness, Dangerous Offenders, and the Criminal Justice System, sponsored by Harvard University and the John F. Kennedy School of Government, Boston, February 11–12, 1982, Tables 6a–b, pp. 16–18.
45. Ibid., Tables 8a–b, pp. 16–18.
46. For example, see Donna M. Hamparian, Simon Dinitz, R. S. Schuster, and John P. Conrad, *The Violent Few: A Study of Dangerous Juvenile Offenders* (Lexington, Mass.: D. C. Heath, 1978); Lyle W. Shannon, "A Longitudinal Study of Delinquency and Crime," in *Quantitative Studies in Criminology,* ed. Charles Wellford (Beverly Hills: Sage, 1978).
47. Mulvihill, Tumin, and Curtis, *Crimes of Violence,* 11: 117–20, 123–25.
48. Ibid., Figures 50a–b, pp. 118–19.
49. Ibid., Figures 54–56, pp. 123–27.
50. Ibid., p. 124; emphasis in original.

# 2

# Crimes of Violence and Public Policy: Changing Directions

ELLIOTT CURRIE

Writing in 1969, in a time of extraordinary social upheaval and frightening rises in the reported rate of violent crime, the Violence Commission offered a fearful scenario of what American cities might look like in "a few more years" in the absence of "effective public action."

Central business districts, surrounded by zones of "accelerating deterioration," would be reasonably protected even in the daytime only because large numbers of people would be working or shopping under the watchful protection of the police. Except for police patrols, the districts would be largely deserted at night. "Upper-middle and high-income populations" would huddle in "fortified cells"—high-rise apartments and residential compounds complete with elaborate security devices and private guards. Homes would be "fortified by an array of devices from window grilles to electronic surveillance equipment"; armed citizen patrols would supplement inadequate police in neighborhoods near the central city.

The more affluent would speed along heavily patrolled expressways which—in the Vietnam-era military language that often popped up, consciously or otherwise, in discussions of domestic social policy—would be "sanitized corridors" connecting "safe areas." Cars and taxis would be "routinely" equipped with unbreakable glass and even "light armor." Armed guards would ride "shotgun" on public transportation. Ghetto slums would be "places of terror" that might be entirely out of police control after dark. Schools and other public facilities would be patrolled by armed guards. Those who had business in or near the central city would have access to inside garages or valet parking.[1]

When the commission's *Final Report* was released in late 1969, this scenario was one of the things that interested the media and the public most strongly. I can remember, in fact, thinking at the time that it was a usefully overwrought portrait—one that exaggerated the terrors before us considerably, but did so deliberately, in the wholly justifiable cause of spurring public action against the roots of urban violence.

But the "few years" have passed, and what most strikes me today about the commission's scenario is that, with some exceptions, it came true to such an extent that we now simply take most of it for granted. There are a couple of false notes; the bit about "light armor" on the cars *was* over-wrought, and though there have been some armed patrols in areas threatened by high crime, they haven't been a *common* response in the cities.

But much of the rest of the portrait has, by the 1980s, become simply the stuff of routine urban life. Not all cities fit the picture, but many do. I was struck by this during a recent foray into the newly "revitalized" downtown area of a large, high-crime western city that shall remain nameless. The high-rise buildings were there, all right. Most of them seemed, indeed, to be banks; they gleamed and glittered and fairly oozed urban prosperity. But the guards were there, too—inside the buildings, in the lobbies *and* in the elevators; outside the buildings, in the parking garages (imagine the commission, in 1969, thinking it worthy of note that downtown visitors would insist on protected parking!) and in the immaculate, if mainly deserted, plaza between the buildings.

Almost literally a stone's throw away is a towering new jail that, along with the banks, has been the *other* big architectural transformation downtown. Unlike the banks, the jail is built of gray stone with narrow slits for windows, not wide expanses of tinted glass and steel, but it is almost equally imposing.

A few blocks from downtown you can indeed find armed guards in school yards and in the housing projects and in some of the remaining neighborhood stores as well. In some of the better-heeled suburbs, you can indeed find electronic home security devices on a scale and sophistication reserved for military operations back in the sixties. Meanwhile this city's ghettos *are* "places of terror," though there are cities that are considerably worse in this regard. The "sanitized corridor" metaphor is probably a little strong for this city, but it is not for some others, where people do sometimes lose their lives because their cars stall in the wrong part of town. In a neighboring big city, the police department politely, but officially, tells tourists simply to avoid traveling through the ghetto areas nearest to downtown if at all possible and, if not, to keep windows rolled up, doors locked, and avoid stopping their cars at all costs.

The figures, of course, tell the same story. In 1968, when the commission began its deliberations, the national homicide rate as measured by the Uniform Crime Reports was 6.8 per 100,000. In 1981, there was much celebration in the media because the rate had fallen slightly—to 9.8—from 10.2 of the year before.[2] The jump between 1968 and 1980 in this, the most reliable of indicators of criminal violence, amounted to exactly 50 percent.

Overall rates of criminal violence have apparently fallen slightly from their peak in 1980, but the comfort we can take from this is small. So far, crime rates haven't fallen below their usual late-1970s' levels; they've only returned to a more typical course after the sudden upward surge at the close of the decade. More important, though the recent decline is certainly welcome, its sources are mysterious. We don't know why it happened nor whether any particular policy or set of policies can take any credit for it. It's sometimes said that the decline reflects the effect of community crime prevention programs, but it isn't clear that such programs are, nationally, more widespread or much better designed than they were in 1980, when violent crime apparently rose sharply. The recent decline is also sometimes attributed to tougher sentencing, and it's certainly true that we have locked more offenders up than ever before in recent years. But that trend began *well* before the fractional decline in violent crimes in the past two years, and it coincided with the opposite trend—sharply *rising* criminal violence— in the late 1970s.

Moreover, looked at more closely, the *pattern* of this decline is also somewhat mystifying. If we look at age-specific rates of homicide victimization, for example, from recent vital statistics data, we learn a puzzling fact about the slight decline in homicide between 1980 and 1981. That decline took place for some age groups but not others. It was sharpest among infants under one year, while homicide death rates *rose* slightly both for other children under fourteen and for adults aged thirty-five to forty-four, as well as for some older adults, including those sixty-five to seventy-four and over eighty-five (but *not* those aged seventy-five to eighty-four).[3] What do we make of this? Someone may have an explanation, but I don't. What it suggests to me is that we know very little about the meaning of either the recent decline or the only slightly less recent upward spurt in violent crime that preceded it.

Meanwhile, our more general situation is clearly, and painfully, apparent. Overall, violent crime has risen substantially since the Violence Commission's report. Even then, as the commission noted, with irony, the United States was the "clear leader" among otherwise comparable societies in its high levels of criminal violence.[4] In many cases, those disparities have *risen* since the sixties. Even more than when the commission wrote, the United States more closely resembles some less developed countries of the Third World in this respect than it does any other advanced industrial society.

What's especially troubling about our present situation is that it exists in the face of a decade and a half of extraordinarily intensive anticrime efforts. Indeed, the seventies and early eighties have been unique in the degree to which vast social and economic resources, as well as a good deal of human ingenuity, were poured—sometimes recklessly, sometimes with considerable care and creativity—into the fight against crime. Since the commission wrote, we have doubled the national incarceration rate, spent enormous sums on police hardware and software, instituted thousands of local crime prevention programs, "hardened" our "targets" through the extensive application of security measures to homes and businesses, and, not least, changed our daily routines in a multitude of ways to avoid victimization. All this, according to common sense and even to some criminological theory, *should* have helped the crime problem a great deal more than it did.

Instead, by the early eighties, we had reached what was widely regarded as a frustrating and depressing impasse. *Newsweek*'s cover story on crime in 1981 reflected the sentiment well, noting that the response to violent crime had become a "dispiriting malaise" and that we had lost the "old optimism proclaiming that we know what the problems are and that we have the solutions at hand." *Newsweek* concluded its gloomy review with the suggestion that we learn "not to expect too much,"[5] a quietism that was echoed by the Reagan administration's Task Force on Violent Crime, which opted out of even seriously *considering* the causes of crime as a possible subject for public policy, citing the "risks of assuming that the government can solve whatever problem it addresses."[6]

Is this impasse inevitable? I don't think so. As I have elsewhere argued,[7] I think we know a great deal more about the causes of crime than much fashionable argument since the mid-1970s has suggested; and that we also know a great deal more about what, broadly, we might do about it. Out of the increasingly sophisticated research and program experience of the past several years, there is emerging what, I think, promises to be a fruitful series of new directions in dealing with violent crime. In what follows, I won't attempt to give a detailed description of those directions; some of them are treated in other chapters in this volume. Instead, I want to sketch what I take to be some of their broad, thematic outlines, the guiding principles that seem to me to distinguish them from the dominant approaches to violent crime in the recent past. One way to begin is to consider briefly the outlines of what has gone before.

Since the mid-1970s, the strategy most consistently adopted against crime in America has been one designed to increase the levels of incarceration of serious offenders. In the most superficial sense, this strategy has been an enormous success. We have doubled our rate of state prison incarceration in the past decade, and our often noted world prominence in this regard has grown; if we were the world's leader in imprisonment rates a decade ago, we're now leaving most of the competition in the dust, despite the pale efforts of some of our would-be competitors, like Mrs. Thatcher's Britain.

What this has done to the fabric of institutional life inside the correctional system is well known. What it has done to the fabric of community life in the high-risk areas that disproportionately supply the recruits to the swelling inmate army is less well understood. But it must be considerable, given the astonishingly high proportions of young men from disadvantaged communities—particularly minority communities—who have been signed up.

What is clear is that it hasn't done much about *crime*. This is especially clear, because—unlike most other social experiments—this one has been implemented on such a large scale and with a single-mindedness bordering on ferocity.

At the best interpretation, it could be argued that it has simply taken all these years for the strategy of raising the "costs" of crime to really hit its stride and that the recent decline in crime attests to that strategy's emerging success. Yet even if we were to grant that the recent decline is both significant *and* largely due to the incapacitative and/or deterrent impact of doubling the incarceration rate—both of which are not altogether unreasonable, but do require a substantial leap of faith of a sort not usually permitted in the evaluation of social experiments—we are left, at best, with a remarkably meager payoff for the enormous, costly, and disruptive investment of social resources involved.

Moreover, this has been a thoroughly unsurprising outcome. Virtually all the serious research available to us—best summarized in the National Academy of Sciences's review of the deterrence and incapacitation literature in 1978[8]—suggested that very large increases in incarceration might result in small decreases in serious crime. I, for one, would be quite surprised if our putting an extra fifty thousand young American adults in prison between 1980 and 1982 had *no* effect on the crime rate. But the hard facts tell us that, even on the most generous reading, whatever effect it has had has been small, which is precisely what the research would have led us to expect.

Ultimately, it seems clear that the incarcerative strategy of the past decade failed because its most fundamental premise was simply wrong. Stated most generally—but I don't think unfairly—that premise was that the level of crime was rising primarily because the "costs" of crime in America were too low. In turn, this was at least loosely based on the suspiciously simple, but doubtless appealing, tenets of neoclassical economics that regarded criminal behavior, like all other behavior, as the outcome of a more or less rational calculation of costs and benefits.

Rising crime, from this view, was a clear signal that the costs of illegal behavior were falling; hence the mandate for social policy was to increase the costs by making punishment a more likely and/or more severe consequence.[9]

More was wrong with this argument than can be dealt with in a single article, but two particularly egregious flaws stand out. First, even were we to grant its picture of the nature of the imbalance between the costs and benefits of behavior in the United States, the *resolution* of that imbalance this argument offered didn't follow from the premises. As the Vera Institute's researchers pointed out in their recent review of economic approaches to crime, a strategy that placed most of its bets on increasing the benefits of "straight" behavior is an equally logical outcome of the cost-benefit approach of neoclassical theory.[10] It seems clear that the reasons that path wasn't chosen have little to do with logic *or* theory and a great deal to do with broader social and political agendas that were usually left unexpressed.

The second flaw was, if anything, even worse. For, as has often been pointed out, the United States was already one of the most prison-happy societies in the advanced industrial world. The conjunction of that fact with the American "leadership" in serious criminal violence should have been cause for reflection among those who were partisans of the strategy of increasing crime's costs. Apparently, it wasn't, despite the fact that the paradox of uniquely high imprisonment rates *and* uniquely high rates of individual violence intensified through the 1970s.

By the 1980s, those who still clung to this view were often forced to resort to strategies of argument that were decreasingly credible. Thus James Q. Wilson, confronted with the stark testimony of these international differences, insisted in a 1982 article on the curious point that the concern of social scientists should be restricted to the *similarities* among different countries, not their differences[11]—an adage that may come as something of a surprise to social scientists toiling in the fields of comparative research.

Does the apparent failure of an approach based mainly on increasing the costs of crime suggest that we may simply return to the more complex— and more generous—principles of the sixties? I don't think so, for several reasons. One, not the most important, is that there really wasn't one single, easily identifiable "liberal" approach to crime before the seventies; there were instead several loosely connected strands, not all of them compatible. But more important, the conventional criminological liberalism isn't enough. It had much to recommend it, and indeed, it has been unfairly maligned, along with the rest of Great Society liberalism, in more recent and less humane times. But we will need to move beyond it, incorporating its enduring insights while consciously transcending its limitations, if we are to be both serious and credible about crime in the eighties.

We may better understand both the strengths and the limits of this criminological tradition if we look more closely at the Violence Commission's own treatment of the problem of violent crime. This is not, by any means, to single out the commission's work as either unique or particularly limited in the context of its time. On the contrary, the commission's treatment of violent crime represented the fruits of some of the best, and most representative, thinking and research available in the sixties. Because of that, we can think of it as an important source, along with the 1967 crime commission reports, of the best of the criminological tradition that was at least partly abandoned during the decade of the 1970s. We can still learn a great deal from these efforts. Rereading the reports and materials of both commissions roughly a decade and a half later often produces pleasant surprises, for they are valuable compendia of usually solid and often still illuminating research. (In any case, I should hasten to point out that I do not exempt myself from my own criticisms of this tradition; I was part of it, and I don't regret it.) To hold the commission's treatment of violent crime—and the tradition it represents—up to scrutiny is simply one step toward defining some of the differences between where we were then and where, I think, we are today.

In its *Final Report,* the commission adopted what is called a two-pronged approach to the problem of urban violence generally and to violent crime in particular. That is, it recommended a strategy along two broad fronts. It proposed a variety of enhanced measures of "control" encapsulated in the recommendation to "double our investment" in the system of criminal justice. At the same time, the commission insisted that increased control was not enough by itself and that "safety in our cities requires nothing less than progress in reconstructing urban life."[12] This double emphasis put the commission squarely in the tradition of earlier ones, notably the Katzenbach Commission, in both insisting on the importance of an effective system of justice *and* recognizing that crime was emphatically not simply a criminal justice matter. Indeed, one of the enduring contributions of the criminological tradition of which the commission was a part was precisely its fundamental understanding that crime and the criminal justice system are not the same issue, that there are indeed roots of crime above and beyond the reach of even the most effective system of justice we might be able to devise.

But at the same time, seen closer up, both sides of the commission's recommended strategy left too much unanswered. On the "control" side,  the commission's main recommendation was to "double our investment" in the criminal justice system. That is, it saw the problems of that system primarily as resulting from a lack of resources (secondarily, from bad management). And it suggested that a massive infusion of funds into the system would go a long way toward resolving them. It's *this* side of the commission's two-sided strategy that came, in fact, to pass, rather than its equally strong emphasis on "social reconstruction"—an outcome that, of course, is hardly the commission's fault.

The more immediate question is whether the commission's approach to the needs of the criminal justice system itself was the appropriate one. And the answer, I think, is—not entirely. Indeed, some of the commission's own background research suggested a somewhat different emphasis.

Thus, for reasons it made compellingly clear, the commission's discussion of criminal violence focused on the violence of ghetto youth. The commission's Task Force on Violent Crime commissioned several background papers that threw considerable light on the criminal justice system's response to that violence. The overview of the state of knowledge about youth corrections in Lamar Empey's consultant report, for example, ought to have been one of the most relevant in shaping the commission's conclusions. Yet Empey's review led to rather different conclusions than those put forward in the *Final Report*. What Empey showed was that, on the best reading of the available recent research and program evaluation, alternative programs outside the formal criminal justice system seemed to do no worse, and perhaps better, than formal corrections for delinquent youth. And since most of the alternatives were cheaper substitutes for more formal processing for many less dangerous offenders, the net result of a more careful, selective use of the correctional apparatus might well be more efficiency for less cost.[13]

The Empey review, in other words, suggested a strategy of what we could now, I think, call careful targeting of limited criminal justice resources, based on an assessment of the differing requirements of different types of offenders. The *Final Report*, on the other hand, concluded in effect that the most urgently needed response to the problems of criminal justice was to throw money at them.

This attitude was, again, by no means confined to the commission; it was widespread (though of course not universal) in criminal justice thinking in the late 1960s, and it had an unfortunate influence on the growth of the criminal justice system in the 1970s. It helped turn that system into what was often an oversized, underconceptualized set of bureaucracies, which raised expectations about their ability to affect the crime rate that couldn't be fulfilled and which diverted both attention and funds from other alternatives—notably the search for ways of strengthening the infrastructure of local communities and enhancing *their* capacity to deal with problems of crime and disorder, an issue to which I'll return shortly.

Obviously, this wasn't the whole story. As Norval Morris and Alan Gordon point out elsewhere in this volume, much that was serious-minded and creative did come out of federally sponsored research and program development during the 1970s. Some of that research and experimentation will necessarily form part of the base for a more careful and innovative approach to criminal justice in the 1980s. But most of these more creative efforts were *not* ones that called for massive infusions of money, and those that did—prison and jail construction or police technology, for example— brought no discernible results in the reduction of violence.

It's difficult to avoid the obvious, chronologically jarring parallel with the events in Southeast Asia. In both realms, conventional liberal wisdom sought to resolve problems that were fundamentally social and communal in nature through the use of high technology and big money. In both realms, the "solutions" were bound to fail, not least because they misread the nature of the problem.

In the case of domestic criminal justice, it was apparent in the late 1960s that, in crucial ways, the self-regulating mechanisms of many urban communities in America had broken down. The most logical response would have been to think more about how to recreate those mechanisms and less about ways of replacing them with bigger, more distant, and more expensive means of "control"—especially since there was little in the research or theoretical literature to indicate why such a replacement should be expected to lower the crime rate.

Even more important, however, to the fate of what I have called liberal criminology was what seems, with the advantage of hindsight, to have been a fundamental confusion about just what it meant to do on the other side of the ledger—the part of the dual strategy that proposed to deal with the social "roots" of crime through what the Violence Commission called "social reconstruction."

The *Final Report*'s opening remarks about this were strong ones; it declared that "the way in which we can make the greatest progress toward reducing violence in America is by taking the actions necessary to improve the conditions of family and community life for all who live in our cities, and especially for the poor who are concentrated in the ghetto slums."[14]

This was surely a worthy goal, hard to improve upon. It was also, as Clarence Shrag noted in his background review of sociological theories of criminal violence, "a large order."[15] But the commission was notably vague about how to do this—about exactly what points of intervention would offer the most leverage in improving the lives of the disadvantaged in ways that might reduce crime. Indeed, the *Final Report*'s main recommendation in this regard seemed, again, to be somewhat tangential to the more detailed analysis the commission developed elsewhere, particularly in its staff report on crimes of violence.

For once again, the commission's most emphatic and clear-cut proposal was more money—in this case, $20 billion in increased federal spending for the "general welfare." In the commission's discussion, the "general welfare" was apparently meant in its broad sense, to encompass virtually every category of nondefense spending.[16] The commission was certainly correct in arguing that the then-current levels of spending on the Vietnam War were draining funds from domestic purposes. But the proposal to fight crime on the reconstruction side of the ledger by finding $20 billion to spend at home left too much unclear. Would we spend the $20 billion on summer job programs? On higher income-maintenance payments? On higher police salaries? On housing subsidies? All these possible uses of money for the "general welfare" were at least implied at one or another point in the report. But there was little analysis of how exactly such sums would be used to "reconstruct" community and family life.

The *Final Report* did reaffirm a number of broad and worthy goals, including giving every American a decent home, taking "steps" to fulfill the mandate of the Employment Act of 1946, providing "better educational opportunities" for all our children and basic income maintenance for those who could not care for themselves, and restoring the "fiscal vitality" of local governments.[17] But these goals, while well intentioned, were very general indeed. The report's chapter on crimes of violence, moreover, explicitly shrugged off the responsibility of suggesting more detailed programmatic responses to the reconstruction of urban communities. Those programs, the commission insisted, "must be worked out in the normal functioning of our political processes."[18] While that was certainly a realistic depiction of how social programs do in fact get worked out, it left us with nothing very tangible by way of programmatic analysis to bring to the political process, no solid sense of what programs might, on the basis of the evidence, be worth fighting for. Though it offered a strong vision of social responsibility to deal with the roots of violence, in short, the vision was relatively unfocused. As a result, the recommendations tended to blur a variety of somewhat different aims without a clear sense of the theoretical or empirical rationale behind them.

Here again, there was material in the commission's other reports that could have provided the basis for a more focused response. The Task Force on Crimes of Violence, for example, had placed considerable emphasis on the specific impact of the labor market on the ghetto. The task force pointed out that, in addition to blacks' having twice the white unemployment rate, "71% of all Negro workers are concentrated in the lowest paying and lowest skilled occupations."[19] As one response, the task force called for macroeconomic policies to maintain high levels of employment and income. But it also noted that "general macroeconomic policies will not alone suffice" to bring deprived groups into the mainstream and that we would also need private and public work programs, "vigorous" antidiscrimination policies, and programs to develop ghetto business. Even more cogently, it pointed to the criminogenic effects of "changing job technologies, agricultural overproduction, vast migrations of rural blacks and whites to cities." And it insisted that all these issues (and others) were "not individual problems with separate solutions," but "one problem."[20]

Both insights were remarkably prescient and, I think, correct. Properly understood, both pointed to concrete, if still broad, areas for policy intervention. The emphasis on the inadequacy of employment in the ghetto pointed, as the task force noted, to the crucial need for direct intervention into the labor market. The recognition of the larger disruptive impact of regional and technological change pointed squarely to the need for at least rudimentary economic planning. Both points got somewhat lost in the commission's *Final Report*. It is fruitless to speculate about why, and in any case it would take us off the point, for this anomaly, as I have already argued, was by no means unique to the Violence Commission. Indeed, the commission went further than most public policy analysis of the sixties in its farsighted recognition of the relationship between urban crime and rural economic transformation. It therefore raised more seriously than most previous discussions the need to think, in policy terms, about the linkages between crime and broader patterns of economic development.

The difficulty was that the commission did not systematically draw out some of the most important *policy* implications of these linkages. Again, this was traditional. For one of the central characteristics of much of the serious policy-oriented literature in crime in the 1960s was some version of this curious split between analysis and program, between description and prescription. The well-known, and indeed stirring, declaration of the Katzenbach Commission—that warring on poverty and poor housing was warring on crime, that money for schools was money against crime, that "*every* effort to improve life in America's inner cities is an effort against crime,"[21] which the Violence Commission took as an honored predecessor of its own views—illustrates the same problem. First, in its scattergun quality—was *every* effort to improve inner-city life really likely to be equally productive of reductions in crime? Second, in its vagueness—war on poverty *how*? Through higher welfare payments? Community economic development? And third, again, in its bias toward viewing most solutions as fiscal ones. Were we so sure, for example, that the *main* problem with urban education was simply a lack of money, and were we sure we knew what we'd use the money for?

All of this, multiplied throughout many discussions of public policy during the 1960s, gave an impression of something less than analytical rigor and something less than fiscal realism, and both helped speed the downfall of what I have loosely called the liberal approach to crime in the 1970s. That the dominant approach that followed also lacked both rigor and realism doesn't detract from the real vulnerability of an approach to crime that often at least seemed to say that giving people more welfare or more new school buildings or sending some ghetto families to live in new housing in the suburbs would necessarily reduce crime.

That sort of position left this tradition in criminology wide open to attack in the 1970s, most importantly because it could indeed be shown that public money for such archetypical liberal urban programs as school construction, income maintenance, and urban renewal didn't stop crime. Indeed, this wasn't really surprising, since there was, in fact, little grounds in either the theoretical or empirical literature to suggest that they would.

Put in another way, the social side of the liberal criminology of the 1960s often seemed unable to distinguish between a reactive, welfarist strategy toward what it understood to be the socioeconomic roots of crime and a more active approach that would focus most heavily on the twin issues of economic development and stable employment. To be sure, the latter was—and is—a large order. But it is also a more realistic strategy over the long run and one that accords much better with most of the theory and empirical evidence we have—much of which we also had in the 1960s.

By tackling head-on the forces that both destroyed livelihoods and split family and community ties, such a strategy would have held out the promise of something like the genuine reconstruction of community life the Violence Commission (and many others) rightly called for. As it was, with important exceptions, much social policy toward the urban disadvantaged necessarily took the form of picking up after what the British social theorist Richard Titmuss used to call the "diswelfare state"[22] had done its dirty work. People whose chances for a decent and productive working life within a recognizable community had been shattered were certainly better off with income support and publicly supported housing and food stamps than they were without them. But while these other measures cushioned the suffering and boosted the income statistics, they did little to reduce the harsh inequalities of urban life or to create conditions of communal cohesion or integrative work—all of which were the more relevant problems in criminological terms.

Something similar may be said about another key strand in this earlier tradition, the idea that crime would be reduced by improving "opportunities" for the disadvantaged. With hindsight, it seems clear that this idea was susceptible to different interpretations which had importantly different consequences for public policy. It could mean improving opportunities for individuals to rise out of a generally unsatisfactory environment into something better; or it could mean transforming the structure of the unsatisfactory environment itself and thus upgrading the entire scale of opportunities. (Such a distinction bears some resemblance to the one in economic theory between "human capital" and "dual labor market" theories.)[23]

With important exceptions, notably in some of OEO's community-based programs and in local economic development strategies funded through CETA or the Economic Development Administration, the first interpretation most often guided public policy toward the disadvantaged. Indeed, one of the most common phrases in the lexicon of liberal criminology in the 1960s was the idea that crime might be reduced by developing means of helping individuals "escape their environment."[24] But the problem was, of course, what would happen to those who were—virtually by definition, in this model—left behind while others "escaped." If anything, there might be good theoretical reasons to believe that this kind of fragmentation of urban communities into more and less "successful" segments would tend to make urban crime worse, not better.

Much more might be said about these matters, but I don't want to labor the point. I've tried to suggest that both the dominant "conservative" criminology of the past decade and the more "liberal" approach that preceded it are no longer adequate responses to the realities of crime in the 1980s. But this needn't lead to the pessimism and shoulder shrugging of the past few years, for there is, I think, another direction available to us. For want of a better name, let me simply call it, for the moment, a "third stage." It is a direction that fits much better with the evidence we possess from empirical research and program results. It isn't yet, by any means, a thoroughly developed, clear-cut strategy against violent crime. But I do think we know enough to be able to sketch out some of the most important broad components of such a strategy, within which there is considerable room for debate, theoretical argument, research, and experimentation.

Most of those components have already been suggested. Some of them involve ways of looking at what we can expect from the criminal justice system. Others involve the role of alternative strategies of intervention with high-risk individuals, families, and communities. And still others involve ways of thinking about the kinds of larger social and economic interventions without which much of the rest will be limited at best, fruitless at worst.

1. *Criminal Justice: Not the Solution.* As I've already argued, time has not been kind to the idea that much can be gained by way of crime reductions through the sheer expansion of criminal justice resources.

It is possible to argue, of course, that we can do better in this regard by increasing the efficiency with which we channel the most serious offenders into incarceration. In the past few years, much attention has been given to the notion of selective incapacitation, the idea that we can develop methods to better predict those (relatively few) offenders who are at high risk of continuing careers of serious criminality.[25] On the basis of such prediction, we can isolate those extremely high-risk offenders for tougher sentencing, meanwhile presumably lightening up on the less dangerous. On the most abstract level, it is hard to quarrel with this as a general strategy. It is true that there are strong limitations on our capacity to predict "dangerousness" or future criminality. But it is also true that, for example, the research evidence indicates that an offender's past record is an important, if rough, predictor of that person's likelihood of serious criminality in the future.[26] I think it would be rash to say that *no* improvements in our ability to sort out selectively and process such people are possible. But it is even more rash to hope that we will achieve great strides in crime reduction through such improvements.

Why not? Primarily because we already—of course—use the principle of selective incapacitation, and we use it with both considerable logic and a level of success that usually doesn't leave very large margins for improvement. Every careful study we have indicates that once repeat offenders have been caught often enough for us to know that they are, in fact, dangerous repeaters, their chances of conviction and, once convicted, of incarceration are quite high.[27] Judges and prosecutors already (for the most part) do their best to selectively target their resources on the offenders they regard as most dangerous, and with exceptions, their best is not typically so bad—at least, not bad enough to justify the expectation of great improvements. Since we already incapacitate selectively, the real issue is whether the kinds of predictors of future offending developed in recent research would be substantially more effective than the less hard-and-fast ones used already in various jurisdictions. We don't know this, since we lack prospective experience with them. But some other factors also weaken the potential effects of selective incapacitation. One is that, as even its most ardent advocates acknowledge, it is useful, if at all, only for some crimes and not others; some of the most serious of violent crimes, especially homicide, are not very responsive to strategies of incapacitation.[28] Another is that such a strategy can only be invoked fairly late in an offender's career where it does the least good, since many of the predictive factors on which the strategy relies are measures of prior encounters with the criminal justice system.

Most of the best research developed in recent years suggests that the main locus of slippage in the criminal justice system is at its front end—especially at the stage of apprehension—rather than at the rear. If we are looking for *dramatic* improvements in the deterrent or incapacitative capacity of the formal justice system, they will have to come in increasing the risks of getting caught. This suggests that such improvements will come, if at all, through changes in police practices and, perhaps, in methods of integrating police and community efforts in more effective ways. But it's not yet clear how to do these things, and this isn't for want of trying.

A number of innovative strategies were carefully fielded and evaluated in the 1970s, without, on the whole, resounding results. Take foot patrol, a strategy specifically promoted by the Violence Commission in its *Final Report*.[29] It's a sound idea in principle, but the Police Foundation's recent experiment with increased foot patrol in Newark turned up no significant impact on serious crime. It may be true, as George Kelling and Mark Moore have argued, that such practices can help achieve a more diffuse goal of order maintenance in a community.[30] But this is a long step away from reducing crime. There is some suggestive evidence from the Hartford experiment that aggressive policing coupled with close police-community involvement may have some localized impact on the crime rate.[31] But we need to know much more before we can state with any confidence what, exactly, the police can do to stop crime that at least some of them are not doing already.

These limitations have sometimes been taken to mean that we can't expect *any* reductions in crime through changes in the courts or the police. I think that's exaggerated and needlessly stretches an already powerful point. What the evidence most clearly tells us, I think, is that any very helpful changes in the functioning of the criminal justice system are likely to be incremental ones, whose effects on the crime rate—while obviously impossible to predict—are unlikely to be large ones. Again, to believe otherwise requires us to believe that the justice system (as a whole) is now doing something dramatically *wrong,* something that it's within our capacity to correct through better programs, better management, or more money. It requires us to believe, in other words, that the margin for improvement is both wide and closeable. I do not think the available evidence supports either point. This does not, of course, foreclose the search for incremental reforms in efficiency or in equity within the justice system. It only forecloses magical thinking about what we may expect from them in terms of domestic tranquility.

2. *Strategies of Intervention: Individual, Family, Community.* One of the most damaging effects of an anticrime strategy that puts virtually all its chips on increasing the costs of crime through incarceration is that it allows only the most peripheral attention to other kinds of social intervention into the institutions of family, socialization, and community which we have good reason to believe are powerfully influential in generating crime. Even at best, as I think we've learned with much pain in recent years, such a strategy usually forces us to wait until one or several sometimes fearsome crimes are committed before we do anything to alter the course of personal and social development that the crimes represent.

Partly, I think, because of the wide promotion during the seventies of the idea that "nothing works" on this level,[32] we've lost considerable ground in the development, analysis, and careful evaluation of more preventive programs of this nature for individuals and families. And our understanding of preventive programs on the level of what I've called rebuilding the community infrastructure is even less developed. But I think some general points are warranted.

A. First, a revitalized criminology in the 1980s will necessarily pay renewed attention to the potential—sharply attacked on many sides during the 1970s—of what used to be called rehabilitation. The phrase was probably an unfortunate one, but the more general concept—of systematic intervention beyond simple punishment in the careers of high-risk individuals—can't simply be abandoned. To do so requires us to believe either that there is no such thing as serious individual pathology or that the threat of punishment is the only feasible way of dealing with it. Stated so flatly, neither stance seems credible.

Perhaps surprisingly, some of the same evidence often presented to support an anticrime strategy that relies heavily on incapacitation also supports (indeed more convincingly) an intensified search for more effective programs of intervention outside the correctional system.

As a recent California Youth Authority study of the prospects for early identification of "chronic" offenders points out, our ability to predict (within very broad limits) which offenders are most likely to continue in careers of serious crime does not lead, necessarily, to a strategy of selective incapacitation. It can just as easily lead to a strategy of selective treatment.[33] The logic of early identification, that is, lends itself just as easily to an emphasis on alternatives to incarceration as it does to correctional solutions. The key here, according to scattered but interesting research, is probably the *intensiveness* of alternative programs for offenders. A careful rereading of the full range of recent research (as the National Academy of Sciences panel on rehabilitation pointed out in 1979) leads to a more complex assessment than the one offered by the mid-1970s platitude that "nothing works." We know for sure that poorly conceived, inadequately funded programs for high-risk individuals don't work. But we have reason to suspect that some kinds of intensive and carefully designed and implemented programs might.[34]

B. A second realm of intervention is the family, and here, as in some other areas, the fit between theory and policy in the recent past has sometimes been difficult to discern. Both the Violence Commission and its predecessor, the Katzenbach Commission, surveyed existing literature on the relation between the family and crime and concluded that it was an important, if complex one. More recent research, both here and in England, has reaffirmed the connection. Families that are burdened by the stresses of poor income, lack of responsive social networks, internal conflict, and parental violence are, not too surprisingly, less able to ensure the kind of supervision and guidance that, in families with better resources, reduce the risks of youth criminality and violence.[35] Again, in fact, this is not an area of really substantial disagreement in the serious criminological literature. But its translation into effective policy has been uneven and intermittent. One reason, at least since the mid-1970s, has been the curious but widespread belief that "government" is powerless to affect the conditions surrounding family life,[36] a belief promoted most enthusiastically among some criminologists.

Fortunately, that belief didn't stifle other efforts during the 1970s to learn something about the potentials of active programs to provide resources and support to the kinds of families, particularly among the poor, for whom these problems—as we've known since the 1960s—are typically most severe. Much of the careful evaluation of some of the HEW-sponsored family support programs of the seventies, for example—notably the Child and Family Resource Centers—suggests that very substantial benefits in enhanced family functioning can be achieved with remarkably little cost. These programs provided a gamut of services ranging from child care and child-abuse counseling to family planning—and they apparently provided them well, achieving notable gains in parents' capacity to better manage their lives and to cope adequately with the demands of raising children.[37] Because these were not programs explicitly designed to test theories about the family and crime, their significance has not, I think, been adequately acknowledged by criminologists. But that's an unnecessarily circumscribed response; these programs are suggestive, deeply relevant from the viewpoint of criminological theory, and well worth pursuing.

C. A third line of intervention outside the formal justice system points toward the community. The theoretical underpinning for such an approach has several sources. One involves what we know about the importance of what in the criminological literature have traditionally been called informal sanctions. Throughout all the heated debate about the deterrent effects of various "tough" criminal justice policies, there has been, as far as I know, no convincing challenge to the more fundamental and long-standing argument in criminology that informal sanctions applied by family, peers, and community have more effect.[38] As I've suggested, that awareness doesn't logically lead us to ignore the potential uses of the criminal justice system, but it does point us strongly in the direction of enhancing the ability of these more informal, communal institutions to do their job.

From another angle, the same point is upheld by our growing recognition of the salience—for crime control as well as other social issues—of what have come to be called mediating structures.[39] From several disciplines at once, we are learning that there is something about the individual's degree of integration into local structures of kinship, neighborhood, and organization that is fateful for their prospects of mental health, physical well-being—and criminality. By now, it seems clear that an effective approach to criminal violence will have to pay far greater attention than it typically has in recent years to the health and functioning of these environing institutions.

Not that the importance of something called community is a new idea in criminology. On the contrary, it has long been a staple of classical criminological thinking, and it underlay, to some extent, the innumerable efforts at community crime prevention during the 1970s. Paul J. Lavrakas and Lynn A. Curtis review the promises and pitfalls of these programs elsewhere in this volume, so I'll only offer a couple of cautionary remarks.

The general impulse behind the idea of community prevention is a sound one, but I think it often carries more problematic baggage. The danger in the notion of community crime prevention is that it sometimes grants an almost mystical, idealized efficacy to an abstractly defined community altogether detached from the larger, environing forces that, in fact, make or break living communities in the real world. At its worst, this can degenerate into a kind of pulling-the-wagons-in-a-circle mentality, most likely to result, at best, in displacing crime from more "organizable" communities to those with fewer mobilized resources. Too often, this involves a peculiarly American tendency to place responsibilities on the local community that it cannot feasibly meet. And it sometimes comes packaged as part of a broader agenda aimed at dismantling the public sector in the name of a presumably healthier "voluntarism."[40] The fact that most comparable industrial societies with much lower crime rates also devote much more, not fewer, resources to the public sector does not, apparently, diminish the zeal of those who would turn most social functions over to cheerful volunteers. It's well to remember that what most clearly distinguishes the United States from other industrial societies with far lower rates of violent crime is not the lack of community crime prevention programs, narrowly conceived. It is, more significantly, the relative lack of some degree of social control over the broader socioeconomic context of community life that stands out most clearly in the United States—an issue to which I'll now turn.

3. *Social Reconstruction Reconsidered.* The other side of the Violence Commission's strategy was social reconstruction, or the transformation of the conditions of family and community life, especially for the disadvantaged. With some exceptions, the thrust of public policy since the commission wrote has not been congenial to that vision. But—given what I think we know about the connections between inadequate employment, harsh economic and racial inequality, and violent crime—it is time to say flatly that without some such vision there can be no believable strategy against crime.

But the vision needs to be somewhat more sharply focused than it was in the sixties, as I've already suggested. In the eighties, the evidence is clear enough that we won't make substantial progress against violent crime by strategies of merely increasing income and other material supports for the disadvantaged if that means allowing whole communities to fall into welfare dependency. Nor are we likely to make great strides by opening up "opportunities," through education and training, for offenders and potential offenders if there is no functioning labor market beyond the school or the training program.

I do not know of any serious empirical challenge to the assertion of the Task Force on Crimes of Violence in 1969 of the importance of inadequate labor markets in shaping the cycle of deprivation and crime in the cities. The best research since then—much of it summarized in the Vera Institute's recent review, *Employment and Crime*[41]—suggests that there are powerful links between the prospect of a life of intermittent, unstable, poorly paid employment and the risks of criminal violence. I don't think this is surprising, and for that matter, I don't think there is very much serious disagreement with it from any point on the political spectrum (except its more curious fringes).

I've argued elsewhere that "if there is a way to cope with violent inner-city youth crime while the official jobless rate for black youth hovers around 40 percent, we have yet to hear what it is."[42] A year later, the only difference is that the jobless rate for black youth now hovers around 50 percent. Just as there is no long-range criminal justice solution to the problem of violent crime, there is also no solution that does not include the restructuring of the labor market in the inner cities and depressed rural areas. Again, I don't think there is a serious argument that denies the strength of these connections. The argument really lies around whether—if at all—it's possible or desirable to transform those labor markets through explicit public policy. In practice, this boils down to a difference between those who, for whatever reasons, wish to keep the inner cities hostage to the vagaries of the private market and those who believe that reconstructing urban life will require substantial—and enduring—commitment to public funding and planning for employment, training, and local economic development.

I've noted already that the criminology of the sixties often raised these issues on the level of analysis only to drop them, for all practical purposes, on the level of policy. Some of the reasons no doubt have to do with the imperatives of politics; but others have to do with more fundamental conceptual questions—questions that, I think, must lie at the heart of a credible approach to criminal violence in the eighties.

Let me give a specific example. As I have noted, the Violence Commission pointed out at several places that the economic transformation of the rural South was intimately related to the problems of the cities and that, more generally, the rural-to-urban migrations of recent decades were deeply implicated in rising crime rates. Yet the commission's response to this crucial recognition was revealing: it described these problems as broad "demographic" ones.[43] Despite some brief nods to the notion that such matters might become the focus of policy, the most common posture of both public and private authorities at the time was that these issues of regional, economic, and technological change were things about which no one felt responsible.

The economist Geoffrey Faux has described this phenomenon as he witnessed it among Washington policymakers during the sixties. Faux notes that the infusion of federal aid to agriculture from the 1940s to the 1960s created an enormous increase in agricultural mechanization, which, on one side of the social and economic ledger, raised farm productivity greatly, but on the other side, threw millions of tenant farmers and farm workers out of livelihoods and into the cities. "During that time," Faux writes,

> I attended a briefing at the Agriculture Department at which researchers predicted (accurately it turned out) the rough magnitude and destination of the large numbers of Southern farmworkers who would be forced out of the tobacco fields. When I asked what was being done to create jobs for them, the answer was that the Agriculture Department's job was to increase farm productivity, not to alleviate urban poverty. Efforts to get other departments to address the problem were in vain; it wasn't their problem yet.

The social costs of this mentality, as Faux points out, were (and are) enormous.[44] In terms of understanding America's violent crime problem in the sixties, seventies, and eighties, they are crucial. But we are no further today than we were in the sixties to accepting public responsibility for them.

It's here, I think, that a third-stage criminology must distinguish itself most sharply from its counterparts in the past. In both its earlier recent stages—one humane, the other not so humane—the forces that make for the migration of whole populations, that structure their chances for reasonably meaningful employment, and that either maintain their local communities in relative stability or disrupt and fragment them are typically viewed, either tacitly or explicitly, as facts of life rather than matters over which a rational society may exert some systematic control. As Jeff Faux also observes, "National economic policy remains the only significant organized human activity in America where planning ahead is considered irrational."[45] But if we are to be serious about reconstructing—or constructing—the context of family and community life for the urban disadvantaged, we will have to bite the bullet and think directly about public planning for urban economic development. Without that focus, we can expect, at best, to recapitulate the default of the more progressive criminology of the sixties. With it, we may begin to achieve a major impact on violent crime in America—not tomorrow, not next year, but in the not-so-distant future. And we may begin, finally, to roll back the long-term deterioration in the quality of American life that the Violence Commission predicted, with such unfortunate foresight, at the close of the 1960s.

## NOTES

1. National Commission on the Causes and Prevention of Violence, *To Establish Justice, To Insure Domestic Tranquility, Final Report* (Washington, D.C.: U.S. Government Printing Office, 1969), pp. 44–45 (hereafter, *Final Report*).

2. Federal Bureau of Investigation, *Crime in the United States—1981,* Uniform Crime Reports (Washington, D.C.: U.S. Government Printing Office, 1982), p. 6.

3. U.S. National Center for Health Statistics, *Monthly Vital Statistics Report, Annual Summary of Births, Deaths, Marriages and Divorces; United States, 1981* (Washington, D.C.: U.S. Government Printing Office, December 1982), p. 21.

4. *Final Report,* p. xv.

5. "The Epidemic of Violent Crime," *Newsweek,* March 23, 1981, pp. 44–53.

6. Attorney General's Task Force on Violent Crime, *Final Report* (Washington, D.C.: U.S. Department of Justice, August 1981), p. 2.

7. Elliott Currie, "Crime and Politics," in *Rethinking Liberalism,* ed. Walter T. Anderson (New York: Avon Books, 1983).

8. Alfred Blumstein, Jacqueline Cohen, and Daniel Nagin, *Deterrence and Incapacitation: Estimating the Effects of Criminal Sanctions* (Washington, D.C.: National Academy of Sciences, 1978).

9. For one fairly early statement of this position, see Gordon Tullock, "Does Punishment Deter Crime?" *Public Interest* 36 (Summer 1974).

10. James W. Thompson et al., *Employment and Crime: A Review of Theories and Research* (Washington, D.C.: National Institute of Justice, 1981), ch. 2.

11. James Q. Wilson, "Crime and American Culture," *Public Interest* 70 (Winter 1983): 39.

12. *Final Report,* p. 46.

13. Lamar T. Empey, "Contemporary Programs for Convicted Juvenile Offenders," Appendix 30, in *Crimes of Violence: A Staff Report to the National Commission on the Causes and Prevention of Violence* by Donald J. Mulvihill, Melvin M. Tumin, and Lynn A. Curtis, vol. 13 (Washington, D.C.: U.S. Government Printing Office, 1969).

14. *Final Report,* p. xxi.

15. Clarence C. Schrag, "Critical Analysis of Sociological Theories," Appendix 26, in Mulvihill, Tumin, and Curtis, *Crimes of Violence,* p. 1285.

16. *Final Report,* p. xxvii.

17. Ibid., p. xxii.

18. Ibid., p. 48.

19. *Crimes of Violence,* p. xxxiv.

20. Ibid., p. xl.

21. Cf. *Final Report,* p. 55.

22. R. M. Titmuss, *The Welfare State and Equality* (Boston: Beacon Press, 1968), p. 148.

23. A useful review of these theories may be found in Thompson et al., *Employment and Crime,* ch. 2.

24. For example, President's Commission on Law Enforcement and Administration of Justice, *The Challenge of Crime in a Free Society* (Washington, D.C.: U.S. Government Printing Office, 1967), p. iv.

25. See especially Peter Greenwood and Allan Abrahamse, *Selective Incapacitation* (Santa Monica: Rand Corporation, 1982).

26. For an especially strong discussion of these issues, see Jean Floud and Warren Young, *Dangerousness and Criminal Justice* (London: Heinemann, 1981), Appendix C.

27. Cf. the research cited in Peter Greenwood, "The Violent Offender in the Criminal Justice System," in *Criminal Violence,* ed. Marvin Wolfgang and Neil Alan Weiner (Beverly Hills: Sage, 1982).

28. Cf. Greenwood and Abrahamse, *Selective Incapacitation,* p. xv.

29. *Final Report,* p. 272.

30. Mark H. Moore and George L. Kelling, "To Serve and Protect: Learning from Police History," *Public Interest* 70 (Winter 1983).

31. Floyd Fowler, Jr., and Thomas W. Mangione, *Neighborhood Crime, Fear, and Social*

*Control: A Second Look at the Hartford Program* (Washington, D.C.: National Institute of Justice, 1982).

32. D. Lipton, R. Martinson, and J. Wilks, *The Effectiveness of Correctional Treatment* (New York: Praeger, 1975).

33. Rudy A. Haapanen and Carl F. Jesness, *Early Identification of the Chronic Offender* (Sacramento: California Youth Authority, 1982), p. 131.

34. Lee Sechrest et al., *The Rehabilitation of Criminal Offenders: Problems and Prospects* (Washington, D.C.: National Academy of Sciences, 1979).

35. For some reviews of these issues, see Donald West, *Delinquency: Its Roots, Careers, and Prospects* (Cambridge, Mass.: Harvard University Press, 1982), ch. 3; Michael Wadsworth, *Roots of Delinquency* (New York: Barnes and Noble, 1979), ch. 4.

36. For a recent version of this stance, see Travis Hirschi, "Crime and Family Policy," *Journal of Contemporary Studies* 6, no. 1 (Winter 1983).

37. Abt Associates, *Child and Family Resource Program Evaluation, Executive Summary of CFRP's Infant-Toddler Component* (Cambridge, Mass.: Abt Associates, 1982).

38. For a recent review of these issues, see Charles Tittle, *Sanctions and Social Deviance* (New York: Praeger, 1980); for a recent investigation affirming the salience of informal sanctions, see Raymond Paternoster et al., "Perceived Risk and Social Control: Do Sanctions Really Deter?" *Law and Society Review* 17, no. 3 (1983).

39. See Robert Woodson, *A Summons to Life: Mediating Structures and the Prevention of Youth Crime* (Cambridge, Mass.: Ballinger, 1981).

40. Cf. Woodson, Ibid.; Nathan Glazer, "Towards a Self-Service Society?" *Public Interest* 70 (Winter 1983).

41. Thompson et al., *Employment and Crime,* esp. ch. 2.

42. Elliott Currie, "Fighting Crime," *Working Papers,* July–August 1982, p. 21.

43. *Final Report,* ch. 2.

44. Jeff Faux, "Who Plans?" *Working Papers,* November–December 1982, p. 13.

45. Ibid., p. 12.

# 3

# Black Violence and Public Policy

JAMES P. COMER

Americans, as a group, are more violent than any other developed country in the world. Black Americans, as a group, are more violent than white Americans. And the incidence of violence has continued to grow during the past two decades despite a spectrum of policies and programs designed to combat it. The purpose of this discussion is to suggest a perspective that will enable us to better understand violence—black violence in particular— and to respond to it more effectively.

I was first confronted with the complexity and multiple issues involved in crime and violence through an interaction with a twelve-year-old black student. He was one of five youngsters in a therapy group I conducted in an inner-city school in New Haven, Connecticut, in 1965–66. He was the school's leading "bad boy"—easily provoked, often in fights, suspicious, sullen, and angry; he was a low academic achiever because of his inattention and in spite of his average and possibly above average intelligence. After several months, however, he grew comfortable enough to confide in me.

He told me that he occasionally walked through the nearby college dormitory and "ripped off" student rooms. (He considered the students to be fair game because "they got everything.") He complained disappointedly that on one occasion when he got caught the judge did not send him back to the residential juvenile detention program where he had spent several months a year earlier. On inquiry, it turned out that he wanted to be returned to the residential program because there was more order, structure, predictability, and consistent care there than in his home.

My own background—a black family economically as poor as this youngster's but with a rich social, emotional, and psychological texture— could have led me to the easy conclusion that family life was the cause of his delinquent and violent behavior, and indeed it probably contributed. But I grew up with youngsters from equally chaotic backgrounds who did not become criminal or violent. It is often said, also, that many youngsters from difficult backgrounds could be successful in school and, in turn, in

life if their teachers cared more or were less racist. This youngster's teacher
was a well-educated, talented black woman from one of America's most
successful families. She cared, and most of the teachers before her had
cared and had tried to help. They had not succeeded.

About fifteen years later, I met him again, working at a menial job in
the housekeeping service of a hospital. He was scarred from violent encounters over the years. He had served two jail terms, held four or five
jobs (he couldn't remember the number), and had five children, although
he was not married. At twenty-seven, as at twelve, he was well intentioned
and not a deliberate bad guy. He simply did not cope adequately with the
demands of his life, and this eventually led to acts of violence and other
behavior that contributed to social problems.

His experience, juxtapositioned with that of other black, poor people
from both troubled and stable families, suggested to me that there is no
obvious or easy way to understand violence among blacks. Research by
professional students of crime and violence reveals the same paradoxes and
problems I encountered in trying to understand that single case. But when
problems are as prominent and troublesome to society as violence is, significant action is taken regardless of our level of understanding.

As violence began to escalate in the 1960s, voices calling, on the one
hand, for "get tough" policies and, on the other, for "be fair" policies were
both heard. The evidence of national wrongdoing against blacks by American society, highlighted by the civil rights movement of the 1960s, soon
provided a plausible explanation for the disproportionate number of social
problems, including anger, alienation, and violence, among blacks. This led
to greater support for policies designed to overcome past injustices in housing, education, employment, preparation for employment, and the like.
Despite many successes, however, violence rates continued to climb. This,
and other forces, contributed to a change in attitude among almost every
segment of the society—politicians, academicians, average citizens—which
weakened the thrust for justice and opportunity and favored the "get
tough" policies. But now, after almost a decade of "toughness," violence
rates are still high.[1]

The issues involved in the case of the twelve-year-old in my therapy group
suggest that neither approach—be fair or get tough—alone is sufficient.
Many youngsters like him were the prime targets of compensatory education and job-training programs. Many families like his were involved in
family and neighborhood development programs. Again, some benefited.
But my patient, unsuccessful in school with a talented and caring teacher,
was not likely to be helped by compensatory education and job-training
programs. His family was too troubled to benefit from most intervention
efforts. Both the youngster and his family were products of relationship

and developmental conditions in society that will not yield to information, advice, and skill training.

Locking him up didn't help. Indeed, *he wanted to be locked up!* (The use of correctional institutions for their own control by people who know they are dangerous to themselves and others is more common than liberal thinkers would care to admit.) While this particular youngster may not have become a hardened criminal because of his sojourns in prison, it is well known that many do. Locking him up more often and for longer periods—as his juvenile court judge understood—would only have added to the problem of overcrowded facilities without serving as a crime and violence deterrent or incapacitator. If he had been put away more often and for a longer period of time, other youngsters with a similar constellation of problems would probably have committed similar crimes and acts of violence.

If neither toughness (punishment) nor justice and opportunity is the answer, what is? And what lies behind our difficulty in understanding and addressing our violence problem?

## BARRIERS TO UNDERSTANDING

Our understanding of and response to crime and violence are rooted primarily in religious ideology. Politicians and undereducated, and even too many well-educated, Americans regularly think of crime and violence as willful, even sinful, bad behavior that will yield only to punishment. This attitude is seductive, because crime and violence are often, as an end product, the consequence of deliberate acts. But such acts are, at the same time, the consequence of a complex social process that involves more than the individual. This is suggested by the fact of lower rates of violence in other reasonably developed white and mixed racial societies such as Sweden, Switzerland, West Germany, and Cuba.[2] This is not to suggest that a particular social and economic order necessarily produces more or less crime and violence. But it does suggest that students of American crime, violence, and other social problems must adequately consider and respond to adverse factors in our society that are beyond the control of the individual, the family, and its primary social network (most meaningful associations).

Also, social and behavioral scientists, less influenced by religious or democratic ideals, have employed an unfortunate focus in their thinking about crime and violence. They have tended to look for a root, or primary, cause rather than develop an adequate conceptual framework to deal with the multiple forces involved. In one study, over twenty of the biological, social, and psychological factors usually suspected as causes of crime and violence (from brain dysfunction to unfavorable family conditions) were analyzed in order to find a predictor of dangerousness among 122 juveniles. The factors did not systematically predict dangerous behavior nor did they show a primary, or root, cause for violence.[3]

Clusters of suspected causal factors often show up among those who manifest dangerous behavior. But similar clusters show up among many who do not. Because of our focus on the individual and root causes and the absence of a conceptual framework that deals with multiple factors, we cannot explain why the same or similar conditions have different outcomes within a particular family, among families in the same neighborhood and social network, and among different racial and ethnic groups of similar income levels.

But wasn't the response of the government and other elements of society in the 1960s an acknowledgment of multiple causal forces—injustice, poverty, racism—and the adverse role of factors beyond the individual's control?

It was. But this response was hampered first by the absence of an understanding of the precise way in which multiple factors beyond a family's control interact to create and maintain crime and violence in vulnerable individuals. The effort, particularly with respect to black crime and violence, was further hampered by guilt, denial, and ignorance of the consequences of the past experience of blacks in America. There was, and still is, a desire to let unpleasant bygone conditions be bygone without understanding their effects and present-day manifestations and addressing them in intervention programs.

To understand crime and violence, a perspective is needed that takes into account the complex way in which multiple factors interact to adversely affect particular individuals, families, and their social networks or groups. The perspective must include a consideration of historical, present, and future interactions among families, their primary social network, and the larger society. (Human behavior, unlike that of other animals, can be affected by future social conditions.) The perspective must also include the peculiar ability of the human individual not to be affected in a predictable way by family and social network conditions.

No single traditional social and behavioral science discipline provides such perspectives. But a parallel in medicine—epidemiology—and principles from the budding science of human ecology do provide the necessary perspectives.

Epidemiology is the study of disease patterns in natural populations such as communities or nations. Crime and violence, as used here, is a parallel of disease, even when disease is defined as a harmful development in social institutions or civilizations. Human ecology is the study of the totality of the pattern of relations among and between people and the social institutions and environment they create. Principles and concepts of both are applicable to the study and understanding of crime and violence and can help suggest possible policies and practices of intervention.

An important concept of epidemiology—the web of causation, or the notion of multiple interacting factors, rather than a root, or primary, cause—is particularly useful in thinking about crime and violence. Empirical evidence from epidemiological studies indicates that while it would appear to be most beneficial to search for a major and direct cause of disease, it is often more useful to attack a causal web at a distant but critical, even generative point. A key principle of human ecology is that families and the social networks in which they are enmeshed are generative of both anti- and prosocial individual and group behavior. These concepts and principles, and knowledge from child development, suggest that the family is the institution of society—more than the justice and correctional systems—that a nation must focus on to attack crime and violence and other social problems, even though the justice and correctional systems are more directly involved with violent and criminal people.

There is much discussion among politicians, religious leaders, and social and behavioral scientists alike about the importance of the family. But again this is done without adequate consideration of the complex but precise way in which the key structural elements in the society—political, economic, educational, and religious institutions and their policies and practices— affect the family function most related to crime and violence—child rearing and consequently child development. Let us, then, examine the child-rearing function of the family.

## CHILD DEVELOPMENT

Through adequate child rearing, normal and potentially violent and otherwise harmful human forces are brought under control. The child-rearing competence and motivation of the parent, parents, or caretaker is, in large part, determined by past, present, and future conditions in the society and the child rearers' peculiar adjustment to them. Thus, economic, educational, religious, political, and other conditions can affect people of the same race, class, ethnic group, or intelligence differentially, though similar conditions *tend* to result in similar behavior among people of the same general intelligence and experience. Also, the innate capacities, temperament, and psychological responses of a child can result in different developmental outcomes despite similar child-rearing and other environmental conditions.

I will return later to the issue of developmental outcomes. But let's first consider the basic tasks of parents and society and the nature of child rearing and development.

Children are born completely dependent. To maintain a technologically and scientifically based civilization, such a society must make certain that children are reared to become adults capable of holding a job or following a career; capable of living in and rearing a family or of living as an adult without a family; capable of self-expression and finding meaning and worth in life without compromising the rights and needs of others; capable of accepting and acting on citizenship responsibilities. Parents are the agents of the society in promoting such outcomes.

The newborn, aside from its biological makeup, is equipped only with the capacity to establish relationships and with an aggressive and/or survival energy. This energy drives the development of the child and is capable of negative and destructive or positive and creative expressions from the standpoint of others. In the process of meeting the dependent child's basic needs—food, warmth, protection—the parent or caretaker establishes an emotional tie or bond with the child. This enables the caretaker to assist the child's development along important pathways to the point that he or she can cope with society's basic expectations.

There are many developmental pathways. Several are critical: cognitive (thinking), speech and language, social, moral, and psychological. Cognition and speech and language permit learning and skill development needed for meaningful expression, life appreciation, and earning a living. Social, moral, and psychological development permits the same, and in addition, enables the individual to manage internal desires, wishes, and impulses and to interact with others in a way that makes civil human relations possible. *Adequate development along the psychological, social, and moral pathways, in particular, are necessary to keep crime and violence at a level that is tolerable in society.* In short, these pathways are society's primary crime and violence prevention sites.

As providers of basic needs, parents become most important to their children. They model behavior—children identify with them and imitate the behavior. Parents also encourage or discourage certain behavior through approval or reward and disapproval or punishment. It is through these mechanisms that parents push, pull, and cajole children along developmental pathways. Schools assist (or should) in the child-rearing task, particularly in the intellectual and social areas. Other people and institutions in the primary social network of a family can and often do greatly affect development. And even if there is a biological basis for a predisposition to violence, our current understanding of human behavior indicates that its expression can be socialized and/or controlled through adequate child rearing.

## PRIMARY SOCIAL NETWORKS

The quality of child rearing—at home and elsewhere—is usually directly affected by social conditions through a complex but modifiable individual, family, and societal interactional dynamic.

Parents or families exist in social networks—primary, and in certain stratified societies, secondary and tertiary. They belong, by birth or choice, to religious groups, social organizations, and groups of friends and kin. This is their primary social network and is usually most important to them. It is the place or group of associations from which member families gain a sense of belonging, meaning, and security. Thus, they identify with and are most influenced by the attitudes, values, and ways (culture) of this social network. This includes attitudes and behavior relative to child rearing, learning, opportunity, work, religion, relationships with people and institutions in and outside their primary social network, and much more. In our society there is often an ethnic or racial configuration to primary social networks.

In less stratified—though complex—and often preindustrial societies, the work place, organized education, government, and other structural elements are an intimate part of the primary social network of a family. The programs and leaders of these institutions—religious, educational, political, economic—are meaningful and a powerful source of identity for *all* the members of the society. It is through identification with leaders that persons of relatively modest ability and achievement can feel adequate, successful, and reasonably secure. In turn, this gives institutional leaders great power to influence individual and group behavior. Thus, social pressure for meeting societal expectations can be great and the reward for conformity—belonging and security—can be equally great.

Also, the ability of heads of households to provide basic needs for oneself and one's dependents is a major source of a psychological and social sense of adequacy and well-being. Various social beliefs can serve a similar purpose, but in this age they are usually not as powerful as economic well-being. The latter may be minimal, and even provided by others, as long as the head of household can experience a sense of adequacy from the way his or her needs and dependents' needs are met.

*When parents are able to meet basic family needs, identify with institutional leaders, and experience a sense of belonging, they are likely to be adequate child rearers and to promote the social, psychological, and moral development of their children to a level that enables them to cope as young people and adults and reduces the likelihood of crime and violence to a minimal and manageable level in society.*

## SECONDARY AND TERTIARY SOCIAL NETWORKS

Let us turn now to the cause and effect of greater social stratification, or secondary and tertiary social networks, on families and child-rearing conditions.

Social stratification on some basis—birthrights, possessions, perceived ability to control the body or environment—has always existed. But interaction with powerful leaders was local and rigidly prescribed. Early technology and resultant industrial development, more recent and rapid scientific and technological development, and postindustrial conditions facilitated change. The way heads of households earned a living and cared for themselves and their families changed greatly—most sharply between the 1860s and the 1960s. The change was greater and more rapid than ever before in the history of the world. Important social arrangements changed—increased interaction and interdependency among physically removed but powerful people and institutions in society—without sufficient attention to the effects of these changes on families, child rearing, and, in turn, crime, violence, and other social problems.

Prior to the 1950s, expectations and controls in a local community were clear. Without rapid, visual communication, high mobility, and a high level of education, knowledge of "the way things are and must be" was confined to local people with economic and related political power. Families and groups had little recourse but to accept "their place" in the local social order, with varying degrees of resistance and efforts to bring about change. And a limited amount of acting out and criminal, violent, and disruptive social behavior was displayed by those who were poorly reared or who felt excluded and abused. But with only a local community vision of what could or should be, even the abused felt some sense of belonging and security— in their place—in the pre-1940 communities.

The pace of industrial development in the 1940s changed the society from one of predominantly small towns and rural areas to a mixture of small towns, rural areas, and predominantly middle-sized and large cities. Technological development—cars, roads, and the nature of work—removed the work place from the field or factory to sometimes quite distant places. Schools and sometimes churches and other primary social network institutions became physically distant. The interaction between authority figures or leaders of critical institutions—parents, administrators, teachers, employers, government officials, the police—was reduced. Social and emotional bonds among families and their institutions began to loosen. (And even though there was always physical distance among people in rural areas, social and emotional bonds tied them together more tightly prior to the 1940s.)[4]

Better transportation, communication by radio, and improved public education reduced the knowledge monopoly held by local leaders. By the 1950s, the emergence of television and other technology significantly increased the information from outside local communities, challenging local social orders. Economic and social arrangements were no longer automatically accepted and identification with institutional leadership was less complete. Indeed, this had never been completely the case. But now institutional leaders, once physically and emotionally close, were more dis-

tant physically and more clearly potential allies or sources of income, justice, education, and security for families and groups *or* potential enemies,
denying such needs. Local government, economic, and educational networks were now outside the primary social network of more families or
were part of the secondary social network of most families and individuals.

With the growth of national government, economic, educational, communications, and transportation institutions and systems, a third or tertiary
level of leadership emerged. Identification with leaders after the 1940s was
across often less emotionally positive and binding social and psychological
space. With industrialization, local leaders increasingly had less to offer
families in the way of assurances of economic and resultant social and
psychological well-being.

But the primary mechanism of social order cannot ever change. Social
order is a function of heads of households identifying with meaningful others, especially the leaders of critical institutions, and resultant motivation
to meet societal standards. Also, they must be able to meet their basic
needs, feel adequate, obtain the skills and incentives to rear their children
so that sufficient social, psychological, and moral development takes place.

On the other hand, in industrial and postindustrial societies, it is possible
for an individual to reject immediate places, people, and their attitudes,
values, and ways and identify with those in less close physical and social
proximity. It is even possible to identify with the perceived enemy of one's
apparent primary social network or group. Likewise, the individual child
has the capacity to reject the attitudes, values, and ways of his or her family.
Indeed, it is these mechanisms or capacities that make crime and violence
and other social problems so difficult to predict on the basis of family and
other social experiences. But identification with and patterning after one's
parents and primary social network is more common because of the sense
of belonging and psychological security it provides. This is the reason that
the family and the primary social network is the most important potential
violence prevention site, more important than secondary or tertiary social
networks.

Industrial development and the changes just described were driven by
the acquisition of wealth, economic development, and the acquisition of
additional wealth, in a circular fashion. Those able to participate in the
process became the leaders of institutions in the secondary and tertiary
social networks of the society. Most of the major wealth of the nation was
distributed by legislative acts before the 1870s; this distribution was almost
completed by the 1940s. Mining rights, railroad subsidies, land for schools,
military compensation, homestead grants, and a variety of other allocations
to states and individuals gave great economic and, in turn, political power
to those who already had enough economic and political power to effect
such decisions.[5]

These beneficiaries, as they industrialized the nation, were able to determine who would have secondary and tertiary wealth and power—who would control local, regional, and national politics, and economic, educational, and social institutions; who would work and who would not work; who would determine national attitudes, opportunities, and mobility; who would serve as authority figures, leaders, or identification models at every level of society.

The manner and speed in which wealth was acquired and the competitive nature of and attitude about the acquisition (or nonacquisition) of wealth were the seeds of inadequate, often negative social binding within American society. The frontier nature of early American society, the absence of a strong central government or an entrenched economic power structure, and certain dominant religious precepts fostered a national ideology of individualism and competition rather than cooperation and concern about society's need to develop children.

Even more troublesome was, and is, the notion that economic success is due to divine favor and personal ability rather than to chance and the presence of opportunity for development and expression of talents. This attitude has promoted exclusionary social policies and practices. It has increased the probability of intergroup conflict, made identification with leaders beyond one's primary social network more difficult, and forced groups of like interests or needs to turn in on themselves and struggle for social and economic well-being, often in the process scapegoating more vulnerable groups.

Groups that were able to obtain sufficient economic power were able to participate in leadership positions in the critical institutions and areas of American life beyond the primary social networks. The movement of leaders from various ethnic, religious, and racial groups—an aspect of the primary network of many people—into the secondary and tertiary social networks set up linkages and networks of information, money, political contacts, experiences, and other support for sometimes the most talented—but often just well-connected—families. This permitted such groups to have significant representation and influence at the secondary and tertiary social network levels and made it possible for members to meet basic needs and identify positively with secondary and tertiary social network leadership, attitudes, values, and ways. It gave the groups power to influence information and communication—and, thus, national attitudes toward themselves. It also facilitated a kind of three-generational development of groups that parallels the three-generational development of affluence and industry in this country.

Prior to the 1900s, it was possible to be uneducated and unskilled and still earn a living—to care for oneself and one's dependents and experience the psychological and social sense of well-being from doing so. This increased the probability of family stability and made it possible for a large number of families to carry out the kind of child rearing that prepared their children for the moderate educational and skill level needed in the generation between the 1900s and 1940s. This was particularly true when groups were able to experience a reasonable degree of cultural continuity with their country of origin. Such continuity led to cohesiveness and social organization even when groups experienced ethnic, racial, religious, or class prejudice. Families able to compete successfully in the job markets of the 1900s to the 1940s were better able to adequately rear their children and, because of group cohesiveness, organization, and power, take advantage of increasing opportunities in public education, particularly in the North and West, which prepared them for the job markets of the 1940s through the 1970s.

Also, social programs after the 1940s—thirty-year mortgages, education and training benefits, the G.I. bill, and other government subsidies that were possible because of increasing national affluence—facilitated stability. This three-generational development of families, within primary social networks that included a larger ethnic, racial, and religious affiliation, organization, and power, is what enabled them to meet their needs, rear their children adequately, and greatly reduce group violence, crime, and other social problems over the past century. But national attitudes facilitating individualism and exclusionary policies did not change greatly—in fact, they were reinforced by apparent group mobility—and perpetuated the need for an out group and the continuation of scapegoating of the most vulnerable groups.

In the late 1960s, the nation began to enter the postindustrial period. Even a high level of education and training did not guarantee success on the job market. Nonetheless, families that had gained stability and had become a part of social networks in the past were best able to prepare their children for the new demands.

The talented members of groups that had experienced active and severe societal exclusion were not able to work their way into positions of influence in the political and economic institutions of the secondary and tertiary networks of the society. Families from such groups were not able to undergo the same degree of three-generational development as did other groups. This made it difficult for a disproportionate number of such group members to meet basic family needs. While some families were able to do so and to identify with the secondary and tertiary network institutions, the sense of belonging and security could not be complete in the face of denial of basic opportunities and fundamental rights to themselves and people like themselves. Excluded groups experienced increasing ambivalence about and alienation from the institutions, leadership, and people of the secondary and tertiary networks.

As a result, some families that were functioning well in a less complex socioeconomic order began a three-generational downward trend, functioning less well each generation. Crime, violence, and other social problems could not be reduced in the same fashion that it was reduced in more advantaged groups who experienced the three-generational opportunity and family development trend. Black Americans were a disproportionately large part of the negative family development pattern because of their peculiar experience and resultant vulnerability.

## THE BLACK EXPERIENCE

Disproportionate crime and violence among blacks in America can best be understood by examining the interaction among families and primary, secondary, and tertiary social networks over time. This perspective will also suggest the reasons that some corrective approaches show promise and others do not. Because of the generation-to-generation transmission of culture, experience, and parental adaptation to experience, it is necessary to begin with the preslavery, or West African, experience of Afro-Americans.

West Africa was organized into kinship groups that were the core of all political, economic, and social activities.[6] Each kinship group was composed of a collection of extended families or lineages in which nuclear families were enmeshed. Each lineage had a particular history, ancestral shrine, rituals, and taboos which provided members with personal and group organization, a belief set or systems, direction, purpose, and sense of security. Each age group had clearly defined roles, and the responsibility of parents and other adults to children and vice versa was clear.

West African culture was communal in style. Land was held in common within a lineage and as a result, no lineage member worked for hire. Sharing and mutual support was a prominent attitude and style in the life of West Africans. The effect of these conditions was that families and children had a very powerful sense of belonging in their society. There were differences of status within and between lineages, but identification with leaders, customs, values, and ways was very strong among all. And through identification, every member of the society had a sense of being valued, a sense of purpose and power. In return, leaders and institutions had a strong influence on the behavior and performance of members.

Because of these conditions, families were highly motivated to support the development of their children in order to prepare them for participation in their society as adults, to pass on skills, attitudes, values, and ways that would enable them to be successful. This task was not complicated by identity conflict, ambivalence, role confusion, and a sense of marginality within and alienation from institutions and leaders of the society. The entire social system facilitated parental ability to promote a child's development along important pathways and to promote prosocial behavior.

I am not suggesting that West Africa was Utopia. I am suggesting that the relationship between children and parents-adults, and social networks beyond the parents and children were critically important in influencing the behavior and development of children, including intragroup control of crime and violence. (Indeed, such social organization can make groups vulnerable to intense conflict with and violence against outside groups.)

Slavery disrupted the kinship and related governmental, judicial, religious, social, and economic systems.[7] Because of the kinship and communal nature of West African society, this break was even more important and troublesome than the separation of individual families that Western social scientists are more prone to be concerned about. In kinship and communal societies, personal adequacy and a sense of power are more highly dependent on the operation of societal institutions. Thus, West Africans, for this and other reasons, were more susceptible to control during slavery and more foreign to the individualistic culture they entered after slavery than groups who had not experienced communal and kinship social organizations prior to immigration.

In the United States, the master was all the social organization the slave had. The basic necessities of life were provided or determined by the master—food, clothing, shelter, religion, companionship, and sex. All executive functions necessary for self-determination and the promotion of skills, such as planning, organizing, developing, and carrying out long-range programs, were not allowed. Only the remnants of the aesthetic components of African culture that did not threaten the slave system—language and body style, self-expression through music and dance, and so on—were allowed to remain. Without cultural continuity, self-determination, and related power, the slave was forced to identify strongly with the master—positively, negatively, or both.

The overall effect of American slavery was the creation of negative psychosocial conditions for the slave. Some were infantilized, or rendered passive, apathetic, or depressed. Many became passive-aggressive, devious, and deceptively rebellious. Some ran away. Some became defiant, hostile, and aggressive, and struck out against the oppression, violently and directly, whenever possible. The latter behavior brought punishment or violence and created an atmosphere of violence. Slavery provided little institutional or cultural bases for responsible slave interaction.

Families were not a part of a primary social network of their creation or choosing. Under the slave system, children were reared for the use of the master and not for the glory and self-expression of the parents within a network of prideful and supportive lineage members. The children were not to grow and develop to carry on traditions and values; to hunt, fight, or farm; to support or maintain the integrity of the lineage. There was no glorious lineage future. After one generation, in most cases, there was no glorious lineage past. Under these circumstances, the master's approval or disapproval was the only source of a sense of value, worth, and purpose. And under the best of circumstances, both approval and disapproval were a statement of inferiority. Nonacceptance of such feelings promoted rage, often hidden, but capable of being triggered into violence.

The negative family-life and child-rearing consequences of these conditions are obvious. Children were sometimes the victims of anger and violence displaced from the dangerous target of the slave master or other whites. Children were not reared to participate in the political, economic, social mainstream of the society. They were reared to be slaves, and slavery was a system of forced dependency and negative feelings about the self. It was a system that promoted powerful forces for identification with the aggressor (slave master and other whites) and depreciation of and often ambivalence and antagonism toward one's self and group.

Blacks in slavery composed a group formed by force rather than by cohesive affiliation and common cause. Oppression of a potentially cohesive group promotes a sense of common cause, organization, and often sustained rebellion. Oppression of a group that has had its organizing institutions and systems destroyed usually results in sporadic and ineffective efforts to rebel. But more often it results in serious intragroup *and* intergroup relationship problems, promoting violence and crime against the self and people like the self. In the absence of an opportunity to constructively channel angry feelings, violence against perceived oppressors increases when the oppressed feel more positive about themselves and when external conditions are less threatening.

American slavery existed for about 250 years. Unlike Nazi Germany concentration camp victims and other violated groups, Afro-Americans did not bring a largely self-determined culture into an oppressive system, hold on to it as much as possible, and then return to supportive and reorganizing cultural conditions. The instrumental, executive, and organizing aspects of West African culture were broken in the enslavement process and replaced by the powerlessness and degradation of the slave culture. This culture was then transmitted from parent to child generation after generation. The conditions after slavery, for about 100 years, reinforced among some much of the psyche and behavior that was established during the slave period. The master-slave relationship is the basis of symbolic and underlying conflict and violence—individual and collective, covert and overt—in black-white relationships even today.

When slavery was officially abolished in 1863, American society was in the early stage of industrial development, more in the North and East than in the South and West where most blacks were located. Some carried with them the burden of the slave culture—the attitudes, values, and ways related to being a slave, such as dependency, few long-range planning and organizing skills, little independent family management experience, and so on. Some, because of opportunities during slavery or various adaptive mechanisms, had managed to acquire adequate or even highly developed social skills and were prepared to undergo three-generational development like other groups.

Blacks with ability, however, were denied opportunities in the secondary and tertiary social network institutions of politics, government, and education on the basis of race, backed up by government sanctions and social policies and practices.[8] And leaders in the secondary and tertiary social networks not only permitted violent and nonviolent intimidation and denial of black rights and opportunities, but often promoted it. Public officials and leaders who should have been positive identification models, the source of social and psychological well-being, and the basis of motivation for responsible family and citizenship behavior were the opposite. Many such leaders played insecure whites against blacks for political, economic, and other advantages.

Like other groups experiencing exclusion, blacks turned in on themselves for social organization and a sense of adequacy, belonging, and security that could not be acquired in institutions in the secondary and tertiary social networks. The black church was the only major primary social network institution available for such purposes, and in the black community it became more than a place of worship and a faith and belief system. It was a substitute society, providing what the larger society provided most other groups except economic and political opportunity. The black church came under attack when it moved to address political and economic inequities. Thus, it was not able to adequately address these issues, though it often tried.

The church, and later church people in derived organizations such as colleges, clubs, and group advancement organizations, provided a significant number of families with the basis for stability and adequate child rearing.[9] It was from this group that the first generation of better educated black Americans emerged. Second, third, and further generations of successful family development and functioning followed in many cases. It was from the black church that the attitudes, discipline, and power to sustain the civil rights movement derived. But the denial of opportunity after slavery put a disproportionate number of blacks out of phase with industrial development and the three-generational economic and political opportunities and educational development that other groups experienced.

Blacks were still in slavery when most of the primary wealth of the nation was all but given away. Blacks were closed out of the labor movement by the 1900s and even the high-level blue-collar skills learned in slavery were lost; high-paying, easily acquired blue-collar skills were denied, and employment was primarily in the secondary job market characterized by no-training, no-advancement, often seasonal and inconsistent, low-paying work.[10]

Until the 1940s, at least four to eight times as much money was spent on the education of white children as black children in the eight states with 80 percent of the black population in America—twenty-five times as much where blacks were greatly disproportionate in number.[11] A similar disparity in support for blacks and whites existed in the land-grant colleges.[12] In the mid-1960s, the endowment of all the one hundred plus black colleges put together was less than one half that of Harvard University alone![13]

The consequences of these policies and practices was that the society failed to create a large enough black middle- and upper-income group. It failed to make blacks a part of the network of secondary and tertiary institutional leadership with its related influence on money utilization, information, political contacts, skills, experience, and so on. The black middle-income group that did emerge was largely in professional service areas, often themselves excluded from larger society institutions and power. The black middle-income community was not in a position to make it possible for its group to meet basic needs and to serve as powerful identification models and links to the larger society. As a result, the black middle-income group had less influence on group behavior than it might have had; it was able only to petition the larger society for justice and opportunity.

When black and white leadership did begin to gain limited economic and educational opportunities for uneducated, unskilled blacks in the 1940s, the society had already moved into a period in which at least moderate education and skills were needed. If not education and skills, certainly contacts with friends, kin, and influential others were needed to obtain better paying jobs. Racist social practices eliminated almost all blacks from better paying job opportunities. By the time overt and massive political, economic, educational, and social injustice toward blacks was considered unacceptable in the 1960s, the society was almost through the last stage of the industrial revolution and its related social conditions.

As a result, over the last century, many black heads of households worked at the margin of the economy, barely eking out a living wage that would enable them to care for themselves and their families and to experience the related sense of well-being that would have motivated them to be adequate child rearers and citizens. Many were not able to earn even a living wage. It was for this reason that many competent families in the agricultural South and the unskilled-labor North became less successful in the next generation and even disturbed and disturbing in the third—a three-generation downhill spiral.

In black and white communities alike, economic, educational, and other opportunities served to reduce family size. Indeed the average family size of middle- and upper-income blacks is smaller than that of whites.[14] Family size, however, is larger among poor and socially marginal families. And unsuccessful families in each of the last three generations often contributed double to triple the number of unsuccessful families in the subsequent generation. Thus, a disproportionate number of black families were poor and socially marginal.

Moreover, unable to identify positively with institutions and leaders beyond primary social networks and black community organizations, many blacks were not able to experience the sense of adequacy from minimal personal gains that many whites experience through identification with white leaders and institutions of the larger society. Frustration, powerlessness, and rage existed for many more blacks. Many experienced alienation and antagonism toward the larger society. Even successful black families experienced ambivalence and rage about secondary and tertiary social network institutional policies and practices toward blacks. This is aggravated by the larger society's need not to know or understand its contribution to black community problems, such as violence, crime, or welfare dependency.

The black experience is antithetical to the Judeo-Christian and democratic principles on which the nation is founded; it is a blemish on the majority culture image. Thus there is a tendency, even a need, to blame blacks for problems created, in large part, by societal institutional policies and practices. Even when injustice is acknowledged, the extent of economic denial and the social and psychological consequences is not fully examined by scholars nor does it become a part of the information base of the average American citizen through education or the mass media. As a result neither the public nor the policymaker is in a position to support or develop programs and practices based on the effects of troublesome past policies and practices. Economic hard times increase the need not to know, increase the need of marginal white groups to scapegoat blacks, and increase social pressures on and problems in the black community.

## SOCIAL POLICIES AND BLACK VIOLENCE

Social policies and practices toward blacks over the years have promoted a disproportionate amount of black violence at several sites and through several long-standing and continued mechanisms.

Larger-society social policies—welfare, housing, employment preparation, economic development—were not and are not now designed to take advantage of the critical adaptive function of the black church and other black community organizations. These programs are delivered and controlled by outsiders, often professional and well paid but with little positive relational tie to the recipient community. Such programs often leave little economic power in the hands of black community leaders. Aside from the issue of economic benefits to larger-society service givers, the implicit assumption is that there are no residual black-white relationship problems that must be addressed in developing programs to assist the most traumatized segment of the black community; that attitudes of dependency, short-range goals, limited motivation for responsible family behavior—all the legacy of slavery and years of oppression—will disappear with training and job opportunities.

The less traumatized black families were able to take advantage of the increased opportunities in government, education, employment, and business, thereby experiencing improved economic conditions in the 1960s. But the most traumatized families, which were unable to secure social and economic well-being or a sense of adequacy through identification with either larger-society or black community institutions and leaders, deteriorated most in the face of a changing economy. Such families are the primary site of a disproportionate amount of violence, crime, and other social problems. The twelve-year-old youngster with whom I worked in 1965–66 and remet fifteen years later was from such a family. These families appear to be increasing.

Traumatized families often overwhelm institutions and programs based on the notion that no previous trauma took place, that success as families and in the economic system is merely a matter of will and hard work. Housing programs that isolate the poor and then systematically remove the best organized and most effective families from the neighborhood or housing project through income limits are an example of such thinking. Still another example is that of teacher and administrator education programs that focus on content and methods and do not prepare educators to promote the movement of underdeveloped children along critical pathways other than the intellectual. There are many other examples of "policies of denial."

Children from the most traumatized families more often fail in school—unnecessarily—and begin a downward trend of failing in later school, often dropping out or attending without hope and purpose, and then failing in life.[15] In reaction to failure, the most vibrant and reactive often become disruptive and violent in and out of school, both individually and in groups or gangs. Neighborhoods and communities of adequately functioning families are then overwhelmed by the reactive and most troubled individuals and families. Models of violence and other troublesome behavior for children abound in relatives, friends, and neighbors unsuccessful in previous generations.

Those less prone to strike out at others in frustration and anger often develop self-destructive (self-violent) habits—alcoholism, drug abuse, and so on. But for some, financing such habits and finding supplies has become a way of life—providing ironically a sense of purpose, personal organization, achievement, and adequacy. And financing drugs in particular is a major source of violence, robbery, and other crimes in our society.

The mechanism of displacement used so frequently in slavery and throughout the period of overt oppression persists. Much black-on-black violence is in reaction to an inability to cope with the larger society or to identify with black and white leaders and institutional achievements. Frustration and anger is taken out on people most like the self. But while technology and social change has increased social distance, they have also weakened the notion that "the universe is unfolding as it should." The have-nots can more often ask, "why not?" They can more often strike out against the haves in crime and violence because the social and psychological constraints related to limited information and other social conditions no longer exist. This has increased and will continue to increase black-on-white violence.

While social change has affected blacks and other vulnerable minorities most, many marginal white families also have been less able to cope since the 1940s. Black success in the highly visible areas of athletics, entertainment, and media news contributes to the notion that blacks are getting ahead. This threatens the ability of marginal whites to identify—use the fact of being white—with the achievement of the white leadership group. Among less well-functioning whites, this increases the need to scapegoat blacks. Economic hard times intensifies their anxiety and increases incidents of white violence and threats against blacks. This accounts for the increased Ku Klux Klan and other hate-group activity across the country. And while the least well functioning act out in violence, the threat and resistance to change within the larger society has increased up and down the larger-society socioeconomic ladder.

Blacks at every socioeconomic level sense and directly experience the resistance. Black organizations and better educated and connected black people respond with programmatic efforts to maintain basic rights and opportunities obtained during the 1960s, despite considerable anger and alienation. Blacks less well controlled personally and less well connected to black or white institutions providing economic and psychological security more often respond with violence. Triggering incidents, such as questionable police action in black neighborhoods, have set off several major and minor riots, including acts of violence against people and property, during the last two or three years. These blacks are reacting to more than the incident. They are responding to a general sense of unjustifiable exclusion from reasonable opportunities to meet basic physical, social, and psychological needs. The police are symbolic of the larger-society forces perceived as responsible for the exclusion.

Some social policies and practices by government and private institutions and individuals have come closer to what is needed. Programs designed to try to overcome extreme economic powerlessness in the black community, knowingly or inadvertently, go to the heart of the problem in a society in which economic, political, educational, and other social opportunities are so intertwined. A variety of programs to promote black businesses have been developed, and a small black business leadership group has emerged. But overall these programs have been a matter of too little, too late; they have been based on white community development patterns rather than on the peculiar experience of blacks and the resultant need to promote broad-based black economic development as well as individual opportunity and wealth.

The amount of money allocated for such programs has been relatively small. The commitment of too many in government and private agencies is merely token and moreover is devoid of much understanding of the urgency and degree of need. To be widely and greatly successful, black business people, like immigrant groups before them, would have to be supported by a rising tide among their own group while they make significant links with the larger-society business networks. But overall black community opportunities have come in a trickle rather than a tide and there are no real links to the larger business community. Affirmative-action policies were designed to address this problem. But resistance based on a lack of understanding of the need and fear of the loss of a competitive edge has greatly limited the effectiveness of this policy.

Also, and again, the nature of the postindustrial economy does not facilitate easy identification with local leadership and community development in the natural way it once did. Thus, black political, economic, and social leaders would have to create ties to all segments of their community to have the same trickle-down economic and bubble-up social effects that white business developed two and three generations ago. The black community, never as cohesive as some other groups and subjected to a century of attitudes and values favoring individualism, may not fully appreciate the necessity for broad-based group economic and social development; it may not appreciate the degree to which group cohesion, strong organizations, and power, in addition to individual effort, is necessary to achieve widespread black development. Appreciation of this need is even more unlikely to occur among blacks born after the height of the civil rights movement in the 1960s. The result may be that the gap between black haves and have-nots will grow wider. Should this be the case it will be even more difficult to link the most troubled black families to the mainstream of the society.

Finally, the only tried and true road to reasonable economic opportunity for blacks has been education. Societal neglect of predominantly black colleges has put their future in imminent peril. The across-the-board reduction in assistance for higher education has hurt families from groups that were most excluded from economic opportunities in the past and are now least able to support skyrocketing higher education costs for their children. The neglect and threatened abandonment of public education will have the same effect.

The consequence is that the nucleus of black leadership, already less than 10 percent of what is needed, will shrink even more. And the ability of talented young people to identify, learn from, and be influenced by people like themselves, to be emotionally attached and therefore powerful motivators, will be reduced. It already appears that the flow of blacks into new career areas and opportunities does not come from poor or previously excluded families, but from families of people who managed to obtain a reasonable education and income level in the previous generation.

Should these trends continue, positive black community growth and development can eventually be outpaced by downward spiraling families. This will worsen violence, crime, and every other social problem, including black and white conflict.

## THE REDUCTION OF BLACK VIOLENCE

To reduce black violence will not be easy. It will require a significant change in larger-society understanding, attitudes, policies, and practices. The motivation to change is not great, because the connection between larger-societal conditions and violence, crime, and other social problems is not widely understood or accepted. As mentioned earlier, barriers to understanding are rooted in long-standing religious beliefs and defensive responses. No one can list the specific programs that must be created to promote black community development and resultant violence reduction. But the areas that must be addressed can be articulated.

First, mature nations have long recognized that violence, crime, and other social problems are not simple acts of bad will or sin, that promoting prosocial behavior and relying heavily on families and their support systems is far more effective than police action, justice, and correctional systems. The notion of inherent badness and laziness must be put to rest. Perhaps people from all groups experiencing the serious social and psychological effects of unemployment, business failures, near riots of thousands of people over the mere rumor of available jobs, and other economic recession–related problems will help improve our understanding and permit more mature responses to our social problems.

The critical role of the family and its dependence on economic opportunities and positive relationships to institutional leadership cannot become common knowledge until information sources and decision makers make it so. Violence and crime scholarship must focus more on the family, child rearing and development, and issues of community relatedness than on justice and correctional issues. School academic programs must allow young people to understand the critical role of family and community relations and the past and present deterrents to successful family functioning. Political leaders and mass media executives have the same responsibility. Because of television, top political and/or government leaders have become extremely important in establishing national understanding and attitudes.

No social program, public or private, designed to address black community economic and educational underdevelopment can be successful unless the negative consequences of past government and private-sector social policies are as well understood as the devastating consequences of national disasters. Also, the negative consequences, for blacks and whites, of not addressing past and present problems must be understood. Otherwise, public support for programs such as affirmative action, adequate support for black education, community development, and the like will not be great or sustained long enough to be helpful.

Second, a national family program and focus is needed. Indeed, until all American families understand the importance of child rearing and development and feel reasonably supported and appreciated in that effort, material success and other achievements will remain more important. The emphasis on material gain will remain a source of destructive competition and scapegoating. Hundreds of public and private family support programs—child care, health care, education, recreation and character development—exist. But most are fragmented and uneven in quality. Many families fall through the cracks and receive no support at all. This means that in one of the most highly developed scientific and technological nations in the world—where effective functioning requires a high level of social, psychological, and intellectual development—child development is left to chance.

Third, the more tightly knit communities of the past cannot be restored, but government and private attention must be given to how local communities can restore a reasonable "sense of community." Ironically, in some places, the violence and crime problem and resultant neighborhood watches and the like have spawned the kind of interaction and concern that is needed. But such approaches must be less defensive and negative in orientation and more in the spirit of promoting a positive, supportive community climate. Numerous school programs across the country have decreased violence and crime with this approach. Even some cities have done so.

All the above approaches would positively affect black violence and crime. But it will be necessary to go one step beyond to address black community needs. The most troubled and troubling segment, and the not so troubled but excluded segment, of the black community must be linked to the larger society through black community institutions that *themselves* must be linked to the institutions of the larger society. Programs in housing,

employment, employment preparation, general education, economic development, and the like must have a significant black community input,
sponsorship, or other arrangement that allows for residual benefits, primarily money. But skills, such as planning, organizing, and implementing
long-range programs and goals and the confidence, contacts and know-how
to participate in larger-society activities, are also needed.

I am not suggesting that white people can't be helpful in black communities. Indeed many blacks now operate effectively in predominantly white
settings and whites in predominantly black settings. But I am saying that
black institutions and people who are sensitive and emotionally attached
to, and dependent on, the outcome of programs in the black community
can and must serve as important primary social network identification
models and links to the larger secondary and tertiary social networks. A
low-income black parent in a school improvement program that was floun-
dering singled out the only black person among the several leaders involved
and said, "I want my son to grow up and go to work with a shirt and tie
and briefcase, just like you!" The black participant's commitment and sense
of responsibility had to go beyond rational program planning, work, and
concern.

The evidence that groups link and support their members and thereby
reduce violence and other social problems can be seen in the experience of
immigrants a generation or two ago. The success of black programs that
anchor violence-prone youth and other people in need in programs promoting ethnic pride, concern, care, and guidance suggests the same. Black
groups that developed businesses, group pride, and cooperative, communal
supports were even more powerful in positively influencing people that
social workers and probation officers couldn't touch. But such groups are
often seen as threatening, do not receive support, and are perhaps even
undermined, so that they wither and die. Genuine efforts to link such
groups to black and white institutions would give the society a mechanism
for reaching the unreachables.

Finally, I am not suggesting that nothing can or should be done to improve and support police work and justice and correctional activities. Much
must be done. I am suggesting that we will never be able to mop the water
off the floor unless we turn off the faucet that is causing the tub to overflow.
And time is running out. Unlike decaying streets and bridges, the tear in
the fabric of human social systems somewhere down the line will be beyond
repair.

## NOTES

1. See chapter 1 of this volume.
2. Elliott Currie, "Crime and Ideology," *Working Papers,* May–June 1982, pp. 26–35.

3. S. E. Schlesinger, "Prediction of Dangerousness in Juveniles—A Replication," National Council on Crime and Delinquency, *Crime and Delinquency,* January 1978, pp. 40–48.

4. Staff of the *Wall Street Journal, Here Comes Tomorrow: Living and Working in the Year 2000* (Princeton, N.J.: Dow Jones Books, 1966).

5. James P. Comer, *Beyond Black and White* (New York: Quadrangle/New York Times Book Co., 1972), ch. 3.

6. Jacob Drachler, ed., *African Heritage: Anthology of Black African Personality and Culture* (New York: Macmillan Co., 1969); James L. Gibbs, Jr., ed., *Peoples of Africa* (New York: Holt, Rinehart and Winston, 1965).

7. Daniel Mannix and Malcolm Cawley, *Black Cargoes: A History of the Atlantic Slave Trade, 1518–1865* (New York: Viking Press, 1962).

8. John Hope Franklin, *Reconstruction after the Civil War* (Chicago: University of Chicago Press, 1961).

9. E. Franklin Frazier, *The Negro Church in America* (New York: Schocken Books, 1962).

10. Phillip S. Foner, *Organized Labor and the Black Worker: 1619–1981* (New York: International Publishers, 1981).

11. David Blose and Ambrose Caliber, *Statistics of the Education of Negroes, 1929–30; 1931–32,* U.S. Department of Interior, Office of Education, bulletin no. 13 (Washington, D.C., 1936), p. 16.

12. Federal Security Agency, Office of Education, *Land Grant Colleges and Universities,* bulletin 1952, no. 21 (Washington, D.C., 1952), p. 12; Edward Danforth Eddy, Jr., *Colleges for Our Land and Times: The Land Grant Ideas in American Education* (New York: Harper Bros., 1957), pp. 257–58.

13. "1964–1965 Voluntary Support of America's Colleges and Universities" (New York: Council for Financial Aid to Education, 1967), pp. 3, 21–59.

14. Bureau of the Census, *Fertility of American Woman: June 1980,* Current Population Report, series P-20, no. 375 (Washington, D.C., October 1982).

15. James P. Comer, *School Power: Implications of an Intervention Project* (New York: Free Press, 1980).

# 4

# Citizen Self-Help and Neighborhood Crime Prevention Policy

PAUL J. LAVRAKAS

Often when people learn that a rape, murder, or other serious crime has occurred in their neighborhood, their typical response echoes an old refrain: "Why didn't the police stop this from happening?" With all the exposure to the Perry Masons and Kojacks of television, it should come as no surprise that many Americans assume that crimes occur because of the *direct failures* of the institutions of the criminal justice system.

In contrast to this notion, it is a major premise of this chapter that the criminal justice system (including the police) can in most instances only *react* to crime, not *prevent* it. While this is not a new idea, it merits constant repeating until its importance has been acknowledged and acted upon. Charles E. Silberman, in *Criminal Violence, Criminal Justice,* has argued compellingly about the limited role of the criminal justice system in preventing crime and maintaining order.[1] But even many of our best known

I have studied citizen crime prevention for the past ten years. In that time many other scholars and practitioners have added to our state of knowledge in this field, one whose roots may be traced to the presidential crime commissions of the late 1960s. Among those many, I would especially like to acknowledge my appreciation to Fred DuBow, Dan Lewis, Janice Normoyle, Dennis Rosenbaum, and Wesley Skogan for the benefits I have gained from exposure to their work and ideas. The same holds true for Fred Heinzelmann and his colleagues at the Community Crime Prevention Division of the National Institute of Justice. Finally, I would like to thank former Chief William McHugh, former Chief Howard Rogers, Chief William Logan, Sgt. Hank White, and Commander Frank Kaminski of the Evanston, Illinois, Police Department for providing me with numerous opportunities to conduct applied research on citizen/community crime prevention.

I would also like to thank a number of persons who provided helpful comments on an earlier draft of this chapter. These include Susan Bennett, Royer Cook, Lynn Curtis, Fred Heinzelmann, Janice Normoyle, Dennis Rosenbaum, Wesley Skogan, James Tien, and Richard Titus.

scholars, such as James Q. Wilson, appear to continue to view the institutions of the criminal justice system (e.g., the police) as the primary vehicles through which crime can be prevented and order maintained.[2] While the criminal justice system is necessary and important, I believe these agencies can at best play only a secondary role to that of an efficacious citizenry.

What seems most clearly needed to prevent most instances of crime and other antisocial incidents in neighborhoods is a caring and vigilant citizenry. Such citizens not only would use the agencies of the criminal justice system to enforce laws but also would strive to improve the quality of life in their communities, especially for those who seem to have the least incentives to conform to the values shared by most of their fellow citizens and thus are most likely to cause problems for them. While arguing this point, I also suggest that the criminal justice system and especially the police must develop and exercise the expertise attributed to them by citizens as "crime prevention experts." They must teach the public that crime prevention is primarily the *public's* responsibility.

Since the presidential crime commissions of the late 1960s, we have learned that crime prevention is best not viewed as an either/or venture. Citizens cannot merely strive to "reduce opportunities" for crime by protecting themselves, their households, and their neighborhoods, and then automatically expect crime to be prevented.[3] Nor is it realistic to expect every American to volunteer time to projects that address the "root causes" of crime.[4] Nevertheless, if we expect to make meaningful reductions in the levels of criminal victimization we have experienced since the 1950s, increased efforts on both fronts must be encouraged. Unfortunately, it appears that not enough of the public or the policymakers realize this, or if they do realize it, not enough have been willing or able to act on it. This, I believe, helps explain our lack of significant progress in stemming crime.

The impact of crime in diminishing the quality of life is far greater than a mere tally of victimizations (whether reported or unreported to the police). Its greatest effect on the psyche of our nation may be its signal that "things are getting out of control."[5] Furthermore, there appears to be a self-feeding spiral at work here—one in which crime and instances of disorderly behavior result from deteriorating social control on the part of community residents, which fuels the loss of control, which in turn speeds the cycle onward. It is this cycle that needs to be interrupted. And it is my contention that the lessons of the past fifteen years teach us that we will continue to miss the mark until we focus our resources not so much on improving the efficiency of the criminal justice system as on nurturing the desire and ability of citizens to help themselves—with the assistance of the criminal justice system—by gaining a measure of control over their neighborhoods.

## CITIZEN PRODUCTION OF COMMUNITY SECURITY

The notion that, collectively, citizens play the greatest role in determining the level of crime and disorder that exists in neighborhoods is not new. Yet it is clear that at present too many citizens do not recognize their responsibilities in these matters. Rather, people seem to have fallen into a "why-do-I-pay-taxes?" mentality. That this has happened probably reflects the basic change our culture has undergone in the past century.

Historically, humans took for granted that *they* were primarily responsible for their own safety.[6] As population density grew and cities formed, institutions such as the police developed, releasing the citizenry from some of their responsibility for keeping communities safe. But even then, it was the behavior of the citizenry, not the police, that ultimately determined community security.

In time, law enforcement agencies and agents became an established part of government bureaucracy, but still it was recognized that these institutions and agents could play only a limited role if for no other reason than their limited numbers. Thus at times, the vigilance of the citizenry was manifested in the vigilante tradition. In a review of American vigilantism, R. M. Brown concluded that at its base this phenomenon strove to enforce the "conservative values of life, property, law and order." Furthermore, when it "represented a genuine community consensus" and was not directed against legitimate "minority" behavior, vigilantism was often a socially constructive movement.[7]

Because of the necessities created by our increasingly more complex and technological society, governments at all levels have assumed more and more of the responsibility for neighborhood security in the last century.[8] While this *is* their legal mandate, a serious mistake was made when we apparently failed to recognize that a democratic government's institutions can provide security only in a very narrow sense. They are our *fall-back* mechanisms when things go wrong. Generally, government institutions can react to criminal events and disorderly behavior and restore normalcy to *specific situations*. But we grievously erred when we also ascribed to them the power to prevent (and thus reduce) crime and disorder, in the broader sense.

Recently, some scholars have begun to write about citizen "co-production" of safety and security. Most of this work has come from those who apply an economic model to crime prevention, treating safety and security as valued goods that are "produced" by police and citizens.[9] These scholars, most of whom have worked with the Ostroms at Indiana University, seem interested in determining what proportion of security is produced by public sector agencies (e.g., the police) versus the proportion produced by the private sector (the citizenry). While no firm estimates are made, it is implicit in their work that a great deal of the internal security we experience in our daily lives is directly attributable to the anticrime behavior in which the public engages. This view is clearly shared by other observers of the crime scene.[10]

What is it, then, that we as citizens do that appears to so determine our own security? From my own research and that of my colleagues at the Center for Urban Affairs and Policy Research at Northwestern University, it appears that citizens' preventive reactions to crime can best be understood as three fairly independent clusters of responses.[11] First, citizens try to protect themselves through a variety of self-precautions (including weapon purchases), but most often by merely restricting their own behaviors to reduce their exposure to possible victimization. Second, citizens take precautions to protect their households against home invasions.[12] These responses most typically represent some form of access control via the deployment of physical barriers (e.g., lights and timers) to the would-be offender. Finally, citizens engage in anticrime activities aimed at increasing the overall security of some territory (e.g., their neighborhood). This latter type of anticrime activity is nearly always a collective effort involving other citizens (e.g., neighbors) and ranges from informal surveillance, citizen patrols, and escort programs to projects directed at the presumed root causes of crime (e.g., providing recreational and employment opportunities for youth).[13]

Our research also indicates that these three basic modes of citizen anticrime responses are driven by different forces. Behavioral restrictions, the prototypical self-protection response, is directly tied to fear of crime. That is why we find that a majority of our central-city residents (where fear of crime is the greatest) place many restrictions on their own movements in place and time. On the other hand, a far fewer proportion of suburban and rural residents restrict their own behaviors, at least not in their own communities.

The security-oriented measures that citizens deploy in their homes appear linked not so much to fear of crime or to experience with victimization as to owner/renter status. Home owners, regardless of where they live, create a more secure environment to live in than do renters.[14]

Finally, we have found strong evidence that participation in collective anticrime activities at the neighborhood level rarely has anything to do with fear of crime, since fear's effect is a restricting one. Rather, this form of citizen self-help appears directly linked to citizens' concerns about the general quality of life in their neighborhoods and to their willingness to voluntarily give some time to "make this a nicer place to live."[15]

All these anticrime measures that citizens use to protect their person, their home, and their neighborhood probably do more to determine the amount of neighborhood crime that takes place each year than the direct effect of all the agencies and agents of the criminal justice system. This, then, is what is meant by citizen "production" of community security. While it is unfortunate that it is necessary in today's world, citizens reduce their levels of victimization when they restrict their own behaviors. (This may well be one of the major reasons women and the elderly have relatively low victimization rates.) It also seems very likely, though definitive evaluation studies have not been performed, that citizens contribute to their own safety and that of their neighborhood when they engage in and/or employ both household and neighborhood crime prevention activities and measures.

Why then have we not seen a massive and sustained policy thrust in support of these citizen efforts at production of neighborhood security? In partial answer to that question, and as a primary purpose of this chapter, let us look at public policy in these matters over the last fifteen years.

## COMMUNITY CRIME PREVENTION PUBLIC POLICY SINCE 1965

The emergence of attention to *citizens as a resource* in the fight against crime was one of the most important outcomes of the commissions set up by President Lyndon B. Johnson. Yet I believe that this approach to crime prevention has failed to receive the level of attention and support it merits from federal, state, and local governments.

In July 1965, President Johnson established the Commission on Law Enforcement and Administration of Justice through executive order, "recognizing the urgency of the Nation's crime problem and the depth of ignorance about it."[16] While today our crime problems are no less urgent, we are no longer as ignorant about solutions. By making this statement, I am suggesting that the process that President Johnson set in motion has done little, in a real sense, to reduce crime, but has done a fair amount to help us learn (or some might say relearn) what must be done to reduce it.

The Katzenbach Commission issued its findings in the 1967 volume, *The Challenge of Crime in a Free Society.* In response, Congress passed the Omnibus Crime Control and Safe Streets Act of 1968. In establishing the action agency, the Law Enforcement Assistance Administration (LEAA), the 1968 act stated "that crime is essentially a local problem that must be dealt with by state and local governments if it is to be controlled effectively." This was a start in the right direction, yet a careful reading of the act finds rather vague directives about what should be done at the local level to control crime; the act merely specified that funds could be allocated to educate the public about crime prevention and law enforcement. Funds could also be spent to employ community service officers (civilians) at the local level to encourage "neighborhood participation in crime prevention and public safety efforts." Other than this, nothing was said by the Congress about citizen involvement in crime prevention.

As such, the Omnibus Crime Control and Safe Streets Act left up to the LEAA the *particulars* of how to support citizen involvement in crime prevention. The agency then received billions of federal dollars to allocate to these and other crime-control ends. In retrospect, we can see that with all the established constituencies of the criminal justice system (e.g., police, attorneys, judges) vying for LEAA money, it is not surprising that insufficient attention and support was given by the top (politically appointed) LEAA administrators to the notion that citizen involvement was critical to the war on crime. Specifically, the Community Crime Prevention Division of the National Institute of Justice has never received sufficient funds to investigate fully how best to promote this notion of an involved citizenry.

All this is not to say that no attention was given to the citizenry's role in crime prevention. Yet as one looks back on the years that followed, it appears that too often the time and resources devoted to citizen involvement seemed more a matter of lip service on the part of top administrators than a sincere and serious effort to develop policy in this direction. Recommendations made by lower level bureaucrats were rarely supported to the extent necessary to give the ideas a fair chance of succeeding.

By 1971, LEAA had established a commission "to formulate for the first time national criminal justice standards and goals for crime reduction and prevention at the state and local levels." The series of reports that were issued by that commission included a volume, *Community Crime Prevention,* that addressed the roles of public- and private-sector agencies and *citizens* in the fight against crime at the local level. For the most part, the volume contained recommendations for community-based programs targeted at presumed root causes of crimes: youth service bureaus, drug abuse programs, and other employment, educational, recreational, and religious strategies.[17]

Apart from this, very limited space was given to *specific* recommendations of what the average citizen could realistically do to prevent crime. One example, though, was a statement on the "reduction of criminal opportunity":

> Combating crime is not solely the responsibility of law enforcement agencies. Crime reduction can come about only if the community, criminal justice personnel and individuals work together. Law enforcement agencies have a responsibility to inform citizens of ways to protect themselves, and their families. Such programs, however, will have little effect unless citizens take such elementary precautions as locking their doors and windows, or reporting suspicious or criminal activities in their neighborhoods. Citizen participation in crime prevention begins at home.[18]

In this statement and in an appendix to the volume, the commission suggested that proper citizen anticrime measures included:

- Locking doors and windows
- Reporting suspicious/criminal activity
- Increasing the "target-hardness" of homes (e.g., special locks)
- Increasing the informal surveillance of one's neighborhood and participating in block watches
- Engraving personal property with an I.D. number
- Patrolling neighborhoods via walking or driving with or without CB radios.

It is important to note that all these recommendations were made in the total absence of valid evaluation research on the effectiveness of any of these measures in preventing crime.

What one finds in this volume is basically a case-by-case citation of "successful" community crime prevention programs that had cropped up around the country in the 1960s.[19] In retrospect, this created a serious problem, because it was assumed by many that programs that purportedly had worked in one community could be automatically taken off the shelf and successfully deployed in another community. Unfortunately, it took the rest of the 1970s to learn that community crime prevention does not work this way! What, at cursory inspection, may appear to be a successful anticrime strategy or program is often only the final visible stage (somewhat like the proverbial tip of the iceberg) of a much more complex process. When a program seemed to succeed in reducing crime, it was probably something much larger than the specific anticrime strategy that changed in the community to bring about the crime reduction. And the complexity of understanding what this much larger something was led one scholar to ponder "what *is* community crime prevention?"[20] (Later I will discuss this larger process, which I believe accounts for successful community crime prevention.)

A further look at *Community Crime Prevention* is called for, because it also illustrates what has been another major barrier to reasoned policy development in this area (one that unfortunately continues to this day). As mentioned earlier, the evidence that was used to make policy recommendations about community crime prevention was little more than a collection of testimonials and "expert opinion." Too often these presumed experts on crime prevention were not expert at all. Nowhere has this situation been more prevalent than within the police field. Most often the police were (and continue to be) thought of as experts on crime prevention, and I will later argue that they should be. But rarely have they been truly knowledgeable about crime prevention in its larger sense, other than knowing how to react to and control specific instances of criminality.

I have argued that a critical mistake was made when we, as a society, began to shift our expectations about who is responsible for crime prevention. When we began to ascribe this responsibility to the police, we also erred in assuming that if they were responsible, then they must also be expert in prescribing solutions. I am not arguing this point so much as a critique of the police (though they share some of the blame) as a critique of ourselves and other officials for shunning a responsibility that should have remained the public's.

All this led to a crime prevention policy formulated on untested hunches. The commission's 1973 report contained many good suggestions, but they were untested. While there were claims that the measures had worked in some communities, no one really knew how or why they worked. If things could be done over, it would have been at this point that Congress and LEAA should have committed a significant amount of funding (say, $50 or $100 million) to *systematic testing* of these ideas to see if they really worked and, just as important, how they worked.[21] This was not done. Instead millions of dollars were committed to implement these "good ideas," and it took a series of national evaluations to point out the shortsightedness of this policy course.

Starting in 1974, the research and evaluation arm of LEAA, then called the National Institute of Law Enforcement and Criminal Justice (NILECJ) and now called the National Institute of Justice (NIJ) began a series of meta-evaluations, using a model developed by the Urban Institute.[22] These evaluations were proposed to NILECJ by evaluators throughout the country, and five were funded that directly related to community crime prevention. Each of these meta-evaluations aimed at documenting the state of existing knowledge about certain kinds of anticrime programs, highlighting knowledge gaps and making policy recommendations. The anticrime strategies that these evaluations focused on included: (1) property-marking projects (Operation I.D.),[23] (2) citizen crime-reporting projects,[24] (3) security survey projects,[25] (4) citizen patrol projects,[26] and (5) streetlighting projects.[27]

Each evaluation found that there was a lot of involvement on the part of citizens in these crime prevention programs (that is, in absolute numbers; not a large *percentage* of the public, though). But each evaluation also concluded that very little evidence was available to decide whether these anticrime strategies really prevented crime and if so, *how* they worked.[28] (And the latter concern is a critical one before we can apply some "successful" strategy in another location.)

Again, in retrospect, it appears clear that a much-needed and proper follow-up to the findings of these evaluations should have been some form of controlled field testing of these community crime prevention strategies.[29] And, in fact, that is what was proposed to LEAA in 1976.[30] In conducting the above mentioned meta-evaluation of citizen crime-reporting projects, it became clear to Leonard Bickman and me that these types of anticrime projects were often used as part of a larger set of strategies that included property marking, security surveys, block watches, and so on (for example, the Community Crime Prevention Program in Seattle). Yet when we presented our findings to NILECJ, we sensed that top administrators were tired of hearing that more testing was necessary, and because of the apparent political agenda of the time, they could not wait for the results of methodologically sound testing. Thus, at the conclusion of this phase of evaluative work, no one knew with any certainty whether these strategies actually prevented crime, and, in what later became a painful lesson, no one knew the best ways to successfully implement these strategies in new settings.

Despite this lack of tested knowledge, Congress supported the use of these and other anticrime strategies at the local level through the creation of the Office of Community Anti-Crime Programs. This office was mandated by the Crime Control Act of 1976, which also made funds specifically available for the "development and operation of programs designed to reduce and prevent crime against the elderly" and for "crime prevention programs in which members of the community participate, and including but not limited to 'blockwatch' and similar programs."

In interpreting the 1976 Crime Control Act, the Office of Community Anti-Crime Programs chose to build its funding priorities around the following distinction:

> Priority will be given to programs and activities that are "public-minded" in the sense that they are designed to promote a social or collective response to crime and the fear of crime at the neighborhood level in contrast to "private-minded" efforts that deal only with the actions of citizens as individuals or those that result from the provision of services that in themselves do not contribute to the organization of the neighborhood.[31]

While this distinction may appear to be a clear one on first reading, it turns out to be ambiguous when put into practice, because the public-minded/private-minded distinction does not hold up as a valid way of differentiating anticrime *behaviors*. Rather it is properly used to identify different *motives* for these behaviors.[32]

The Community Anti-Crime Program (CACP) was mandated by Congress to allocate $30 million to fight crime through direct grants to community groups rather than funding state or local governments. The premise implicit in this funding process is noteworthy. For the first time, the federal government was acknowledging that organized groups of residents were the best vehicle to combat local crime. Dan A. Lewis of Northwestern University noted the importance of this underlying premise in his critique of the CACP when he suggested that "the CACP may be . . . [an] approach to the reallocation of political authority through federal initiative."[33]

Despite what could be considered a good start, at least when it came to recognizing the proper vehicle through which to foster crime prevention, the CACP did not live up to its promise, in part because of the pressures and constraints put on the program by Congress. While the evaluation report on that program is more than four years overdue, what seems to have happened is an example of inadequate program implementation. Rather than providing sufficient crime prevention technical assistance to community organizations so that they could make good use of the CACP funds to devise and implement "their own preferred solutions to locally identified crime and crime-related problems," Marlys McPherson and Glenn Siloway of the Minnesota Crime Prevention Center concluded that the heavy federal involvement so hampered the local planning process as to render CACP ineffective.[34]

The conclusion that should be drawn from the CACP experience is not that the theory of supporting citizen self-help anticrime initiatives will not work, but rather that the theory did not get a fair and proper testing via the CACP. As Carol Weiss pointed out in her seminal book on evaluation research, a clear distinction must be made between a "program" failure and a "theory" failure.[35] And without a program success there can be no valid test of the theory. What happened with CACP cannot be viewed as a program success.

The Justice System Improvement Act of 1979 acknowledged the importance of supporting neighborhood and community anticrime efforts by continuing the Office of Community Anti-Crime Programs and by authorizing formula grants to state and local governments. The act specified that these formula grants could be used for: (1) establishing or expanding community or neighborhood programs that enable citizens to undertake initiatives to deal with crime and delinquency, and (2) improving the police utilization of community resources through support of joint police-community projects designed to prevent or control neighborhood crime.

Here again, no adequate follow-up occurred, in this case, because of politics. Drastic cutbacks in the LEAA budget took place as part of the budget-cutting pressures to which the Carter administration responded in 1979 and 1980. What then followed under the Reagan administration was the effective elimination of most of the planning bureaucracies at the federal, state, and local levels that had arisen since the crime commissions of the 1960s. This cutback in the level of bureaucracy was not all bad, but it also coincided with elimination of funds that could have been allocated to carry out the mandate of the 1979 act.

By 1982, all that remained of citizen anticrime action programs being funded by LEAA was the Urban Crime Prevention Program (UCPP) and the national anticrime public service media campaign that featured the slogan "Take a Bite out of Crime." The UCPP was a joint ACTION/LEAA venture that carried on the funding premise underlying the CACP—that local groups merit direct funding to help plan and implement anticrime strategies. At present it is unclear what actual impact UCPP has had on crime and fear reduction. But a process evaluation of eighty-four projects in nine cities that received $4.5 million in UCPP funds observed the critical necessity of providing technical assistance to these local groups "to help them help themselves."[36] In other words, it is not enough merely to give funds to most community/neighborhood groups and expect them to know how to put them to best advantage. I am not questioning that they, the local groups, must have the final say on what they do, but there are critical information-gathering skills and planning skills that most local groups do not have, but that are often necessary to fight local crime successfully. (I will be returning to this point later.)

Although it has been received with mixed reactions by many criminal justice practitioners and observers of the crime scene and by certain minority groups, I believe the anticrime media campaign featuring McGruff, the crime prevention dog-detective, is an important start in the right direction.[37] As I have stated previously, I believe that the public needs to (re)learn their responsibilities for preventing crime. This is one of the themes underlying the TBOC campaign. Although it is unrealistic to expect the campaign to markedly change the behavior of the American public, the ads can serve a very important legitimizing function for the efforts of local agents (e.g., community organizers and the police) as they take the crime prevention message to their community. I suspect that as more and more of the public is exposed to the campaign's message, it will become progressively easier to convince people at the local level of their crime prevention responsibilities. And it is at the local level where the battle against neighborhood crime must take place.

Apart from these LEAA-sponsored anticrime programs, the Department of Justice has also engaged in major delinquency prevention efforts during the past ten years. With the passage of the Juvenile Justice and Delinquency Prevention Act of 1974, Congress set out to remedy this century's lack of progress in preventing juvenile delinquency. Echoing earlier calls for community involvement, the act's underlying philosophy held that

the responsibility for control, primary punishment and rehabilitation of identified juvenile criminals remains with the court, but the *responsibility for prevention* has been given back to the community. The primary responsibility for preventing youngsters from engaging in illegal behavior . . . has been returned to those "front-line" community institutions—the family, schools, clubs, church, neighborhood—which historically have been responsible for the social integration, socialization, and control of youth.[38]

In addition to the anticrime programs that the Department of Justice has sponsored since the early 1970s, the Department of Housing and Urban Development (HUD) has also supported anticrime demonstration projects, such as the Urban Initiatives Anti-Crime Program. This program provided upwards of $40 million to public housing authorities in thirty-nine cities throughout the country so that they might involve residents (especially youth) in anticrime activities. At the time this chapter is being written, the Police Foundation is in the process of completing its two-and-one-half-year evaluation of this program, so it remains to be seen what new lessons may be learned from the HUD experience.

Looking back, then, at public policy toward community crime prevention for the last seventeen years, we find a number of instances where good starts were made, but often with insufficient follow-up. This has left us with a legacy of both strengths to build upon and weaknesses to overcome. The strengths have sometimes come through lessons learned from mistakes. For example, the CACP taught us that it is not enough to dole out money to local groups and expect positive results; one must also provide adequate crime prevention technical assistance. CACP also taught us that because of politics it is highly unlikely that the federal government can implement such a program without hampering its chance for success. While this is a useful lesson, CACP and other community crime prevention programs that turned out to be program failures have also tainted the underlying theory. We must overcome the *image of failure* that was sometimes left behind by the citizen anticrime action programs of the 1970s before the public and policymakers alike will acknowledge the wisdom of fostering citizen production of neighborhood security.

Fortunately, one of the strengths we now have to build on is the knowledge gained through the support of LEAA's research arm, the National Institute of Justice. Using that knowledge base, we now have a much better idea of how community crime prevention can best be fostered.

## RESEARCH FOR CITIZEN/COMMUNITY CRIME PREVENTION PROGRAMMING

As previously mentioned, a major barrier to the successful implementation of citizen anticrime strategies has been the relatively shallow knowledge base on which many programs have been founded. The political realities of the past seventeen years often forced policymakers to go into the field with programs whose concepts sounded good but actually were untested. Because an anticrime program can be linked to a reduction in crime and/ or fear of crime in some given community does not automatically mean that we can successfully transfer that program to another location. While the practitioners who planned and operated the program may claim to know *why* it works, it often turns out that there was more to the program that accounted for the positive results than even the practitioners realize. That is why successful citizen/community crime prevention is better viewed as a broader process than simply anticrime strategies such as block watches, citizen patrols, recreation programs, or the provision of employment opportunities for youth. This broader process includes those specific anticrime strategies, but just as important, it also includes both subtle and mundane actions by residents that signal that *they are trying* to get back in control of their neighborhoods. As such, it was a mistake when we thought that we could simply fund specific anticrime strategies without also re-creating the broader process.

The series of national meta-evaluations sponsored by NILECJ in the mid-1970s found that most of the action programs that tried to involve citizens in crime prevention were poorly conceptualized, especially in their understanding of how to sustain citizen participation. (This criticism also holds for other federal programs that encouraged citizen participation, not simply those dealing with crime.) The need for research for planning purposes appears to have been of low priority at LEAA compared with the need to "look like we're doing something." It didn't seem to matter that what was being done was wrong, or not especially efficient, as long as some actions were being taken to "fight crime."

Fortunately, at this time, LEAA was beginning to support research that has informed us about the broader process that appears to lead to citizen production of neighborhood security. Simply stated, the process is one that gets citizens to *feel* and *act* as though *they* are in control of their neighborhood! As the twelve-year-old heroine of "Suzy's War" (a superb, but little seen thirty-minute film for television) cries, "People, these are *our* streets!"[39]

The first significant research that helped us understand citizens' reactions to crime after the crime commission surveys in the late 1960s[40] was the seminal work of Frank F. Furstenberg.[41] He was the first to note the important distinction between citizens' *fear* of crime (how personally vulnerable they imagine themselves to be) and citizens' *concern* for crime (how much of a social problem they perceive crime to be in some given locale, such as their neighborhood). He also was the first to suggest that citizens' preventive responses clustered along two basic dimensions ("avoidance" and "mobilization"). Unfortunately, but indicative of the problems at LEAA in the 1970s, Furstenberg was so appalled with the political agendas of Congress and the top LEAA administrators that he quickly went back to academia and gave up his interests in crime research.[42]

Some of the major NILECJ-funded research programs of the 1970s that related to this general topic were: (1) the Defensible Space and the Crime Prevention through Environmental Design (CPTED) programs (the latter included a $4 million contract to the Westinghouse Electric Corporation) and a major environmental design demonstration/evaluation project in Hartford, Connecticut; and (2) the Reactions to Crime project at the Center for Urban Affairs, Northwestern University, which conducted multimethod field research for three years in neighborhoods of Philadelphia, Chicago, and San Francisco.

The CPTED research performed by Westinghouse was intended to be a field test of the crime prevention concepts promoted by the "defensible space" work of Oscar Newman and others.[43] This theory linked crime with the configuration of the physical (built) environment. Although most of the previous environmental design work focused exclusively on architectural aspects of the environment, the Westinghouse work tried to expand the theory to include aspects of the social environment as well.

There were a number of problems and shortcomings with the Westinghouse work with which I and many others who were associated with Westinghouse are all too familiar. Nevertheless, the Westinghouse research did provide some important findings. First, it demonstrated the great implementation difficulties that are encountered when a large anticrime effort is mounted. Westinghouse was involved in the planning of CPTED-type demonstration projects in a residential area of Minneapolis,[44] in a commercial sector of Portland, Oregon,[45] and in a school system in Broward County, Florida.[46] Each of these demonstrations required the coordination of several local agencies, and it was quickly learned that the local political environment often determined what, if anything, would be done as part of the demonstration. Second, the Westinghouse research suggested that modification of the social environment was as important, if not more important, than mere modifications of the physical environment.

One of the most promising specific findings of the Westinghouse research was a marked reduction in commercial burglaries in Portland that was apparently due to the formation of a community organization representing local businesses and to security surveys of all businesses that were made by the Portland police.[47] (These findings were later substantiated in a reevaluation of the Portland commercial demonstration.)[48] As a follow-up to this positive finding, NILECJ moved in a highly commendable direction— a controlled test of the strategies via the Commercial Security Field Test. The final results from this demonstration/evaluation project (in Long Beach, Denver, and St. Louis) are not yet in, but initial findings reinforce the conclusion that having a local community organization (in this case, a business group) serve as the primary vehicle through which to promote citizen/business involvement in crime prevention is of value.[49]

In addition to these CPTED-type projects, NILECJ heavily supported a demonstration/evaluation project in a residential section of Hartford, Connecticut, between 1973 and 1981. What was especially significant about

Hartford was the importance accorded the role of research/evaluation in the *planning process,* that is, the demonstration was based, in part, on the research. In their latest assessment of the Hartford experience the evaluators, F. Jack Fowler and Tom W. Mangione, have concluded:

- Environmental design changes can strengthen a neighborhood.
- Strengthening informal social control in a neighborhood can have a positive effect on residents' fears and concerns, although not necessarily having a *direct* effect on crime reduction.
- Fear of crime is more related to the character of a neighborhood than to actual crime rates.
- Aggressive, effective police activity *within the context of other elements of social control* may play a key role in deterring neighborhood crime.[50]

The legacy of the environmental design research that NILECJ/NIJ has funded has clear implications for programming in the area of citizen involvement in crime prevention. So too have the findings of the $1.5 million Reactions to Crime (RTC) project. That work began in 1975 as the brainchild of Fred DuBow and others at the Center for Urban Affairs, Northwestern University. Basically the RTC project was the first *comprehensive* attempt to conceptualize and then investigate citizens' varied cognitive, affective, and behavioral reactions to crime. The data base for the research included over ten thousand pages of field notes by on-site observers in ten neighborhoods in three central cities, thousands of random telephone surveys with residents of these cities, and detailed content analysis of all crime-related stories in each of the major daily newspapers in each city over the course of three months while the surveys were being conducted.[51] There was also a follow-up project that investigated the underlying motivations for citizens' preventive responses to crime.[52]

The implications for citizen self-help and neighborhood crime prevention that our work at Northwestern University suggested are:

- Citizens' attempts to prevent crime are of three basic types—personal, household, and neighborhood.
- The concepts of "private-minded" and "public-minded" can be useful in describing citizens' motivations, but not their behaviors.
- Fear of crime is only partly related to local crime rates and seems to have a good deal to do with the presence or absence of "signs of incivilities" in a neighborhood.
- Most persons form their fears, concerns, and other perceptions about local crime, not through the media or even exclusively through direct experience with victimization, but also through "vicarious victimization."
- Fear of crime and crime itself appear to be lower in those neighborhoods with relatively higher social cohesion.

- Citizens' involvements in neighborhood-based anticrime efforts are most often associated with their participation in multipurpose community organizations, including local church, school, and business groups.

In addition to the RTC research, others have made significant contributions to the current state of knowledge. Two of the larger research programs include the ongoing work of Stephanie Greenberg and her associates at Research Triangle,[53] and Ralph Taylor and his associates at Johns Hopkins,[54] both of whom are investigating the role of territoriality and informal social control as these concepts relate to lower rates of crime and fear of crime in neighborhoods.

In closing this section on research that can and should be used to help increase citizen involvement in producing community security, I would like to mention some recent work Dennis Rosenbaum and I have conducted with the Evanston, Illinois, Police Department in starting to apply the lessons of community crime prevention research to help a community deal with its crime problems. As part of the police department's Comprehensive Police-Community Crime Prevention Program,[55] detailed information was gathered from residents and community organizations to help identify the nature and extent of crime-related problems and to identify existing community resources that could be built upon in planning solutions. Following this empirical planning phase,[56] the implementation process commenced by convening a Residential Crime Prevention Committee made up of citizens and police representatives. The committee has gone on to produce an anticrime newsletter "Alert" to inform citizens about local crime and crime prevention[57] and to develop various strategies in which the police and local community organizations play pivotal roles in getting the citizenry involved in producing community security. Our preliminary evaluation of the Evanston experience has been quite positive, and like the Hartford project, it serves as an example of the broader process that is needed to involve the citizenry in a successful battle against the causes of crime.

## NEIGHBORHOOD SECURITY THROUGH CITIZEN SELF-HELP: SUGGESTED DIRECTIONS FOR THE FUTURE

In concluding this review of citizen involvement in the crime prevention process, I want to set forth what in my judgment is a course of action that should now be followed. There are a number of themes that are central to my recommendations:

- First, it is the citizenry, not the police or other public servants, who bear the prime responsibility for the security of neighborhoods.[58]
- Second, the government and the private sector (e.g., corporations) must

help citizens actualize this responsibility, and the police can and should play a critical role in bringing this about.

- Third, it is in everyone's best interest, including the police, that citizens assume their responsibility for the security of neighborhoods and properly use public servants such as the police to enhance this end.
- Fourth, it is not enough merely to encourage citizens to engage in anti-crime measures that are thought to reduce criminal opportunity; citizens must be encouraged to take direct actions against the root causes of crime.
- Fifth, although there are important supportive actions that can be taken at the federal, state, and local municipal levels, the focal point for successful crime prevention is the neighborhood/community level.[59]
- Sixth, multipurpose voluntary associations of citizens should be the vehicles through which opportunities are made available to the public for involvement in crime prevention.[60]
- Seventh, although there is a basic process that is common to all successful involvement of citizens in crime prevention, the process manifests itself in a variety of specific ways across different communities.[61]

To begin to teach the public their responsibilities for producing their own security, we should first recognize that most Americans assume that the police are our crime prevention experts. While in most instances this simply is not true, I believe the police *must develop and actualize* crime prevention expertise. As I stated earlier, most police have been too busy reacting to specific crimes to step back and take a long, hard look at how to prevent crime in the larger sense. While money and rhetoric supported the formation of many community relations units and crime prevention units during the past seventeen years, too often this was viewed by police as simply window dressing and/or merely a good way to bring more LEAA money into a department. Good public relations between citizens and the police is critical to the overall process, but it is not enough. Too often the police have failed to take seriously the notion of involving citizens in crime prevention, possibly because we formerly had little useful information about the citizen crime prevention process. Thus, too few departments developed any real expertise on how to involve the citizenry in crime prevention.

For this policy to work in the 1980s, police administrators must make it clear to their departments, through both words and actions, that they acknowledge that citizens play the crucial role in neighborhood crime prevention and that their department is bent on nurturing this role.[62] Logistically, this means that all departments should have officers who are trained citizen crime prevention specialists. And by training I do not mean simply that they should be schooled in the methods of opportunity reduction through target hardening. More important, these police experts must understand the process of citizen crime prevention, which includes the importance of community organizing.[63] And if for no other than symbolic reasons, these officers should be assigned the title of crime prevention specialists.

Moreover, it should be the mandate of these police specialists to seek out and work with existing citizen organizations in their jurisdiction's neighborhoods to increase residents' capacity to prevent crime. These specialists also should have direct input into the formulation of department policies, including allocation of manpower. Only when police chiefs make it clear to their departments in no uncertain terms that these are to be S.O.P. will the police begin to actualize their potential in the crime prevention process.

It will undoubtedly take a number of years for police administrators to see the wisdom of this course of action. There are just too many "good old boys" at the top levels of police departments to expect rapid change. If the traditional macho image police so often have of themselves serves as a barrier, it will be difficult for them to admit that without the efforts of citizens no real progress will be made in reducing crime. Yet, if for no other reason than that of self-preservation, the police should recognize the corner into which they have painted themselves. Too many of the public hold the police accountable for the amount of crime that occurs. When the police fail, as fail they will without the help of citizens, they get blamed for something that never should have been their responsibility in the first place!

Police who are willing to put these recommendations into practice must also be willing to deal with naturally occurring boundaries (the neighborhoods) within their jurisdictions. In large departments, this will require giving a great deal of autonomy and discretion to local area commanders. Only in this way will police be able to mesh with the varied needs of different communities.

Government can support police involvement in this process by setting it as a guiding policy. This needs to be done from the federal level down. The "Take a Bite out of Crime" (TBOC) media campaign is an example of this. TBOC should be further improved and actively supported, because of the legitimizing effect the campaign can have on the public's acceptance of efforts to get them involved in crime prevention. How much easier it would be for community organizers and the police to enlist the aid of residents in anticrime activities if these residents have already been exposed to the TBOC message.

What I have been proposing regarding the outreach that police should make in developing a crime prevention partnership with residents by working with voluntary associations assumes that these associations already exist. In communities where they are needed but don't exist, or where they exist but aren't working well to represent the interests of citizens, the police could try to encourage the community either to organize an association or to improve an existing group. Here it is crucial for the police to recognize that security is a basic part of the quality of life and that local groups should not simply organize around crime. Research shows that single-purpose anticrime groups are often short-lived, since crime, thankfully, is never an ever-present phenomenon at the local level.

Fortunately, though, multipurpose neighborhood and community organizations abound. And even where they are absent there are almost always informal social networks for resident interaction. Thus, in most instances, we already have in place a mechanism to increase citizen involvement in crime prevention. Many times, though, these groups do not recognize their importance, or if they do, they most often do not know how best to go about fighting crime.

I believe that just about anything that improves the overall quality of life in a neighborhood is likely to have a positive effect on local crime rates and fear of crime. Yet rarely do we see the quality of life miraculously improve because of the intervention of some outside agency. Rather, it is direct and indirect citizen involvement that is most likely to improve neighborhoods. While citizens cannot repave their own streets, they can often get city hall to do it if they are patient and properly organized; moreover, citizens can work to keep local streets free of litter. Residents may not have their own facilities to hold after-school basketball games, but they can usually reach some agreement with local schools and churches to use their gyms for practice and games. Residents then can volunteer time as coaches and referees and donate money for uniforms. Citizens may not be the best choice to stop specific incidents of violent crime, spouse abuse, or child abuse, but they can often get the police to intervene. Then residents can try to provide some social support for the victims. And if police consistently fail to respond when they are called, organized citizens can often pressure the local police commander to remedy the problem.

The American public must learn that if they want to live in safe and secure neighborhoods, *they* are the only ones who will bring this about. At the same time, the struggle is more likely to be successful when residents work in close cooperation with public-sector agencies. To increase the capacity of the public to prevent crime, there are a number of other basic strategies that can be followed.

First of all, we are not likely to increase security and feelings of safety in a neighborhood until we fully understand the nature and extent of the problems facing that neighborhood. Since problems will differ across neighborhoods, planning for neighborhood improvement must begin with an information-gathering phase. Ideally, this would include systematic observations of the neighborhood environment, retrieval of information from municipal archives, and random surveys of residents. Through systematic observation, we can, for example, learn where physical deterioration is most prevalent, where teenagers hang out, where people seem to avoid going, and so on. Through data retrieval from municipal offices, we can gain some sense of how burglaries are distributed in space and time, how owned and rented housing units mix in an area, what the age mix in a neighborhood is, and so on. From random surveys of residents, we can get a good (valid) sense of what residents' concerns and fears are, what anticrime measures they currently deploy, the degree of social cohesion in a neighborhood, residents' willingness to participate in organized neighborhood improvement projects, and so on.

I am not suggesting that neighborhood crime prevention can often be as structured and comprehensive as all this. Rather, my point is that there needs to be an explicit information-gathering phase so that planning for solutions can be based on more than hunches, rumors, and false perceptions. Information gathering is often an implicit step in many successful neighborhood improvement programs. Why not make it explicit so that others will recognize its importance when they try to replicate the process in their own neighborhoods?

It is at this stage that local groups could best use some technical assistance from social scientists to help them gather useful information and then make sense of it once it is collected. Local universities, colleges, and even high schools need to become more involved with community groups in applied study projects like these. In the spirit of sociologist Andrew Gordon's Computers for the People project, scientific methods and technology must be made accessible to the public.[64] And when outside funding is available from business groups, private foundations, or public monies, one of the best investments of these funds can be to aid this information-gathering phase.

I say this because spending some money up front to document local problems can bring in much more money and person-time later on in support of the solutions. If knowledge is power, then local groups need to be well informed about the problems facing them. City councils and other municipal agencies will be more likely to listen (or can be better persuaded to listen) when they are confronted with facts. An important ancillary strategy for the local group is image building via the media. Once local groups document the problems facing their neighborhoods, they should interest the local media with press releases of their findings. Just a little visibility can have an enormous snowball effect. When fellow residents, local business owners, and elected officials see the efforts of a local group publicized, this often bestows some special legitimacy on the group, and support is more readily forthcoming. Other residents are then more likely to become members; the business community is more likely to help finance improvement projects; and city hall is more likely to lend an ear when the group's president calls.

Once information has been gathered to document local problems and identify resources in the community, the planning phase can begin. Groups must begin by assigning priorities to the problems they've identified. Given the number of members that are active in the planning process, the larger membership can be broken down into smaller problem-specific planning groups. At this stage, there are two general categories of problems that may be encountered. Each is a signal to residents that things are getting out of control. First, there are the problems of serious crime (assaults, robberies, burglaries). Second, there are the problems of incivilities in the social environment (e.g., teenage loitering) and the physical environment (e.g., poor property upkeep). It is beyond the scope of this chapter to detail the myriad of responses available to combat incivilities, but I will discuss the range of anticrime responses a group might consider.

To begin with, the group must appreciate the basic difference between strategies targeted at the root causes of crime and those aimed at opportunity reduction. I have recommended that groups need to consider both types of action programs. I believe not only that both approaches are critical to crime prevention but that there is an important practical consideration here: groups must be realistic in the goals they set for themselves so as not to create expectations that are impossible to meet, thereby losing the good will of active members. This means that solutions should be planned as a sequence of small steps, with some sure "taste of success" built into the early steps so as to reinforce the motivations of participants. And it is usually easier to see quick successes along the opportunity-reduction pathway than the root-causes pathway.

Depending on the needs of their neighborhoods, groups should consider what types of personal, household, and neighborhood anticrime opportunity-reduction strategies they will advocate. Do women in the area need simple self-defense training? Are there times when it simply is not prudent for certain types of residents to be in certain places? Do houses and apartments need more secure doors and windows? Does lighting in backyards, alleys, and streets need brightening? Do sufficient numbers of residents watch out for one anothers' property at vacation time? Do children need escorting to school along certain routes? Do elderly people need shopping escorts? Do parks require citizen patrols on summer nights? It is wrong to think that every local group can and should encourage each and every possible anticrime measure. Nor should they choose some strategy because it worked somewhere else without first determining the similarity of this "somewhere else" with the local community.

Along the same lines, groups need to grasp some sense of the causes of local crime so that they can adopt a realistic approach that begins to deal with these causes. Since so much of the criminogenic process is linked to the developmental stages of youth, a community must squarely face the needs of its young. How can educational, employment, and recreational opportunities available to youth in the community be improved? Can't business groups be approached to help, even if for no other reason than self-interest? Do the social and health curricula in the local schools devote enough attention to the problems of youth, including drug and alcohol abuse? Are there enough after-school activities to keep youth off the streets while parents are still at work? Are parents properly supervising their children, especially at night and on weekends? (The Office of Juvenile Justice and Delinquency Prevention has published a series of reports that should be of great help to a local group facing youth problems in its community.)

No voluntary community effort can deal with all these issues simultaneously, but once problems have been identified and evaluated, a local group can begin some small-scale realistic effort as a start. Succeeding in this first effort can also have a snowball effect. It is trite to say "nothing breeds success like success," but it seems clear that when a group has demonstrated tangible accomplishments, members will find it easier to gain support for new programs, in terms of both volunteer time and donations.

All this discussion has been focusing on the local citizen group as the vehicle through which crime can best be prevented. As such, it is incumbent upon us to understand how to better nurture these groups.

There is no question that outside funding has the potential to help, whether from the private or public sector. But it is not a necessary, and certainly not a sufficient, condition for success. In fact, outside funding can be the bane of a local group if the group then loses its ability to make its own decisions about proper solutions to its community's problems or if the funds undermine the true strength of the local group—unpaid voluntary person-power. Too often in the past, local groups received government funds for certain programs regardless of whether the programs addressed their chief needs. Many times we have also seen local programs flounder when external funding is withdrawn. That this happens so regularly points up the problem of losing track of the importance of committed citizens. With this in mind, there are a number of specific recommendations (based on research NIJ has funded) that can help strengthen local citizen organizations:

1. It is of paramount importance that a local organization begin by addressing manageable tasks so that enough success is experienced to reinforce and sustain citizen action.
2. The organizations can request the regular attendance of a local police officer to serve as a security adviser to the group and as a facilitator on matters related to crime prevention.

3. Organizations in high-crime areas (typically ones with higher population density, lower per capita incomes, and greater minority population) will be faced with problems different from those in lower crime areas. In high-crime areas, organizations will not only have more serious problems to deal with, but will typically have fewer resources to apply to the problems; they will also have greater difficulties in getting citizens involved. This suggests that a good deal of person-time will have to be devoted to organizational maintenance and membership recruitment in such areas. In these instances, it may turn out that the organization cannot function entirely through voluntary workers; in such areas, funding may be necessary in order to employ at least a part-time administrator.

4. As more people move to the suburbs and as suburbs age, their crime and incivility problems are likely to increase. Suburban populations, however, seem readier to take a proactive stance toward problems, and suburban community organizations should capitalize on this by addressing issues and mobilizing citizens before problems become serious.

5. Voluntary organizations must recognize the life-cycle demands placed on their members and the varying levels of attachment to the community among local residents. This should help the organization develop realistic expectations about the amount of time people are willing to donate. Furthermore, recruitment strategies should recognize that home owners have property interests, parents have child-related interests, and young adults have recreation interests and that it is on such vested interests that the organization should build.

6. Organizational resources may be better invested in maintaining the involvement of the active core of members rather than focusing disproportionately on recruitment of new members. It appears that providing social affiliation benefits and other expressive incentives is especially important in keeping members active.[65]

7. From the standpoint of recruitment, it seems especially important that potential members perceive an opportunity to become involved in helping to solve local problems. This follows from the knowledge that initial involvement in community organizations seems predominantly related to instrumental motives (i.e., problem directed).

8. Fear of crime is not a factor that community organizations should play upon to motivate individual citizens to participate. Instead, residents should be approached by appealing to their interests in being good citizens and working to improve the quality of life in their neighborhood.

As this chapter was written, the Eisenhower Foundation of Washington, D.C., was developing a program that closely parallels many of the strategies

I have recommended for increasing citizens' capacity to prevent crime. This effort is called the Neighborhood Anti-Crime Self-Help Program and is financially supported by the Ford Foundation and over forty other institutions. The Eisenhower Foundation's program will strive to work with established community organizations in urban settings. The client organizations will receive technical assistance, first, to facilitate the gathering of sound information for planning their anticrime strategies and second, to plan and implement their own best solutions. The foundation will also provide seed money directly to the organization and negotiate matches from local foundations, corporations, governments, and law firms in the city where each organization exists. We, at the Center for Urban Affairs and Policy Research, are working in partnership with the Eisenhower Foundation both to help implement and to test the self-help concept. By 1986, we hope to be able to report that this model has been a documented success!

## CONCLUSION

I have argued that, in general, public policy in the United States toward crime prevention has failed to place sufficient weight on the importance of citizen involvement, or self-help. Too many of our supposed crime prevention experts and policymakers may well be expert about the workings of criminal justice system agencies, but they do not appear to recognize the implications of acknowledging the limitations of these agencies in our democratic society. Until we change the emphasis of our public policies away from considering the police, courts, and prisons to be the primary mechanisms for reducing crime, I believe that we will continue to experience the tragic levels of victimization with which our citizens now live. These criminal justice agencies are our means of *reacting* to crime—they should not be expected to *prevent* it by themselves.

I have argued that too many of our citizens need a severe awakening to their own responsibilities for neighborhood security. (Like the "slap in the face" shown on television, citizens may eventually conclude, "Thanks, I needed that.") Citizens must also learn to avoid the temptation to think, "If we only got better service for our taxes, we wouldn't have these problems." While it seems to be in the short-term interest of many politicians and criminal justice administrators to report their "great accomplishments" in fighting crime, this too perpetuates our crime problems by serving as a barrier to long-term solutions. And the media add to this barrier by confusing success in solving or prosecuting specific criminal events with crime prevention.

I have outlined a number of strategies that many others feel should be followed, if not exactly as set forth here, at least in this spirit. I have been purposefully idealistic, because I am optimistic that we have the capacity to change. I recognize that the struggle to involve citizens in crime prevention will face its greatest difficulties in just those neighborhoods where predatory crime is worst. Nevertheless, with adequate support from public-sector agencies, even the resource-poor should be able to *begin* the slow process of gaining control over their neighborhoods.[66]

The strategies I have outlined treat local multipurpose citizen organizations as the primary mechanisms through which neighborhood crime is most likely to be prevented. At the same time, I have stressed the importance of the direct and indirect roles of the police and other criminal justice agencies. In the past fifteen years, we have learned a lot that can now be used to plan a comprehensive strategy to prevent crime. (And a good deal of this knowledge can be traced to LEAA funding.) Yet we need to continue to learn what does and doesn't work and under what circumstances. We need, but are currently not getting, substantial support for field testing of the community crime prevention process. At the same time, we have passed the point where we should wait until more definitive answers are available. We need a major and sustained thrust, from the president on down, to wake America up to the critical importance of citizens helping themselves by helping their neighborhoods become safer places to live.

## NOTES

1. C. E. Silberman, *Criminal Violence, Criminal Justice* (New York: Random House, 1978).
2. J. Q. Wilson and G. L. Kelling, "The Police and Neighborhood Safety," *Atlantic*, March 1982, pp. 29–38.
3. Opportunity-reduction approaches to crime prevention refers to all efforts that strive to lessen the likelihood that instances of criminal victimizations will occur, or if they occur, to lessen the likelihood of success. For example, opportunity reduction includes the use of locks and lighting to discourage burglary.
4. Efforts that address the root causes of crime include programs that provide educational, employment, and recreational opportunities to youth to lessen the likelihood that they will turn to crime. These root-causes approaches also include the formal and informal socialization processes manifest in the actions of families, schools, and churches to regulate public behavior.
5. J. Conklin, *The Impact of Crime* (New York: Macmillan, 1975); J. Q. Wilson, *Thinking about Crime* (New York: Basic Books, 1975); P. J. Lavrakas, organizer of symposium, "Crime's Impact: More than a Mere Tally of Reported Victimizations," American Psychological Association, Annual Convention, Washington, D.C., 1982.
6. L. W. Sherman, "'Watching' and Crime Prevention: New Directions for Police," in *Crime and Public Policy,* ed. J. Q. Wilson, in press; D. Black and M. P. Baumgartner, "On Self-Help in Modern Society," in *The Manners and Customs of the Police* (New York: Academic Press, 1980), pp. 192–208.
7. R. M. Brown, "The American Vigilante Tradition," in *Violence in America*, ed. H. D. Graham and T. R. Gurr (Washington, D.C.: U.S. Government Printing Office [hereafter GPO], 1969), pp. 121–180.
8. cf. L. W. Sherman, "'Watching.'"

9. C. T. Coltfelter, "Urban Crime and Household Protective Measures," *Review of Economics and Statistics* (1977): 499–503; F E. Pennel, "Private versus Collective Strategies for Dealing with Crime, Citizen Attitudes toward Crime and the Police in Urban Neighborhoods," *Journal of Voluntary Action Research* 7 (1978): 59–74; S. L. Percy, "Citizen Coproduction of Community Safety," in *Evaluating Alternative Law-Enforcement Policies,* ed. R. Baker and F. Meyer (Lexington, Mass.: Lexington Books, 1979); M. S. Rosentraub and K. S. Harlow, "The Coproduction of Police Services: A Case Study of Citizens' Inputs into the Production of Personal Safety" (Arlington, Texas: Institute of Urban Studies, 1980), mimeo.

10. R. K. Yin, "What Is Citizen Crime Prevention?" in *Review of Criminal Justice Evaluation: 1978* (Washington, D.C.: GPO, 1979); D. A. Lewis, G. Salem, and R. Szoc, *Crime and Urban Community: Towards a Theory of Neighborhood Security* (Evanston, Ill.: Center for Urban Affairs, 1979); F. DuBow and A. Podolefsky, *Citizen Participation in Collective Responses to Crime* (Evanston, Ill.: Center for Urban Affairs, 1979); W. G. Skogan and G. E. Antunes, "Information, Apprehension, and Deterrence: Exploring the Limits of Police Productivity," *Journal of Criminal Justice* 7 (1979): 217–41.

11. P. J. Lavrakas, J. Normoyle, W. Skogan, E. J. Hera, G. Salem, and D. A. Lewis, *Factors Related to Citizen Involvement in Personal, Household, and Neighborhood Anti-crime Measures* (Evanston, Ill.: Center for Urban Affairs, 1980); F. DuBow and A. Podolefsky, *Citizen Participation*; Lewis, Salem, and Szoc, *Crime and Urban Community*; W. G. Skogan and M. G. Maxfield, *Coping with Crime: Individual and Neighborhood Reactions* (Beverly Hills: Sage Publications, 1981).

12. Ironically, property is more often lost each year through household larceny than through household burglary. In the former, the thief is someone who has been given permission to enter the home (e.g., an acquaintance, repairman, babysitter, etc.), while in the latter the offender gains entrance unlawfully. Furthermore, while a good number of people appear to fear physical harm from a home invasion, this type of crime is an extremely rare event. In other words, of all the people who are assaulted, raped, or murdered each year by strangers, only a very small percentage of these crimes takes place in the victim's home (see M. Rand, "The Prevalence of Crime," *BJS Bulletin NCJ-75905.* Washington, D.C.: GPO, 1981).

13. A fourth type of response to crime is moving to some place of residence that is perceived as safe. Our research indicates that despite the attention this type of response has received, only a small proportion of the citizenry has chosen to "flee" their neighborhoods as a *direct* response to crime (see W. Skogan and M. Maxfield, *Coping*).

14. Paul J. Lavrakas, "On Households," in *Reactions to Crime,* ed. D. A. Lewis (Beverly Hills: Sage Publications, 1981), pp. 67–86. The actual security that one enjoys by deploying many of the available access control devices/systems is questionable. What seems most effective as a deterrence to burglary is the appearance that someone is at home. See I. Waller, "What Deters Residential Burglary?" Third International Symposium on Victimology, Muenster, West Germany, 1979.

15. P. J. Lavrakas and E. J. Herz, "Citizen Participation and Neighborhood Crime Prevention," *Criminology* 20, nos. 3–4 (1982): 479–98.

16. *The Challenge of Crime in a Free Society* (Washington, D.C.: GPO, 1967).

17. National Advisory Commission on Criminal Justice Standards and Goals, *Community Crime Prevention* (Washington, D.C.: GPO, 1973). It appears that this was one of the first usages of the phrase "community crime prevention," which went on to become a buzzword that included all programs oriented at involving the public in self-help, anticrime activities.

18. National Advisory Commission, *Community Crime Prevention.*

19. By "successful," I mean that no one at the time had scientific (sound) evidence that these

programs were a success. Furthermore, when "experts" were confident of successes, it was not clear *what* it was about the programs to which the success should be attributed.

20. Yin, "What Is Citizen Crime Prevention?"
21. The reader should keep in mind that for a number of years LEAA's budget was well over $500 million.
22. A meta-evaluation is a study that collects a broad spectrum of information about a topic area (including past research/evaluation reports) and then critically examines the validity of the information sources to determine what can be said to be *known* about the topic area and with what degree of confidence.
23. N. D. Heller et al., *Operation Identification Projects: National Evaluation Program Summary Report* (Washington, D.C.: GPO, 1975).
24. L. Bickman, P. J. Lavrakas, et al., *Citizen Crime Reporting Projects: National Evaluation Project Summary Report* (Washington, D.C.: GPO, 1976).
25. C. Girard et al., *Security Survey Programs: National Evaluation Program Summary Report* (Washington, D.C.: GPO, 1976).
26. R. K. Yin et al., *Patrolling the Public Beat* (Washington, D.C.: GPO, 1976).
27. J. Tien et al., *Street Lighting Programs: National Evaluation Program Summary Report* (Washington, D.C.: GPO, 1977).
28. It is not surprising that little valid evidence was found by these meta-evaluations. As late as the mid-1970s, there was basically no skilled or interested research/evaluation community in the area of citizen involvement in crime prevention. Through LEAA support, though, such a constituency now exists.
29. By "controlled field testing," I refer to the systematic implementation of an anticrime strategy in target communities, with thorough research to test the impact of the strategy, including taking measures in comparison communities that do not have the anticrime project operating.
30. L. Bickman and P. J. Lavrakas, *Community Crime Prevention Phase II Recommendations* (Chicago: Loyola University, 1976).
31. U.S. Department of Justice, *Guidelines Manual: Guide to Discretionary Grant Programs* (Washington, D.C.: GPO, 1977), pp. 58–63.
32. P. J. Lavrakas et al., *Factors Related to Citizen Involvement in Anti-Crime Measures* (Washington, D.C.: GPO, 1981), p. 15.
33. D. A. Lewis, "Design Problems in Public Policy Development: The Case of the Community Anti-Crime Program," *Criminology* 17 (1979): 172–83.
34. M. McPherson and G. Silloway, "Planning to Prevent Crime," in *Reactions to Crime*, pp. 149–66.
35. C. Weiss, *Evaluation Research* (Englewood Cliffs, N.J.: Prentice-Hall, 1972).
36. Personal communication from the evaluator, Dr. Royer Cook, Institute for Social Analysis, Reston, Virginia, November 1982.
37. The national evaluation of the TBOC campaign found that half the American adult population had been exposed to McGruff as of fall of 1981. Furthermore, the results of that evaluation indicate that for the most part McGruff is having a positive impact on the public. See G. O'Keefe, H. Mendelsohn, et al., *The Public Impact of a Crime Prevention Information Campaign and Implications for Communications Strategies* (Denver: Department of Mass Communications, University of Denver, 1982).
38. J. G. Weiss and J. Sederstrom, *The Prevention of Serious Delinquency: What to Do?* (Washington, D.C.: GPO, 1981), p. 2 (emphasis added).
39. T. Robertson, *Suzy's War* (Cincinnati: Multimedia Productions, 1980).
40. P. H. Ennis, *Criminal Victimization in the United States* (Washington, D.C.: GPO, 1967); A. J. Reiss, *Studies in Crime and Law Enforcement in Major Metropolitan Areas* (Washington, D.C.: GPO, 1967); A. D. Biderman et al., *Report on a Pilot in the District of*

*Columbia on Victimization and Attitudes toward Law Enforcement* (Washington, D.C.: GPO, 1967).

41. F. F. Furstenberg, "Public Reactions to Crime in the Streets," *American Scholar* 11 (1971): 601–10; F. F. Furstenberg, "Fear of Crime and Its Effects on Citizen Behaviors," in *Crime and Justice: A Symposium,* ed. A. Biderman (New York: Nailburg, 1972).

42. F. F. Furstenberg, "Political Intrusion and Government Confusion: The Case of the National Institute of Law Enforcement & Criminal Justice," *American Sociologist* 6 (1971): 59–62.

43. O. Newman, *Defensible Space: Crime Prevention through Urban Design* (New York: Macmillan, 1972); C. R. Jeffery, "Criminal Behavior and the Physical Environment," *American Behavioral Scientist* 20 (1972): 249–274; S. Angel, *Discouraging Crime through City Planning* (Berkeley: University of California, 1969).

44. Westinghouse National Issues Center, *CPTED Final Report on Residential Demonstration in Minneapolis* (Arlington, Va., 1978).

45. Westinghouse National Issues Center, *CPTED Final Report on Commercial Demonstration in Portland* (Arlington, Va., 1978).

46. Westinghouse National Issues Center, *CPTED Final Report on Schools Demonstration in Broward County* (Arlington, Va., 1978).

47. P. J. Lavrakas, J. Normoyle, and J. Wagener, "Evaluation of the Portland Commercial CPTED Demonstration," Evanston, Ill.: Westinghouse Evaluation Institute, 1978), mimeo.

48. J. Kushmuk and S. Whittemore, *Reevaluation of CPTED in Portland* (Portland, Ore.: Office of Justice Planning and Evaluation, 1981).

49. Personal communication from the evaluator, Dr. James Tien, Public Systems Evaluation, Cambridge, Mass., November 1982.

50. F. J. Fowler and T. W. Mangione, *Neighborhood Crime, Fear and Social Control: A Second Look at the Hartford Program* (Washington, D.C.: GPO, 1982), emphasis added.

51. DuBow and Podolefsky, *Citizen Participation*; Skogan and Maxfield, *Coping with Crime*; M. Gordon and L. Heath, "The Newsbusiness, Crime, and Fear," in *Reactions to Crime.*

52. The "Citizen Participation in Community Crime Prevention" project, funded under NILECJ Grant #78-NI-AX-0111; P. J. Lavrakas and W. G. Skogan, coprincipal investigators.

53. S. Greenberg, W. Rohe, and J. Williams, "The Relationship between Informal Social Control, Neighborhood Crime, and Fear," presented at the American Society of Criminology Annual Meeting, Toronto, 1982.

54. R. Taylor, S. Gottfredson, et al., *Toward a Resident-based Model of Community Crime Prevention: Urban Territoriality, Social Network and Design* (Baltimore: Center for Metropolitan Planning and Research, Johns Hopkins University, 1979).

55. F. Kaminski, D. P. Rosenbaum, and P. J. Lavrakas, "Community Crime Prevention: Fulfilling Its Promise," *Police Chief,* February 1983.

56. D. P. Rosenbaum, "Towards a Model of Empirical Program Planning to Prevent Crime," Academy of Criminal Justice Sciences Annual Convention, Louisville, Kentucky, 1982.

57. P. J. Lavrakas, D. P. Rosenbaum, and F. Kaminski, "Transmitting Information about Crime and Crime Prevention to Citizens: The Evanston Newsletter Quasi-experiment," *Journal of Police Science and Administration* 11 (1983): 463–73.

58. This tendency to ascribe such responsibility to some professional group pervades our society. Too many Americans hold public schools totally accountable for the education of their children, without acknowledging their responsibilities as parents. Too many Americans expect physicians to keep them from becoming ill, without recognizing the primary role their own behavior plays in determining their health. Fortunately, in the field of

health, we seem to have recognized the role of actively promoting prevention to the public and have begun to see more and more informed citizens acting accordingly.

59. While definitions and distinctions for the terms *neighborhood* and *community* abound, I refer to them as identifiable *geographic* entities, for the purposes of crime prevention programming.
60. By "multipurpose voluntary associations" I mean formal and informal citizen collectives that may or may not have a paid staff and that in a broad sense strive to improve the quality of life in some given locale. These include neighborhood groups, community organizations, and school, church, and business groups.
61. This process in many instances is not explicit. It includes an accurate recognition of the problem and a feasible strategy whereby citizen participation will be targeted to the remediation of the problem. When it succeeds, the active force underlying the success is very likely to include changes in the everyday behavior of average residents, not merely the observable behaviors of citizens who participate in the overt anticrime strategy. For example, if a local organization forms a citizen patrol and over time street crime is reduced, I would argue that the reduction should probably be credited to the process that was set in motion by the citizen patrol, not merely to the patrols themselves. This process, which the patrols hypothetically set in motion, includes all those subtle changes in the everyday behavior of the nonoffender population that signals less tolerance of crime and is responsive to the fact that a relatively small number of fellow-residents were willing to patrol the neighborhood.
62. cf. K. M. Golden, "The Police Role: Perceptions and Preferences," *Journal of Police Science and Administration* 10, no. 1 (1982): 108–20.
63. cf. Sherman, "'Watching.'"
64. The Computers for the People project is an ongoing research study at the Center for Urban Affairs and Policy Research, Northwestern University, under the direction of Professor Andrew Gordon.
65. For a discussion of expressive incentives, see J. Q. Wilson, *Political Organizations* (New York: Basic Books, 1973).
66. For a discussion of the resource-poor, see Lavrakas et al., *Factors Related to Citizen Involvement,* pp. 16–17.

# 5

# Presidential Commissions and the Law Enforcement Assistance Administration

ALAN R. GORDON AND NORVAL MORRIS

Some years ago, one of us was excoriated as unpatriotic for writing that "to the student of comparative criminal statistics America may or may not be the land of the free, but she is certainly the home of the brave." Such flip commentary may be in bad taste, but it underlines an abiding truth that has frequently been demonstrated earlier in this policy review. Though the rates of criminal violence vary dramatically from area to area in this country, though they vary dramatically from one social, ethnic, and economic group to another, there is uniform agreement that they are everywhere too high for cultural health and social ease. They have led to a situation wherein rates of violence condition where and how Americans live, how they travel, where they go to school, to work, to recreation; they deeply influence race relations; they have created a burgeoning new industry of private policing that surpasses in numbers and resources its official counterparts—in short, there is too much violence in this country, and everyone, particularly every politician prior to an election, wants to do something about it. But what? And how? And how much else would have to be given up if those somethings were indeed done?

These are large questions, larger than we can address in this chapter. Our focus is much narrower, but relevant we hope to those larger questions. We will concentrate on the role of national commissions of enquiry in suggesting public policies to be followed in relation to the diminution of criminal violence, and their success in attracting acceptance and governmental support. Of the several national commissions we will devote central attention to the Katzenbach Commission and its report *The Challenge of Crime in a Free Society* since from it sprang the Law Enforcement Assistance Administration, the largest and longest federal effort to respond to the problems of crime in America. We shall set the discussion in the context of consideration of the sweep of rates of criminal violence over time and place in this country and conclude with some reflections on possibilities for the future.

As a preamble, it may be helpful to state our skepticism about the relationship between national crime commissions and the diminution of crime. National crime commissions are political techniques of *not* addressing the reality problems of crime; they are political gestures, not governmental commitments. They may lead to good, and often do, but it is a mistake to think they do anything except buy time for the formulation of what one hopes will be more rational policies. Perhaps a personal experience may be allowed to underline this obvious but generally forgotten point. Years ago, in another country as will be obvious, the prime minister telephoned a dean of a law school to ask him to serve as chairman of a royal commission (the commonwealth equivalent of the presidential commission—though the latter is also often given the honorific "blue ribbon," which surely partakes of royalty). The law dean expressed himself as overwhelmed by the honor, but regretted that for the next six months he was inexorably committed to a state governmental task that would, together with his decanal duties, preclude this offered opportunity. Try as he would, he could not start work on the royal commission for six months. "The very man I've been looking for" came the reply from an unusually direct and wise prime minister.

## TRENDS IN VIOLENT CRIME

The most careful overview of the sweep of violent crime in this country and abroad is an essay by Ted Robert Gurr, "Historical Trends in Violent Crime: A Critical Review of the Evidence," which appeared in volume 3 of *Crime and Justice: An Annual Review of Research*. Studies such as Gurr's generally excite little attention in the popular press and, regrettably, scant interest even in the community of criminological scholars. But Gurr's was an exception. He stated a truth that ran counter to the conventional wisdom and hence attracted the usual vigorous criticism for such veracity. He agreed with the conventionally wise that there had been an upsurge of criminal violence in the 1960s and 1970s, but he also offered and compellingly demonstrated the view that this increase had been preceded by a much longer period of steady decline in rates of criminal violence not only in this country but throughout the Western world. This surely annoyed the doomsayers of the media who rejoice only in catastrophe or sentimentality.

Gurr went further and suggested the causes of both the long-term decline and the shorter-term increase, seeing the former as "a manifestation of cultural change in Western society, especially the growing sensitization to violence and the development of increased internal and external controls on aggressive behavior" (p. 295), and finding the prime causes of the recent upturn in the legitimization of violence by war, the stresses of rapid urbanization and industrialization, the pressures of economic prosperity and decline, and rapid changes in the demographic structure of the population—all causes of violence noted by the successive crime commissions of the past twenty years.

By pressing these realities of the long-term decline and short-term upturn in violence, we are by no means intending to suggest that the problems of criminal violence in this country are other than severe and important. They are. They strike deep into our culture and particularly into our race and class relationships. All that is intended is to implant a balanced view of the problem that rejects the likelihood that a phenomenon as deep-seated in American culture as a high rate of criminal violence will respond swiftly even to the implementation of recommendations of successive national crime commissions, let alone to their adumbration.

From the historical and comparative viewpoint, it is proper to conclude that there is an excess of criminal violence in the United States; that over time it could and should be reduced; that in the broad we know the etiology of criminal violence, because we know where and among whom it is disproportionately to be found; that its diminution will involve aspects of our culture far outside the ambit of interest of the criminal law; and that we should stop paying attention to the politicians who promise a swift surcease of this evil. Much will have to be done in many areas of social organization, and much of it will not command any immediate popular support. Within the sphere of influence of the criminal law, our major purposes in relation to violent crime will be ameliorative and marginally reductive at best. That does not mean they will be unimportant. It is clearly important to improve the efficiency of our fact-finding and guilt-deciding processes, to make our sentencing system both more fair and more community protective, to be solicitous of and helpful to the victims of violent crime—in brief to fulfill the great precepts of justice under law. These are large purposes that relate closely to much else that must occur in our social organization if criminal violence is to be reduced and the broad historical sweep of its steady reduction continued and expedited.

Let us now look more closely at the increase of violent crime during the past twenty years and then at the response of some of the crime commissions to it.

## THE TWO-DECADE RISE IN CRIMINAL VIOLENCE

By 1980 here is how matters stood. The Uniform Crime Reports suggested a continuing increase in rates and amount of criminal violence, a doubling of the rate per 100,000 over twenty years; the National Crime Surveys indicated that there had indeed been substantial increase but suggested a recent cessation of that increase, even a decline. By the end of 1982, these two measuring instruments had come into broad accord, confirming that over the past two years there has been a stabilization and possibly a decline in rates of criminal violence, but that this stabilization or decline relates to the peak of the very steep increases of the sixties and seventies.

So at a time of generally increasing prosperity and increased governmental concern and effort in relation to crimes of violence, we find a sharp increase in those crimes, and then with the deepening of economic adversity into at least a recession, we find a cessation of that increase in criminal violence. What is to be made of such paradoxical results? And, in particular, how explain the combination of greater governmental effort and worsening results other than in terms of the general perversity of the human species?

A first suggested insight is this: it is probably a mistake to aggregate crime rates as these national statistics do. It is well to remember that there are vast swathes of America with crime rates comparably low to those found in countries in Western Europe with which we like to compare ourselves. The logical and true corollary is, of course, that we have pockets of violent criminality far surpassing in intensity anything to be found in those countries, with racial and ethnic minorities locked into cultures of violence that skew our national aggregate statistics. It is tempting but dangerous on this topic to commit the sin of false unity; nevertheless, as aggregates, such figures do tell us at least this: aggregate rates of violent crime in the United States doubled in the two decades of the sixties and seventies.

Some suggested that this doubling of violent crime was in substantial part a statistical artifact, that the statistics had changed very much more than the underlying reality. Here, in brief, are some of the arguments that were advanced to suggest this misperception.

As more and more rural police jurisdictions joined the FBI crime reporting system, confidence in that system grew and crime reporting became more complete. Likewise, in the big cities, improved communication systems, improved crime accounting systems, automation generally, led to a similar increase of the proportion of crime that was recorded and reported. Further, as the community gained more confidence in the police, as the police improved their efficiency and their courtesy, so more crime would have been reported to them even if the incidence of crime did not change. And finally, on this theme of increased confidence in the police and their criminal statistics, there was during the two decades of our enquiry a steady pressure to make the police more responsive to the needs of the ghettos and barrios of urban industrialized America, and to the extent that such pressure was effective, so would there have been increased reporting of crime to the police from these areas of very high incidence of violent crime.

Looking at this possibility of a statistical artifact of increased violent crime from the perspective of the police, as distinct from the perspective of one reporting a crime to the police, similar pressures toward the open recognition of violent crime by the police emerge. The public and political discussion of the problem of crime in America led to a climate wherein it was acceptable for the police, and not seen at all as a failure by the police, for the true and high incidence of violent crime to be reported. And confirming this support of the police in the context of high rates of violent crime was the mercenary reality that much federal and some state funds for the police to deal with crime were attracted by such high rates. It was not only the intensity of patrol that followed high rates of crime; now money did too.

The other broad line of argument to suggest that the burgeoning rates of violent crime did not reflect a change in human behavior was the demographic analysis. Here is how it went. The postwar baby boom entered the crime-prone years in the sixties and seventies, so that without any change in human behavior a higher rate of crime would have to be expected. Further, from 1960 to 1965 and perhaps continuing thereafter, there was a substantial migration from the rural low-crime-rate areas into the urban high-crime-rate areas with a similar though less certain impact on rates of crime generally.

And there were other explanations of the paradox of increased prosperity, increased concern about crime, and apparently increased rates of crime all coexisting and flourishing. Expectations were higher, it was said, so that more was reported. Though there was prosperity for many, some were left further behind in a culture that stressed and gave pervasive publicity to economic success—so that the pressures on those left behind were greater. In Chapter 7, Ball-Rokeach and Short note that the exodus of the middle classes of all races has left an underclass, which is paralyzed economically and frustrated politically (though we observe with some hope the recent resurgence of black political activity in Chicago and elsewhere). But whatever the explanations, it seems to us that the reported increases in violent crime during the sixties accurately reflected an intensification of the problems of crime and violent crime in the United States, that they were not merely statistical and reporting artifacts but did measure a halting place at least on our long march to less aggressive relations between man and man and to the diminution of domestic violence.

And even if we are wrong and those who gathered the numbers misunderstood and misreported them, nevertheless it is certainly clear that during the sixties and seventies, public anxiety about crime increased. It was seen to be spreading from the inner-city areas and minority groups where it was previously concentrated into the suburbs and rural areas; it was seen to be spreading to the white and to the affluent who had previously been largely immune. Hence, apart from the probable fact of the intensification of the social disease of violent crime, there was greatly intensifying public concern which precipitated the political concern of the sixties and seventies and the several crime commissions to whose work we now turn.

## THE KATZENBACH, KERNER, AND VIOLENCE COMMISSIONS

This is not the occasion to rehearse the many recommendations that emerged from these three presidential crime commissions. Together they contain recommendations, general and specific, for addressing the problems of crime and violent crime in America, which, were they followed, would make appreciable advances in justice and decency. The present volume is a continuation of the important initiative of the Violence Commission; for this reason we shall confine ourselves in this chapter to a brief overview of the three commissions and then turn to a more detailed consideration of what happened to the recommendations of the Katzenbach Commission, for it was that commission that laid the political and administrative foundations of the federal government's larger involvement in the problems of crime and their control, at a state and local level, and hence set a frame of reference for all other federal governmental efforts. It fathered the Law Enforcement Assistance Administration (LEAA) through which federal concerns and federal financial involvement were to be expressed for nearly twenty years.

By 1965 the fear of increased crime amidst increasing prosperity had assumed national political dimensions. Senator Goldwater had in 1964 campaigned for the presidency on a platform that included the frequently stressed planks of "law and order" and "crime in the streets." President Johnson responded to this concern after his electoral victory by creating the President's Commission on Law Enforcement and the Administration of Justice, calling on it to "give us the blueprints that we need . . . to banish crime."[1] The product of that commission, *The Challenge of Crime in a Free Society,* and its accompanying task force reports, and many of the research documents on which the report and the reports relied, are of remarkably high quality and remain the most comprehensive and useful collection of information on the problems of crime and juvenile delinquency, their prevention and treatment, that is to be found in any document or report of a study anywhere. The implementation of their recommendations was, however, a quite different matter to which we shall soon turn.

The Kerner Commission was an immediate response to the race riots of the mid-sixties. The Violence Commission was an immediate response to the assassination of Robert Kennedy. Each of these commissions, focusing not only as they did on the issues that led to their appointment but on other outbreaks of violence in the country, increased our stock of knowledge of violent crime and of possible means of minimizing its social impact. But again, knowledge and political will do not always pull in double harness. Let us take the case of the Katzenbach Commission and LEAA as demonstration of the tensions that tend to develop between the way and the will in the politics of crime control.

Wisdom after the event is properly suspect, but prior to the event that was mainly responsible for the misdirection of the initiatives flowing from the report of the Katzenbach Commission, it was not too hard to be prescient. In 1968, in a review of *The Challenge of Crime in a Free Society,* one of us wrote about the "apparently sound mechanism" that was designed to stimulate the achievement of the two hundred recommendations that had been made in that report:

> Through the Juvenile Delinquency Prevention Act and the Safe Streets and Crime Control Act, the federal government would begin to provide leadership and, in particular, funds for those of the 200 recommendations in the *The Challenge of Crime in a Free Society* that local communities, states or cities, might care to adopt on an experimental basis. Thus, funds and the limited expertise in this whole system could be channeled to what was creative and developmental in the system. We could all learn from the critically evaluated, federally supported, local testing of the Commission's recommendations. Yes, Dr. Pangloss.
>
> I was involved in some of the above planning. With twenty or so other academic types as discussion leaders, well-read in *The Challenge of Crime in a Free Society* and acquainted with the Administration versions of the Juvenile Delinquency Prevention Bill and the Safe Streets and Crime Control Bill, a meeting was arranged in Washington with some 700 people from the states, cities, local communities, and rotten boroughs of this vast country. We academics were briefed the night before in the Department of Justice. The plan was, in essence, that outlined in the previous paragraph. Speaking for myself, the next day I was as a child; the "politicians" were gentle and kind, but they brushed me aside with a firm politeness. I learned the truth over my second drink in the bar after the first day's debacle. I had been ingenuous to believe that the backwoodsmen would accept such a role for the federal government. Federal funds, if they came, would be used, my local political advisers assured me, to reduce pressure on state, city, and local budgets. They would be divided not at all unequally—as testing developments clearly requires—but equally, in accordance with a complex relationship between populousness and political influence. Any developments would not come from a bunch of federally recruited intellectuals, but from such local initiative as might emerge. Now, be quiet, drink up, and let us talk about something amusing like women or crime.[2]

Federal funds to achieve business as usual, to meet the steadily increasing demands on the state and local criminal justice systems, preempted a mechanism planned to achieve social change. Nevertheless, much that is of value flowed from this infusion of new funds and a newly concerned bureaucracy, the details of which merit attention.

## THE RISE AND FALL OF THE LEAA

Possibly the most significant and certainly the most costly proposal acted upon by Congress in the Omnibus Crime Control Act of 1968 was the establishment of the Law Enforcement Assistance Administration. Starting with a comparatively modest budget (less than $300 million for fiscal year 1970, the first full year of operations), the LEAA would eventually disburse close to $8 billion over its twelve-year history before its dismantling under the Reagan administration in 1981. These disbursements were largely of the block-grant variety, a genuflection to state and local politics that would plague the LEAA throughout it existence. But LEAA's use of discretionary grants also attracted ample criticism. This section will deal with the goals, the successes, the failures, and the downfall of the LEAA.

The 1968 act defined three goals for the LEAA: (1) to encourage comprehensive planning by states and municipalities, (2) to direct grants toward the improvement of law enforcement, and (3) to encourage research and development programs for the improvement of law enforcement.

The first goal was met by requirements that any requests for funds should come from state planning agencies (SPAs), which in turn had to review the current state of their criminal justice systems and then submit long-range, comprehensive proposals. These proposals had to provide for the administration of the funds, the "passing through" of funds to local agencies, and the development of advanced techniques and technologies, and had to show the willingness of states and localities to fund projects and not merely use LEAA funds to supplant funds already allocated to existing programs. Once these requirements were met, large chunks of money were then sent to the states, which controlled their spending with relatively little supervision by the federal government.

The amount of red tape generated by these requirements caused some initial delays in setting up the state programs, but the LEAA assisted the states both in setting up the SPAs and in drafting proposals. Early critics immediately began attacking these requirements as vague, difficult to meet, and unnecessary; but the SPAs somehow managed to get organized and submit their proposals within six months of the birth of the LEAA, and money began flowing.

If this method of funding sounds loose from a budgetary standpoint, that is because it is loose from a budgetary standpoint. There was a reason for that. When the Omnibus Crime Control Act was being debated, Ramsey Clark was the U.S. attorney general. Mr. Clark was known for his high intelligence and innovative thinking. He was also known for antagonizing conservative members of Congress, including Senators McClellan and Hruska, chairman and ranking Republican member respectively of the Criminal Laws and Procedures Subcommittee of the Senate Judiciary Committee. Although committed to federal funding of state law enforcement, they were worried about having it under the control of Clark, who might start imposing his own ideas on the states. So the LEAA was created as an agency independent of the Department of Justice. However, this would still create the possibility of one highly powerful agency head, so the initial administrative structure of the LEAA was that of a troika, composed of an administrator and two associate administrators, coequal in authority, with unanimity required for all decisions.

The block-grant method of funding stemmed from the same fears of federal influence. These fears even extended to the belief that somehow the LEAA would lead to a national police force, superseding the states' right to enforce their own laws. Finally, it was thought that the states would be in a much better position to know where their law enforcement problems lay and what should be done about them.

In an article describing his experience as one of the initial troika under Nixon, Charles Rogovin discusses many of the problems caused by that form of administration. The unanimity requirement, which even covered things as mundane but essential as staff hiring, slowed administration down tremendously. Fundamental disagreements over long-term strategies tied up disbursements of discretionary grants for months.[3] Ultimately, the troika system was dropped, but between that, the time needed to set up all the SPAs, and Congress's delays in approving funding, the LEAA got off to a very shoddy start.

There were other problems involved in growing up. Although the LEAA in theory was to direct its funding to all phases of the criminal justice system, in practice most of it went to the police. This was partly the fault of the original legislation and partly the natural advantages the police had over other elements of the criminal justice system. The police had already received grants in 1968 from the LEAA's predecessor, which was a model program targeted at riot control. So the police already had an existing structure geared toward obtaining federal funds. The SPAs also favored the police in return for the latter's acceptance of more innovative programs, directed at such areas formerly within the province of the police as narcotics treatment, juvenile delinquency, and rehabilitation within the community. The legislative bias came from a requirement that there be a one-third limitation on how much of a given grant was to go to personnel. Although the original intent behind this requirement was to encourage technological innovation, it had the effect of shutting out programs that were manpower-intensive, including most of the community-based or social work–oriented programs. The police, on the other hand, could easily meet the requirements through expenditures on hardware, such as vehicles, helicopters, computers, communications equipment, and antiriot gear. As a result, 60 percent of LEAA's first funds and 51 percent of the second-year funds went to police. The one-third requirement for programs other than police was abolished in the 1970 amendments to the LEAA act.

Other problems came from the failure to specifically include areas such as corrections and public defenders in the 1968 act. Although a catch-all law-enforcement section theoretically included them, SPAs saw a mandate to emphasize police programs at their expense. Courts as a whole wound up with only 5.7 percent of the total block grants in 1969, 6 percent in 1970, and 9.6 percent in 1971, with only a small portion going to public defenders, while funds for corrections were allocated mainly because of the jawboning of the SPAs by LEAA officials. The 1970 amendments rectified this situation by adding a section specifically on corrections to the act and broadening the definition of law enforcement to bring the public defender programs more firmly within its scope.

A problem that would end up pursuing the LEAA to its grave was the inadequacy of its self-evaluation programs, both in terms of effective budgeting and in determining what programs were actually working. (See Paul J. Lavrakas's chapter for one such series of errors and trials.) Once again, Congress's desire to keep the states free of federal constraints made auditing difficult. Furthermore, as the number of programs funded increased, so did the auditing difficulties, and so also did the incidence of waste and abuse. The latter inevitably garnered heavy publicity and criticism, including Senator William Proxmire's Golden Fleece Award for waste in federal spending, but all this must be put in perspective. The entire LEAA *budget* at the peak of its funding was less than one-sixth of the money *unaccounted for* in 1979 by the Department of Health, Education and Welfare (and we wouldn't dream of taking a cheap shot at military expenditures by comparing the LEAA's to *their* waste and abuse). As Jerris Leonard, administrator of the LEAA in 1971, pointed out, "More than 50,000 separate projects have been funded . . . by LEAA. Compared to that Everest of effort, projects cited . . . as allegedly going sour comprise a very small anthill."[4] Leonard also pointed out that much of the fraud and waste generally cited was first discovered by the LEAA itself, suggesting that evaluation techniques were improving.

So, as its growing pains were overcome, the LEAA finally hit its stride in the early seventies. For the first time, planning for the criminal justice system was comprehensive rather than separated into its different segments. Centralized information-gathering systems were set up. Programs such as the National Center for State Courts and the Institute for Court Management instituted research and training programs that introduced management techniques into the running of courts to improve their efficiency. Similar programs were developed to help prosecutors organize their case loads and develop priorities as to which criminals should be prosecuted first. Many drug treatment and rehabilitation programs began with funds from the LEAA. Internship programs were developed to train fledgling prosecutors and defenders who otherwise would have been thrust without experience directly into the system. And although expenditures on hardware were occasionally notoriously wasteful (Louisiana used funds to buy an armored personnel carrier, ostensibly for antiriot purposes), most police expenditures were for badly needed communications equipment.

After the 1970 amendments, programs for improving corrections and treatment of juvenile offenders proliferated. Efforts in the latter area were particularly broad ranging, covering detention centers, mental health, and educational programs, and diversion of juveniles from the criminal justice system to an alternative that would, it was hoped, cure the problem without leaving any institutional scars. However, programs such as these came under attack for allegedly departing from the goals of the LEAA and for duplicating or overlapping programs in other state and federal agencies. In defense of these programs, people such as Milton G. Rector, president of the National Council on Crime and Delinquency, pointed out that Congress had clearly defined neither the scope of the LEAA nor its priorities and that attacking crime's underlying causes was a perfectly legitimate exercise of LEAA's powers.

In 1971, the Nixon administration set the LEAA's priorities by announcing a war directly on crime. Money was poured into the effort, and the LEAA's glory days began. Ironically, Nixon also thereby sowed the seeds of LEAA's downfall. By raising expectations to such a high level, anything short of an actual reduction in crime would provide ammunition for the LEAA's critics who could point to an agency that spent billions of dollars without achieving any result.

Nevertheless, it seemed clear to everyone at the time that the LEAA was there to stay. As the budget soared to nearly $900 million a year and crime was targeted directly, tangible and dramatic results were produced. The LEAA sponsored Project Sting, providing the wherewithal for the purchase of stolen goods by undercover police posing as fences. The project was hugely successful and led to hundreds of arrests and the initiation of similar operations across the country. The amount of money needed to finance a production like this was beyond the means of most police departments, making this a perfect project for the LEAA.

Other significant programs that came out of this period included the witness assistance programs, designed to facilitate the use of witnesses for court appearances by more efficient scheduling, cutting the number of appearances needed, providing day care for children of witnesses, and so on. Savings were produced both for the district attorneys who wasted much less time with witnesses and for the witnesses themselves who didn't miss as much work. Special witness programs were developed for victim-witnesses, particularly rape victims. Support groups were formed, and the police themselves were trained to handle such matters with a higher degree of sensitivity than they had previously been known to demonstrate. Antiterrorist programs were stepped up in the mid-seventies as a response to attacks on businessmen around the world. A pamphlet published by the LEAA in 1976 containing guidelines for businesses in combating terrorism sold out its initial printing of forty thousand almost immediately. Another antiterrorist effort was the training of police bomb squads, raising the number of police bomb experts from thirty nationwide in 1972 to a point where "no airplane is ever more than one-half hour's flighttime from one of the airports with a detection team."[5] The National District Attorneys Association's white-collar crime program has paid for itself, returning over $45 million in fines and restitution on an investment of $4.3 million through 1978. Programs were directed at career criminals. Corrections facilities were built or renovated. Rehabilitation, prerelease, and reentry programs have been designed and implemented in prisons. Community crime prevention programs brought awareness to the local level, while new media campaigns achieved nationwide exposure. Few, if any, of these projects would have been funded without LEAA.

Yet the crime rate continued to go up, and so did the federal deficit. Although the latter was hardly caused by the LEAA, President Carter, searching for programs to cut, settled upon it, probably for its high visibility. Senator Hollings led the floor flight in the Senate to cut its funding, ostensibly because of its failure to reduce crime and avoid waste, but more likely to find a social program that could be cut in order to keep defense spending high. Representative Neal Smith, chairman of the House Appropriations Subcommittee overseeing the LEAA, said at the time that he felt that most of the waste had been eliminated from the program and that the proposed budget of $486 million for 1980 was a good one, but to no avail. The program's funding was effectively stopped in the last year of Carter's term, and the final nail was pounded into the coffin by Reagan adviser Ed Meese who, although noting that the LEAA had done "a lot of good," once again brought up money "wasted" on "so-called crime prevention and treatment programs" lining the pockets of social workers. Meese did think that funding more prisons was a good idea.

So, despite the opposition of the ABA, the International Association of Chiefs of Police, the Conference of State Court Administrators, the National Association of Counties, the National Association of Criminal Justice Planners, the National Council of Juvenile and Family Court Judges, the National Council on Crime and Delinquency, the National District Attorneys Association, and the Police Executive Research Forum, among others, the LEAA died in 1981.

Or did it? Over 70 percent of the programs sponsored were picked up by the states in one form or another, albeit at reduced funding, and in some cases the structures of the SPAs were absorbed intact into the state governments. The mechanisms for obtaining federal funds have been fully developed and could be revived or continued in other forms easily. Meanwhile, the current administration periodically announces new national efforts to fight organized crime or drug traffickers, complete with federal funding and coordinated efforts, but then fails to find the funds for these high purposes. And crime remains a major concern with the public.

In the meantime, a series of postmortems has been conducted around the country, some regretful, some triumphant. Although many individual programs have been singled out, the most cited accomplishment of the LEAA was getting the various components of the criminal justice system to work and plan together. No longer will one component casually shunt its problems into the lap of another. As Nolan E. Jones of the National Governors Association said, "The meetings of the regional Criminal Justice Councils (formed by the LEAA) were the first time I saw a director of state police talk to a chief justice."[6]

## IS THERE LIFE AFTER LEAA?

It has come to pass that every president must have his own crime commission, and President Reagan is no exception, though it must be admitted that his model was swift in its construction and modest in its innovative capacities. A reasonably fair description of Attorney General Smith's 1981 Task Force on Violent Crime was offered by our colleagues Zimring and Hawkins (*National Crime Commissions*, p. 4). They pointed out that the Task Force on Violent Crime was distinguished from earlier crime commissions since Wickersham in the 1920s, which began the procession, by neither seeking expert advice nor consolidating basic knowledge into policy recommendations. Instead, in 120 days, with hearings in seven cities, a volume of ninety-six pages documenting sixty-four recommendations was suddenly produced. In the words of Zimring and Hawkins, "Many of the sixty-four were off-the-shelf conservative bromides; others were hastily conceived in an atmosphere of high enthusiasm and substantial misinformation." In the result, little more has been heard of the work of that task force—it seems to have done little harm.

What President Reagan's task force did portend and stress was the New Federalism in this field. Here, as elsewhere, but particularly here, the New Federalism seems to be no federalism at all but rather a determined withdrawal of federal support and federal influence in matters that are primarily of local and state concern. But in this highly mobile, interdependent, anonymous society, such a withdrawal seems to us to threaten basic values that undergird the American dream. It remains a scandal that the federal legislature cannot pass a federal criminal code; after fifteen years of serious effort to do so, we have not defined and brought into a principled cohesion the fundamental behavioral prohibitions of federal law. Likewise, if experimentation leading to better knowledge and practice in the prevention and treatment of crime is to be pursued, a federal role is unavoidable.

There will be future initiatives, federally and at the state and local levels. The great charitable foundations of this country will move back to support some of the work of value that was previously to a degree encouraged by LEAA. The valuable products of the Katzenbach, Kerner, and Violence commissions will in due course be brought to fruition. And, immediately, the task is to protect and to encourage those many and varied achievements in decency and efficiency in crime control that have characterized the past two decades. Knowledge has substantially increased over that period; levels of training in the police and correctional services are much improved; the courts remain swamped, but the paths to the reduction of their burdens are clear enough. The three commissions may not have produced what we hoped for but it was perhaps the hope that was excessive.

## NOTES

1. *Public Papers of the President of the United States, Lyndon B. Johnson,* vol. 11 (1965), p. 983.
2. *Law and Society Review* 2, no. 277:281.
3. Charles Rogovin, "The Genesis of the Law Enforcement Assistance Administration: A Personal Account," *Columbia Human Rights Review* 5, no. 117 (1973).
4. Jerris Leonard, *Statement by the Honorable Jerris Leonard, Administrator, LEAA, before the Sub-committee on Legal and Monetary Affairs of the House Committee on Government Operations, Thursday, October 7, 1971* (Washington, D.C.: U.S. Government Printing Office, 1971).
5. LEAA, *Program Results Inventory* (1977), p. 37.
6. David Ranii, "Will New Agency Rise from Ashes as LEAA Goes up in Smoke?" *National Law Journal* 3, no. 6 (November 10, 1980).

## BIBLIOGRAPHY

In addition to the various reports, staff reports, and task force reports of the Katzenbach, Kerner, and Eisenhower commissions, the following sources were used.

Bacon, Selden D. "Alcoholism and the Criminal Justice System." *Law and Society Review* 2 (1968):489.
"Big Changes Ahead for Anti-Crime Agency." *U.S. News and World Report* 81 (1976):82.
Boguslaw, Robert. "Science, Technology and the Criminal Justice System." *Law and Society Review* 2, no. 287 (1968).
"CJN Interviews Rep. Neal Smith on LEAA." *Criminal Justice Newsletter* 11 (May 12, 1980):2.

"Conference Committee Votes Only $50 million for LEAA-OJARS in Fiscal 1981 Budget." *Criminal Justice Newsletter* 11 (May 19, 1980):1–2.

Crime Panel Reassessed as U.S. Unit Nears End." *New York Times,* April 12, 1982, p. B7.

Cronin, Thomas E., Tania Z. Cronin, and Michael E. Milakovich. *U.S. v. Crime in the Streets.* Bloomington: Indiana University Press, 1981.

Gregware, Peter R. "Massachusetts: Experiments in Crime Prevention." *Columbia Human Rights Review* 5 (1973):155.

Gude, Gilbert, and George J. Mannina, Jr. "The Impact on Crime of the Law Enforcement Assistance Administration in the District of Columbia." *Columbia Human Rights Review* 5 (1973):27.

Gurr, Ted Robert. "Historical Trends in Violent Crimes: A Critical Review of the Evidence." In *Crime and Justice.* Edited by Michael Tonry and Norval Morris. Chicago: University of Chicago Press, 1981, 3:295.

Kleps, Ralph N. "Last Rites for LEAA?" *Judges' Journal* 19 (1980):8.

Krislow, Samuel. "Court-related Processes and the Courts." *Law and Society Review* 2 (1968):284.

Lang, Irving, "The President's Crime Commission Task Force Report on Narcotics and Drug Abuse: A Critique of the Apologia." *Notre Dame Law Review* 43 (1968):847.

Lejins, Peter P. "Book Review: *The Challenge of Crime in a Free Society.*" *American University Law Review* 17 (1967):140.

Lehman, Warren. "Crime, the Public, and the Crime Commission: A Critical Review of *The Challenge of Crime in a Free Society.*" *Michigan Law Review* 66 (1968):1487.

Leonard, Jerris. *Statement by the Honorable Jerris Leonard, Administrator, LEAA, before the Sub-committee on Legal and Monetary Affairs of the House Committee on Government Operations, Thursday, October 7, 1971.* Washington, D.C.: U.S. Government Printing Office, 1971.

Lumbard, Eliot H. "State and Local Government Crime Control." *Notre Dame Law Review* 43 (1968):889.

Lynch, Beth, and Nancy Goldberg. "LEAA: The Dollars and Sense of Justice." *NLADA Briefcase* 31 (1972–73):252–.

Morris, Norval. "Random Reflections on *The Challenge of Crime in a Free Society.*" *Law and Society Review* 2 (1968):277.

"Notes on People (The Golden Fleece Award)." *New York Times,* February 1, 1978, p. B2.

Ohlin, Lloyd E. "The Effect of Social Change on Crime and Law Enforcement." *Notre Dame Law Review* 43 (1968):834.

Peskoe, Howard E. "The 1968 Safe Streets Act: Congressional Response to the Growing Crime Problem." *Columbia Human Rights Review* 5 (1973):69.

"President and House Budget Committee Propose to Kill Most of LEAA Program." *Criminal Justice Newsletter* 11 (March 31, 1980):1.

Purcell, John. "North Carolina: Corrections and Juvenile Justice in a Rural State." *Columbia Human Rights Review* 5 (1973):187.

Ranii, David. "Will New Agency Rise from Ashes as LEAA Goes up in Smoke?" *National Law Journal* 3 (November 10, 1980):6.

"Reagan Adviser Edwin Meese Enunciates Administration's Crime Control Goals."
    *Criminal Justice Newsletter* 12 (May 11, 1981):1.

Rector, Milton G. "Renewing the Law Enforcement Agency." *New York Times,*
    January 8, 1979, p. A22.

Rector, Milton G., and Joan Wolfle. "The Law Enforcement Assistance Adminis-
    tration in Perspective." *Columbia Human Rights Review* 5 (1973):55.

Reid, Charles A. "Philadelphia, Pennsylvania: City-State Relations." *Columbia
    Human Rights Review* 5 (1973):117.

Rogovin, Charles. "The Genesis of the Law Enforcement Assistance Administra-
    tion: A Personal Account." *Columbia Human Rights Review* 5 (1973):9.

Rose, Douglas D. "Book Review: *To Establish Justice, to Insure Domestic Tran-
    quility.*" *Tulane Law Review* 688 (1971).

Ruth, Henry S., Jr. "To Dust Shall Ye Return?" *Notre Dame Law Review* 43
    (1968):811.

Schur, Edwin M. "Indecisiveness and Evasion." *Law and Society Review* 2
    (1968):483.

Sliwa, John. "Letter: Flawed Attack on the LEAA." *New York Times,* February 17,
    1981, p. A18.

Slonim, Scott. "LEAA: Marked for Extinction?" *American Bar Association
    Journal* 66 (1980):539.

Stone, Marvin. "A Blueprint to Fight Crime." *U.S. News and World Report* 87
    (July 23, 1979):76.

"U.S. Business Throws Billions into a Fight against Terrorists." *U.S. News and
    World Report* 83 (November 21, 1977):24.

U.S. Department of Justice, Law Enforcement Assistance Administration. *Annual
    Report of the LEAA.* Washington, D.C.: U.S. Government Printing Office, 1969–
    81.

———. *Program Results Inventory.* Washington, D.C.: U.S. Government Printing
    Office, 1977.

———. *Target.* LEAA newsletter.

Varon, Jay N. "A Re-examination of the Law Enforcement Assistance Adminis-
    tration." *Stanford Law Review* 27 (1975):1303.

"What the LEAA Elephant Learned." *New York Times,* April 21, 1982, p. A22.

Zimring, Franklin E., and Gordon Hawkins. *National Crime Commissions.* Un-
    published manuscript.

# Violence and Firearms Policy

FRANKLIN E. ZIMRING

One is tempted to characterize the fifteen years since the Violence Commission finished its research on firearms as an era of more of everything. We have more guns, more gun violence, more research on the relationship between firearms and violence, more public concern about the gun problem, and a sharper focus on handguns as the pivotal issue in the debate that was termed, by the late 1970s, the "Great American Gun War."[1] The investment of attention and political activity on guns produced an increase in the number of citizens who cared deeply about gun control policy—a dramatic increase on both sides of the question.

Blue ribbon commissions should, of course, studiously avoid claiming credit for movements in crime rates or gun ownership. But the work of the Violence Commission did have a profound impact on the focus of the debate about firearms control, the policy options under discussion, and the nature of the data that is available to inform a debate that now concerns questions of fact as well as matters of value.

One substantial part of the legacy of the commission was the empirical work produced by its task force and the effect of that work on subsequent academic empirical study of guns, violence, and gun control. Put simply, there had been no university-based research prior to 1967 on these matters. Almost immediately after the publication of the task force report, the academic community discovered guns. Research to date—while insufficient—is an important part of current policy dialogue. More than twenty researchers, representing a wide variety of social sciences, have made contributions to the empirical understanding of the issues involved.[2] Four or five scholars of major repute have devoted substantial portions of their research efforts to the issue.[3] With the stakes this high, the budding academic interest in firearms and firearms control may seem modest. However, judged against the factual vacuum prior to the late 1960s, any research tradition is of no small importance.

A second contribution of the commission's work was its heavy emphasis on handguns as a discrete problem calling for special emphasis in the discussion of policy options. While not without precedent, the commission's emphasis was the first forceful advocacy of separate policy dialogue about handguns and long weapons since the late 1930s.

Related to the special emphasis on handguns was a shift from recommendations of mild handgun controls, such as registration and permissive licensing, to more drastic methods of reducing the number of handguns possessed by and available to civilians. No proposals for a policy of national handgun scarcity had been made prior to the Violence Commission since the 1930s.[4] The years following the commission report have seen the terms of the handgun debate shift almost entirely to restrictive licensing, handgun "bans," and other strategies to prohibit law-abiding citizens from acquiring handguns except under special circumstances. The commission's rejection of middle-of-the-road proposals of the sort that have been endorsed by earlier national commissions[5] sharpened the debate at the same time that it intensified opposition to handgun control among anticontrol opinion groups.

How should this tripartite legacy be judged? Much, of course, depends on the values of those making the judgment. However, even from the perspective of pro-control advocates, the shift in focus may be seen as bold or foolish depending on the ultimate political result. Fifteen years into a new phase of gun policy as a societal decision, the issue is in doubt. The beginning of this essay discusses some of the changes in ownership, use, costs, and knowledge about guns that have occurred since 1968. The second half, somewhat more speculative, attempts to outline future changes in public attitude that will serve as leading indicators of long-run handgun policy in the United States.

## THEN AND NOW

If commission efforts are to be judged by immediate legislative results, the Violence Commission's prescription for a policy aimed at eventually reducing civilian handguns by 90 percent was a resounding failure. Legislation based on the commission's national handgun proposal attracted seven votes in the U.S. Senate. Highly restrictive handgun policies were adopted by a scattering of city governments, but restrictive handgun policies at the state level—where federal law and geography suggested more promising results—have proved uniformly unpopular.

If the commission findings and recommendations were intended to alter the structure of the gun control debate, they succeeded in that task almost immediately but with indeterminate results. The nature of public dialogue as well as its outcome are dependent on much more than rapidly aging policy analysis. The job of this section is to detail some of the other substantial changes that affect the context in which American citizens now debate what to do about civilian handguns.

## More Guns

The Task Force on Firearms estimated a civilian inventory of handguns of 24 million, a rough estimate based on averaging production rates in the twentieth century with survey research studies that showed a somewhat smaller civilian arsenal.[6] Whatever total ownership value one adopted for the late 1960s, the trend in total handgun ownership during the 1960s was clear. New domestic and imported handguns added to civilian inventories grew from 600,000 in 1962 to well over 2 million in 1968, a fourfold increase.[7]

The significance of this trend, independent of civilian handgun population estimates, was not known until seven years later. Analysis of guns confiscated on the street in several police jurisdictions suggested that the maximum period of risk for illegal carrying or illegal use of a handgun occurred during the weapon's first few years after production.[8] Thus, if the focus shifts from the total number of weapons in civilian inventory to the number of guns at risk, it was clear that the 1960s operated as a near perfect laboratory in which constantly increasing numbers of weapons were introduced as new guns each year. The new-guns finding has two implications when one retrospectively interprets the data about the 1960s. First, whatever the actual civilian inventory of all kinds of handguns of all ages, the large increase in annual introductions to the civilian market could be expected to have dramatic effects on crime and street-carrying patterns. Second, the notion of significant handgun attrition, at least when speaking of weapons at risk for street use, requires analysts to take into account attrition rates even though these are not knowable by any statistical series presently available. One graphic example: If the risk life of a handgun is six years rather than sixty, the introduction of more than 2 million handguns into the civilian market in 1968 replaced one gun introduced in 1962 with four handguns in 1968. By contrast, the introduction of 2 million handguns in 1975 would just replace the average annual introduction figure in 1968.[9]

This complication introduces the problem of calculating the impact of handgun introduction in the 1970s on handgun availability and the proportion of crimes committed with pistols and revolvers. The decade of the 1970s witnessed a high but more stable rate of handgun introductions over time usually at or near 2 million during those years when it could be determined.[10] Unlike the 1960s, *if* attrition rates were high, handguns being shipped into commerce in the mid-seventies were replacing older handguns mysteriously absent from risk categories, such as street carrying and use in crime on a one-to-one basis. If, in fact, a handgun had a risk life of six years, 1975 introduction figures would have counterbalanced only the 1968 bumper crop of handguns previously discussed. This refinement in the notion of guns at risk leaves us with a theoretical structure beyond our present competence to test rigorously. The introduction of 20 million handguns in a decade probably did not leave the civilian inventory undisturbed. The question of how much and when handgun inventories expanded is an open one, inviting further empirical research.

One result of acknowledging the possibility of early and substantial handgun attrition is an increased margin of error when guesses are made about the total civilian handgun inventory in the United States. Recent survey research yields an estimate of from 30 to 40 million pistols and revolvers in civilian hands.[11] When the focus is guns likely to be involved in criminal activity, a lower number of handguns at risk is suggested by the findings on new guns and street crime.[12] Further, careful analysis of fluctuations in the rate of handgun transfers may be more important than trying to estimate the total population of handguns. If attrition is high, interventions designed to minimize transfers of new or existent handguns show promise of earlier and more substantial impact than would occur if most guns, regardless of age or status, exhibited similar risks of being used abusively.

## More Gun Violence

During its first months of research activity, senior Violence Commission staff were divided on the question of whether the United States was experiencing and could expect a sustained increase in serious violent crime. Opponents of this thesis argued that homicide rates had been escalating for a short period of time, and other measures of violent crime were unreliable. Those who thought violence was increasing substantially (and this view ultimately prevailed) pointed to the sharp rate of increase in general levels of violence and the changing pattern of life-threatening violence, principally the growing role of firearms in assault, robbery, and resultant homicides. Hindsight renders that debate moot. The explosive growth in life-threatening violence and the increasing proportion of violent crimes committed with guns continued almost without interruption through the mid-1970s, moderated temporarily, and returned at the end of that decade to rates at or near the highest levels experienced in the twentieth century.

Homicide statistics, the most reliable data available on violent crime, provide a striking example of the growth of violent crime and the disproportionate contribution of firearms. Between 1963 and 1973, the aggregate homicide rate in the United States grew from 4.3 to 9.3 per 100,000, an increase of 116 percent.[13] A more dramatic contrast emerges when firearm and nonfirearm homicide trends are separately analyzed during this period. Nonfirearm homicide increased from a rate of 2.0 per 100,000 in 1963 to 3.1 in 1973, an increase of 55 percent.[14] Firearm homicide rates increased from 2.5 per 100,000 in 1963 to 6.2 in 1973, an increase of 148 percent in eleven years.[15]

Gun crime played a disproportionate role in periods when homicide rates were moderating or declining as well. Between 1975 and 1976, criminal homicides reported by the police decreased by almost 10 percent. Separate analysis of homicide statistics by weapon type revealed that handgun killings decreased at a rate that was over twice that of killings by all other means.[16] National statistical breakdowns on assault and robbery do not permit the separate analysis of handgun involvement. However, area studies suggest the prominence of handguns in big-city firearms robbery and only slightly less handgun dominance for big-city firearms assault.

The number of assassination attempts is too small for elaborate statistical analysis. It may be worthy of note, however, that every assassination attempt publicly reported since 1968 involved a handgun. Further, handguns were involved in three-quarters of all police killings throughout the 1970s and early 1980s.

It would, of course, be interesting to compare trends in handgun violence with patterns of net introduction of handguns into the civilian population over the past fifteen years. The most formidable obstacle to this research strategy is our inability to estimate handgun attrition over time, discussed above. A further difficulty is that estimates of domestic production of handguns for civilian use are extremely weak for the period 1969 through 1972.[17] The best evidence on this matter comes from the 1960s, a period when a sharp increase in annual introductions overpowers any rate of attrition that would be stable relative to the number of guns introduced in earlier years. Less rigorous cues are available in statistics on handgun introduction in the 1970s.

## More Research
The 1970s produced a substantial number of interdisciplinary studies on patterns of gun ownership, the relationship between firearms and crime, and the impact of gun control initiatives. Less encouraging, little research has been undertaken on the relationship between firearms and accidents, the impact of firearms on death rates from suicide, and the costs and benefits of handguns as a mechanism of household self-defense.

Research on acquisition of firearms depends on two data sources: annual government figures on new production and imports of firearms and public opinion polls that periodically ask cross sections of Americans how many firearms they own and what kinds. The aggregate picture of civilian firearms ownership in the late 1970s suggests high numbers of annual introduction and uneven distribution among households in weapon ownership. The proportion of households owning long guns did not change, whereas the proportion of households owning handguns did increase substantially in the 1960s and 1970s. By 1980, about half of all American households report some gun ownership, a rough guess consistent with earlier poll results. However, gun-owning households own more firearms per household than was the case in the late 1960s.[18]

The proportion of all households reporting handgun ownership has increased substantially over a twenty-year period. It is difficult to estimate the increase with precision, because public opinion polls taken at roughly similar times report large differences in the proportion of households owning handguns.[19] During the 1960s, the sharp expansion of household handgun ownership was consistent with an expanding demand for self-defense guns. By the end of 1968, 80 percent of handgun-owning households owned only one.[20] The pattern for the 1970s is somewhat more ambiguous: one 1978 poll estimates that about 60 percent of handgun-owning households own only one, but that represents a significant increase in multiple handgun ownership in ten years.[21]

Survey research has yet effectively to probe motives for handgun acquisition and attitudes about loaded guns in the home among the families that have acquired them and those who have considered but rejected handgun acquisition. We can guess that between a fifth and a quarter of U.S. households own handguns, but rich insight into why handguns are acquired, patterns of household use, and attitudes toward loaded handguns among gun-owning and non-gun-owning citizens will have to depend on future research.

## FIREARMS AND CRIME

The predominant firearms crimes in the United States are assault and robbery. Assault typically involves a victim and offender known to each other in a conflict setting, although random attacks are more than occasionally reported. Robbery is the attempt to gain property by the use of threat of force. Events classified as criminal homicide are an amalgam of assaults and robberies that lead to the victim's death and lethal attacks in which the victim's death was one of the intended consequences of the offender.

Studies of assault with firearms and other frequently used weapons show that gun attacks lead to death far more frequently than attacks using other widely available weapons. The key issue in assault research is whether the differential death rate can be wholly attributed to the different motives of gun and other attackers or whether the dangerousness of the weapon, independent of intention, contributes to the death rate from assault. A series of studies dating back to 1967 but continuing through the 1970s suggest that guns make a substantial impact on the death rate per hundred assaults when they are used.[22] And comparing the proportion of all attacks committed with firearms over time to the death rate per hundred reported attacks gives circumstantial support to this hypothesis.[23]

Lacking the capactiy to perform controlled experiments, students of instrumentality effects have fallen short of a positive proof that guns significantly contribute to death rates. Further, the magnitude of the increase in death rates attributable to gun use rather than knife use cannot be estimated with precision.

Reviewing fifteen years of research, Phillip Cook recently concluded that "the likelihood of death from a serious assault is determined, inter alia, by the assailant's intent and the lethality of the weapon used. The type of weapon is especially important when the intent is ambiguous. The fraction of homicides that can be viewed as deliberate (unambiguously intended) varies over time and space and is probably fairly small as a rule."[24]

Cook's conclusions are worthy of attention and not simply because they accurately reflect the substantial weight of available evidence. The qualifications, puzzles, and unresolved questions generated by a review of existing research suggest a greater research sophistication and greater sense of particularity to be found in recent studies of firearms and crime.

As to robbery, Professor Cook finds "the objective dangerousness pattern applies to robbery as well as assault, for reasons that remain a bit obscure."[25]

Gun use in robbery presents a different set of research issues, because most robberies involve the threat of weapon use rather than an unconditional intention to injure the victim. Guns are the most credible threat available to robbers. And availability may thus encourage a greater number of robberies as opposed to other forms of property crime. Gun availability may also encourage robbery of "harder targets," such as commercial establishments and banks. The credibility of a firearm as a weapon may discourage victim resistance, increasing the success rate of robberies and decreasing the proportion of robbery attempts where victim resistance leads to victim injury. Finally, the lethal nature of firearms may increase the death rate from robbery by escalating the chances that death will result if the weapon is fired.

Serious research on the relationship between firearms and robbery was born in the 1970s. Studies of samples of robberies in metropolitan areas and robbery over time and comparative studies of robbery patterns in a variety of cities were the most substantial research contribution of recent years. Research to date generates two broad areas of agreement and one issue on which the research findings point in opposite directions. The two consensus conclusions are that the injury rate from nonfirearm robbery is higher than the injury rate resulting from gun robbery, although it is not known whether the characteristics of the offending groups or the situations generate that result. Further, the death rate from gun robbery is substantially higher than death rates experienced in other forms of robbery encounters.[26]

Preliminary indications suggest that the conclusion drawn about the influence of gun availability on robbery volume is dependent upon the methods of analysis used. A robbery study over time in Detroit suggests a high correlation between the volume of robberies and the proportion of robberies involving firearms.[27] A cross-sectional study of fifty cities suggests no substantial relationship between gun availability and the total volume of robbery.[28] Both time studies and multivariate correlational cross-sectional analysis are relatively weak tools for examining the complex relationship between gun availability and robbery volume. Yet more rigorous assessments are difficult to design and remain a prime agenda item for future research.

## THE EFFECTS OF GUN CONTROL INITIATIVES

A number of studies of legal or law enforcement changes designed to decrease gun availability, reduce firearms crime, or deter potential criminals from using guns began to appear in the mid-1970s. Almost without exception, the studies were undertaken after a change in law or law enforcement strategy, and statistics on trends in firearms versus nonfirearms crime before and after the change was the measure of whether the initiative succeeded.

One study of the Federal Gun Control Act of 1968 found no measurable impact on gun crime in those tight-control cities where the 1968 legislation presumably would produce its greatest benefits. The failure of the legislation to make a measurable dent in interstate handgun migration could plausibly be explained by a lack of emphasis on this goal by the enforcement agency or it could reflect the structural difficulties of the state-aid approach of the 1968 law, or both.[29] A follow-up study of special enforcement efforts in the District of Columbia and Chicago claimed success for the enforcement initiative, because the drop in firearms crime in the test cities was larger than the drop in nongun crime in those cities or in firearms crime in two comparison cities.[30] There are, however, problems with attributing this drop to the special federal enforcement level. Chicago experienced only a modest special federal enforcement effort, and its crime patterns were compared to those of Los Angeles during one of the coldest winters in Chicago history. More important, the mid-1970s was a period when a number of cities that did not experience federal enforcement efforts had substantial drops in firearms crime.

The coincidence of declining rates of urban violence and periods selected for the "after" measurements of a before-and-after design also bedeviled the most scrutinized firearms control initiative of the 1970s, the Massachusetts legislation requiring a mandatory minimum jail term of one year for defendants convicted of unlawfully carrying handguns.[31] Careful research pointed to a decrease in gun crime in Boston shortly before and after the effective date of the legislation but no measurable impact in the second year of the law.[32] The problem, again, is separating out the effects of the passage of time from the impact of the legislation.

Three basic problems weaken the initial efforts to assess the impact of gun control enforcement. First, social scientists can only study policy changes that occur, and dramatic shifts in gun control policy were infrequent during the early 1970s. Future research will have the opportunity to examine more ambitious undertakings, such as the changes that occurred in the District of Columbia in the mid-1970s.

A further problem with the first-round studies is the extremely short time frame after an initiative covered by the studies. Two years is the longest follow-up period reported for all but one of the studies.[33] Yet efforts to reduce the availability of handguns, if successful at all, should take years before the collective impact of enforcement on handgun availability shows maximum impact.

The third problem of the first-round studies was the exclusive reliance on reported crimes as the measure of legal impact. Future research can supplement trends in crime statistics with information on the age, street price, and origin of confiscated weapons before and after changes aimed at producing handgun scarcity.

The coming decade will provide the opportunity for careful, multiple-measure, long-range evaluations of the experience in the District of Columbia and any other major jurisdictions that attempt to engineer substantial shifts in handgun availability.

## SOME OTHER QUESTIONS

I have previously suggested that the pattern of empirical research through the 1970s has been uneven. This section covers a few of the more important research questions that have been stepchildren in recently published research. The number and determinants of gun accident injuries and deaths was the subject of one scholarly study during the decade, a time series analysis of Cuyahoga County, Ohio.[34] But no sustained attention has been paid to changes in reported firearm accident rates in the vital statistics or the proportion of handgun accident deaths to total gun accident deaths over time. Changes between urban and nonurban areas in the distribution of gun accidents have gone unstudied. There has been no further research on the relationship between firearms availability and suicide rates. Most surprising, the critical issue of the costs and benefits of keeping a loaded handgun as an instrument of self-defense has not received the careful and sustained attention the question demands.

## More Attention

Through the late 1960s, public attitudes toward firearms control were vaguely positive but episodic and unfocused. Within the last decade, the focus has sharpened. The emergence of single-issue lobbies on both sides of the handgun question has created a high level of public awareness and persistent efforts to reform the law. This, in turn, has polarized public opinion: the number of Americans willing to take drastic steps to control handguns has increased, but so has the number of citizens who oppose them. From city councils to the Congress, each new year brings a bumper crop of legislative proposals that range from repealing laws already on the books to an outright ban on the sale and manufacture of handguns to civilians.

Thus, we have *already* entered a new era in the political career of the American handgun. The issue simply refuses to go away. Compromise is not merely elusive; neither side wishes to search for middle ground. The 1980s begin with an acrimonious stalemate in the political arena that accurately reflects a divided and more intense mix of public feelings about handguns than at any time in previous history. Eventually, something has to give.

At the heart of this tug-of-war is a struggle between two competing images of the loaded handgun in the American urban household.

The anticontrol forces, pushed to a specific defense of the handgun, portray it as the individual's last and only resort to defending his household in an environment of predatory crime and ineffective law enforcement. Procontrol groups portray the self-defense gun as futile and dangerous to the household, and argue that it exposes the community to further risk of violence when the gun is stolen. In the antihandgun view, the high level of gun availability produced by household use necessarily results in high availability as an instrument of violent crime.

No matter who wins the debate, the shape of federal, state, and local gun control laws will change over the next decades. But the outcome of the conflict over handguns and civilian self-defense will have an important influence on how far public policy can change. We thus must shift from discussing past developments to guessing about emerging trends in order to outline alternative policy futures. This is the task of the following section.

### NOTES TOWARD A POLICY FUTURE

If the last thirty years are an appropriate guide, forthcoming decades will bring a national handgun strategy composed of three parts: (1) federally mandated or administered restrictions on handgun transfers that amount to permissive licensing and registration;[35] (2) wide variation in state and municipal handgun possession and transfer regulation, with an increasing number of municipal governments adopting restrictive licensing schemes or bans on handgun ownership; and (3) increasing federal law enforcement assistance to states and, more particularly, to cities attempting to enforce more restrictive regimes than the federal minimum. Under such a scheme, federal law will neither set quotas on the number of handguns introduced into civilian markets nor dictate ownership policy to the states. Rather, designated high-risk groups, such as minors, convicted felons, and former mental patients, will be excluded from ownership, as is presently the case.

The two major changes in federal law I anticipate are, first, a registration scheme that will link individual handguns to owners in a central data bank and will require prior notification before handguns are transferred, and second, a federal law prohibiting firearms transfers when the possession of a handgun by the transferee would violate the laws of the municipality in which he resides. Centrally stored ownership data would permit federal law to extend to transfers made by nondealers, and regulations requiring timely prior notice of private transfers through dealers or local officials would be added to existing regulations.[36]

These changes in federal law would facilitate minimal municipal standards for residents acquiring handguns that could not be frustrated by more lenient state government standards. This new power, and a climate favorable to handgun regulations in the big cities, would produce a much longer list of metropolitan or city governments attempting to impose restrictive licensing or bans on civilian ownership among their populations. Presently existing systems in cities such as New York, Boston, Philadelphia, and Washington, D.C., would be emulated in cities such as Chicago and Detroit and in most nonsouthern metropolitan areas. Within the South, municipal or metropolitan governments in areas like Miami and Atlanta might follow suit.

All of this would in turn increase the demand, particularly on the part of cities, for federal law enforcement support to protect city boundaries from in-state guns. Within five years after extension of federal protection to municipal handgun control, the intrastate, rather than interstate, migration of handguns may well emerge as a top priority in federal firearms law enforcement.

It is, of course, one thing to make up a scheme of handgun regulation and quite another to argue that it is historically derived. Why is it that federal regulation will expand? What is the basis for suggesting that municipal handgun controls will increase? The answers to such questions are neither easy nor obvious.

National handgun registration is only peculiar in that it has not yet been accomplished. Public opinion seems solidly behind handgun-owner accountability if registration is viewed solely as an accountability system and not as a first step toward confiscation of all the guns linked to registered owners.

Registration thus seems inevitable if its proponents can make a creditable case that a registration scheme will not be used to facilitate a shift from permissive to restrictive licensing policies. This could be achieved by "grandfathering" all guns registered to eligible owners so that any subsequent shift in federal regulatory policy would exempt validly registered guns.

The momentum toward tighter municipal licensing is easier to demonstrate. In the cities, pressure for handgun restriction has increased dramatically in the past fifteen years, and those cities that have adopted controls almost never repeal them. The momentum toward further handgun restriction in major metropolitan areas appears substantial in all regions except the South and the Southwest.

Substantial changes in municipal regulation of handgun ownership have become the rule rather than the exception in those American jurisdictions that have reconsidered handgun regulation in the last twenty years.[37] This has occurred despite complaints about the power of the gun control lobby.

The most likely trend is toward a patchwork quilt of federal, state, and local regulation. This conclusion is not surprising. Significant variations exist in attitudes toward handguns, and it should only be expected that these attitudinal differences would more quickly lead to a wider spectrum of state and local variation than to a unified national strategy. Or will they?

## Handgun Scarcity as Federal Policy
State and local variation might not work. Federal attempts to protect tight-control cities and states would continue to be frustrated by interstate and intrastate movement of handguns; the large civilian inventory of handguns would make efforts at accountability based on registration data both expensive and easy to evade at the point of first purchase. Under such circumstances, growing dependence on public transportation, and increased residential desegregation that spreads the risk of violent crime more evenly across metropolitan areas, may lead to demand for more substantial handgun controls.

An alternative federal handgun policy would stress reducing, substantially, the population of handguns and thus reducing general handgun availability. Federal standards might require the states to administer handgun licensing systems that would deny most citizens the opportunity to possess handguns and handgun ammunition. The central features of this scheme are the commitment of federal policy to nationwide handgun scarcity, a policy that would be imposed on states and cities where more permissive approaches were preferred, and a policy shift making continuing possession of handguns by millions of households unlawful.

What one calls such regulation is a secondary matter. Federal "restrictive licensing" is the equivalent of a "national handgun ban"! Indeed, many "ban" bills would leave more guns in circulation than would restrictive licensing because the exceptions—for example, security guards—are broad. The thrust of such a policy is the transition from a 30-million-handgun society to a 3-million-handgun society. This is no small step.

Even if a national policy of handgun scarcity were wholeheartedly adopted, there are limits on the capacity of federal authorities to implement policy without state and local cooperation. Handgun production quotas and regulations governing the distribution of new weapons could be administered at the federal level. Individual determination of whether citizens who apply for licenses meet need criteria is best left to local officials, however, and removing unlawfully possessed handguns is a by-product of local police activity.[38] The only way to shift this burden to the federal level is to create a national street police force, a radical departure from current practice that should not be expected or desired. Thus even federal policies that attempt to centralize authority to reduce existing handgun ownership will operate at the mercy of state and local law enforcement.

Still, any such national standard setting would represent two major departures from present federal law. First, the federal government would attempt to limit the supply of handguns nationwide. Second, in order to substantially reduce the handgun population, citizens would be denied the opportunity to own weapons even if they were not part of special high-risk groups and in spite of less restrictive policy preferences at the state and local level where they reside.

This type of plenary federal policy has never been seriously considered in the United States. Early in the New Deal, Attorney General Homer Cummings proposed tight federal handgun controls that received scant congressional attention.[39] In the 1970s, a series of proposals to create federal restrictive licensing was introduced and soundly defeated. The urban experiments with restrictive licensing in New York City and Washington, D.C., both involved jurisdictions with small inventories of lawfully possessed handguns and cooperative local law enforcement. A restrictive national handgun policy would thus represent a relatively sharp departure from previous twentieth-century politics of handgun control.

## A Turning Point?
Many factors can influence the direction of future handgun policy. A sharp decline in public fear of crime would decrease demand for handguns; at the same time, if this resulted in reduced violent crime, it would reduce the need for handgun control. An increase in burglary rates or, more significantly, in rates of home-invasion robbery would work the other way.

However, the most important element of future policy is not the crime rate, but social notions of appropriate crime countermeasures. The social status of the household self-defense handgun in our cities and suburbs will emerge as a critical leading indicator of future federal handgun control. Public opinion research has indicated that self-defense in the home is the most important "good reason" given for handgun ownership.[40] If citizens continue to believe that possessing a loaded handgun is a respectable method of defending urban households, handgun demand and opposition to restrictive policy will continue. If owning loaded handguns in the home comes to be viewed more as part of the gun problem than as a respectable practice, the prospects for restrictive control will improve over time. The residual uses of handguns—informal target shooting, collection, and hunting sidearms—are peripheral to the handgun control controversy.

Early indications of how the debate on handguns will be resolved may be found in the actions and beliefs of key opinion leadership groups in the next ten or fifteen years. My short list of such opinion leaders includes women, blacks, the elderly, the young, and of course, the mass media.

*Women* Rapid change in the status of women is one of the most important social changes associated with America's recent past and near future. At the same time, women have played a remarkable dual role in public opinion about handguns. Female ownership of self-defense handguns has historically been low, but female vulnerability to violent crime has been one of the most persuasive reasons offered as a justification for household handguns. President Reagan wasn't alone when he justified a gun in the dresser drawer as particularly suited for periods when he would be away from the ranch. Generations of men, who are not themselves supposed to be afraid in their own households, have kept handguns "for the little woman."

Two things are striking about women's dual role. First, both low ownership and the woman's role as justification for the gun are based on traditional sex roles and patterns of family organization. Second, it is inevitable that either female handgun ownership patterns or "the little woman" as an excuse for household self-defense guns will have to change in the near future.

The reason for this is simple demographics. In the 1960s, when 7 percent of the people who bought handguns were women, fewer than a fifth of all American households were headed by females.[41] Since the mid-1960s, the growth in female-headed households has been enormous, and the majority of these are women living alone. Since 1969, the number of households without men has gone from under 13 million to over 20 million and from under a fifth to over a quarter of all households.[42] Either these women will acquire weapons at historically unprecedented rates or they will blow the cover on female vulnerability as a justification for gun ownership. The American woman of the 1980s and 1990s will thus be the first and most important leading indicator of the social status of self-defense handguns in the more distant future.

If female ownership of self-defense handguns increases dramatically, the climate of opinion for drastic restriction of handguns can't happen. Women are physically more vulnerable to crime than men, and this special vulnerability, other liberations aside, will be an important part of our culture for generations. Women, predominantly, are targets of sexual violence.

Further, female attitudes toward household burglary, far and away the most frequent form of home victimization, seem to diverge sharply from male attitudes. Many men tend to shrug off burglary as a loss of property; women experience it as a gross invasion of personal privacy that produces high levels of fear and insult. If single women demand guns for self-defense purposes, federal firearms control will, at maximum, require screening, waiting periods, and some registration. The 50-million-handgun society of the future may be foreordained.

But what if a substantial majority of America's single women reject the handgun as a personal option? There are other antiburglary options: dogs, alarm systems, deadbolt locks. And there are indications that women feel differently about gun ownership. One Harris poll showed that total gun ownership in female-headed households was less than half that reported by households including an adult male.[43]

The political and cultural implications of persistently low handgun ownership by single women are potentially enormous: a large and growing segment of the electorate will not own handguns. And the special vulnerability of this group makes them immune to arguments that other groups really need handguns or that they are being insensitive to the fear of crime.

Even more important is the impact of single women's behavior on the sexual politics of handgun ownership within marriage. Women, particularly mothers, don't like to have lethal weapons in their homes. How does Mr. Smith convince Mrs. Smith that a gun is necessary for her "when he is away" if some of her best friends live alone without guns? This is the kind of moral ammunition wives may put to effective use as they become more confident of their capacity to participate in such decisions as equal partners.

Continued low handgun ownership by females is not a sufficient condition to stigmatize handgun ownership, but it will be necessary to any emerging long-range consensus. Already, antihandgun meetings are composed in unequal proportion of emphatic wives and reluctant husbands. Perhaps, in searching for the eventual solution to the American handgun stalemate, we should redirect our attention from the *New York Times* to *Ms* magazine and the *Ladies' Home Journal.*

*Black Americans* White America lives in fear of violence in a rather abstract way. An astonishingly high proportion of black Americans have tasted violence firsthand in the lives of their families and close friends. The enormous difference in levels of crime victimization between urban minorities and the rest of the country makes the issue of the self-defense handgun far more urgent for urban blacks and gives the black community special credentials for teaching the costs and benefits of the handgun.[44]

To date, blacks—absorbed by other pressing problems—have not played a role in the heated debate over handgun control. Indeed, one of the most striking characteristics of both pro- and antihandgun lobbies is their lily-white leadership. This will change. A large and growing black middle class, imprisoned by residential segregation, lives next door to the urban American ghetto and in constant fear. For the black urban family, there is often no middle ground: handguns are either purchased or detested.

Many black women, mothers of sons, are involuntary experts on handguns in the house and on the streets. Their men and male children, living high-risk lives, have better reasons to buy guns than any other segment of American society and better reasons not to buy guns. Handguns loom as a major source of friction between the sexes, between the classes, and between generations in the black community.

The outcome of such conflicts is difficult to forecast. Decisive rejection of self-defense guns on the fringes of the American urban ghetto could be an important message to mainstream America. On the other hand, an increase in self-defense handgun ownership within the black middle class, and particularly among female-headed households, would represent a major obstacle to the political climate that might promote handgun scarcity.

*Older Americans* The numbers and influence of what we used to call senior citizens have increased dramatically in the past two decades and will continue to increase. This segment of the population is politically active and well informed and lives in constant fear of crime in the city. The combination of substantial political clout and special vulnerability to crime has already produced special legislation stiffening the penalties for those who victimize the elderly. There is, to my knowledge, no consensus among Americans over sixty-five on the issue of handgun restriction. But this group, predominantly female, is another source of potential leadership in building social consensus against the loaded household handgun.

In male-headed households, however, gun ownership patterns may tend to persist. Because the loaded handgun in the urban home is a relatively new phenomenon, the coming years will witness the first large generation of urban handgun owners becoming older. The mix of factors that might change ownership and attitudes in an aging population is substantial: an increase in proportion of female-headed households, increasing fear of crime, perhaps a decrease among older men in the need for machismo artifacts, and a general shift in life situations from offensive orientations toward crime to more defensive adaptations.

Whether all this leads to consensus is anybody's guess. However, the potential impact of a unified senior citizens lobby is substantial. For those who view the power of the National Rifle Association as awesome in legislative circles, imagine what would happen if that organization had opposed the last round of Social Security increases. The critical questions, therefore, are whether older America can come close to consensus on the handgun issue and what that consensus will be.

*The Young* Habits are easier to avoid than to break. It is probably much easier to talk a young person out of acquiring his first home self-defense handgun than to persuade his father that the household appliance he has retained, loaded, and kept ready for twenty years is of no use to his family. If this is the case, the emerging generation of late adolescents and young adults is a leading indicator here as in so many other areas of manners, morals, and behavior.

The urban house gun is a relatively recent phenomenon in American urban life. Perhaps it can fall out of fashion. The first leading indicator might be the behavior of the young upper middle class in major urban areas. But antihandgun sentiments must trickle down to middle- and working-class young America before the elements of political consensus fall into place. It is here that the opinion leadership of women, mentioned above, must play a critical role.

*The Media* This is not the place to debate whether the mass media shape opinion or merely reflect it. They do both. But the performance of television and the print media provide a rare opportunity for common ground between antihandgun and prohandgun groups: Both can show that information leadership in this country is suffering from a bad case of scrambled facts and has profoundly distorted information that is basic to comprehending the role of the handgun in American life.

The reason our information industry fails to ask basic questions or to demand real facts is that facts rarely generate Nielsen ratings or sell papers. The sensational and unrepresentative news angle makes the papers and the ten o'clock news.

The paradox is that no matter how bad a job the media do in covering the handgun issue, media coverage will be an increasingly important part of attitude change toward the urban house gun and the prospects of handgun scarcity. If liberal media sources overstate the handgun problem or promise unrealistic cures, they might shift attitudes against household handguns but only at the cost of their eventual credibility. If, on the other hand, the sensational and unrepresentative news angle dominates our television screens, we may experience a self-fulfilling prophecy. If ABC reports an artificial epidemic of female handgun ownership, the false prophecy can move closer to reality as viewers react.

The American handgun is not a hot story; it is a chronic condition. And facts are facts. One of the horrifying glories of American democracy is that no central directorate exists to teach the press professional responsibility. A zealous antihandgun campaign, when dedicated to the sensational and exceptional case, can backfire profoundly. And some recent treatment of the handgun issue suggests a new libertarian radical chic: a celebration of loaded guns as an individual urban solution rather than an urban problem. One can hope that the American information industry will begin to do its homework on the question of firearms control. Misinformation on either side of this explosive issue is a public disservice.

## A Tentative Bottom Line

A realistic view of the future provides hope only for optimists among anti-handgun groups but small comfort as well for the friends of the urban American handgun. Only an agnostic is on safe ground. In the complexities and pace of American social change, there is a potential coalition of opinion that could lead to change in public attitude and public law regarding hand-gun ownership. But potential, of course, is the word we hear most often from coaches of losing football teams. And the bitter rhetoric and inflated claims associated with some current "antigun" propaganda and legislation may retard the evolution toward a constructive consensus.

Opinion-leading groups may identify the boundaries of American hand-gun policies in the next generation far more quickly than they or we suspect. In making this assertion, I do not mean to understate the role of spectacular tragedies in prompting political action on guns. The Martin Luther King and Robert Kennedy killings were absolutely necessary to the passage of the federal gun laws in 1968. The mindless murder of John Lennon and shooting of President Reagan had powerful impact on public opinion. No doubt, some future horror might provide the spur for further legislation. But these episodes explain more about when we pass laws than how far our gun laws can be pushed as an instrument of social change.

## NOTES

1. B. Bruce-Briggs, "The Great American Gun War," *Public Interest* 45 (1976):1–26.
2. See Philip J. Cook, "The Effect of Gun Availability on Violent Crime Patterns," *Annals of the Academy of Political and Social Science* 455 (1981):63–79.
3. Ibid.
4. Carol S. Leff and Mark H. Leff, "The Politics of Ineffectiveness: Federal Firearms Leg-islation, 1919–38," *Annals of the American Academy of Political and Social Science* 455 (1981):48–62.
5. George D. Newton and Franklin E. Zimring, *Firearms and Violence in American Life* (Washington, D.C.: U.S. Government Printing Office, 1969), pp. 151–62.
6. Ibid., pp. 171–74.
7. Ibid., p. 174.

8. See Franklin E. Zimring, "Street Crime and New Guns: Some Implications for Firearms Control," *Journal of Criminal Justice* 4 (1976):95–107.

9. Compare Zimring, "Street Crimes and New Guns," with Newton and Zimring, *Firearms and Violence*, p. 174.

10. Philip J. Cook, "The Role of Firearms in Violent Crime: An Interpretive Review of the Literature, with Some New Findings and Suggestions for Future Research," in *Criminal Violence*, ed. Marvin Wolfgang and Neil Weiner (Beverly Hills, Calif.: Sage Publications, 1982).

11. See, e.g., James D. Wright, P. H. Rossi, K. Daly, and E. Weber-Burdin, *Weapons, Crime, and Violence in America: A Literature Review and Research Agenda* (Amherst: University of Massachusetts, Social and Demographic Research Institute, 1981).

12. See Zimring, "Street Crimes and New Guns."

13. Franklin E. Zimring, "Firearms and Federal Law: The Gun Control Act of 1968," *Journal of Legal Studies* 4 (1975):133–98, fn. 2.

14. Ibid.

15. Ibid.

16. Murders by handguns dropped by approximately 14 percent from 1975 to 1976, whereas murders by all other weapons dropped by only 2.5 percent; Federal Bureau of Investigation, *Uniform Crime Reports, 1976* (Washington, D.C.: U.S. Government Printing Office, 1977), pp. 9–10.

17. See Philip J. Cook, "Gun Availability and Violent Crime," in *Crime and Justice: An Annual Review of Research*, ed. Michael Tonry and Norval Morris (Chicago: University of Chicago Press, 1983), 5:78–81.

18. Ibid.

19. Ibid., p. 78.

20. Newton and Zimring, *Firearms and Violence*, pp. 175–77.

21. See Cook, "Gun Availability and Violent Crime," pp. 78–81.

22. Franklin E. Zimring, "Is Gun Control Likely to Reduce Violent Killings?" *University of Chicago Law Review* 35 (1967):721–37.

23. A flawed version of such a statistical argument is presented in Seitz, "Firearms, Homicide, and Gun Control Effectiveness," *Law and Society Review* 6 (1972):595.

24. Cook, "Gun Availability and Violent Crime," pp. 71–72.

25. Ibid., pp. 74–75.

26. Franklin E. Zimring, "Determinants of the Death Rate from Robbery: A Detroit Time Study," *Journal of Legal Studies* 6, no. 2 (1977):317, 321–23.

27. Ibid., p. 327.

28. Philip J. Cook, "A Strategic Choice Analysis of Robbery," in *Sample Surveys of the Victims of Crimes*, ed. Wesley Skogan (Cambridge, Mass.: Ballinger, 1976).

29. See Zimring, "Firearms and Federal Law."

30. United States Bureau of Alcohol, Tobacco and Firearms, *Concentrated Urban Enforcement CUE* (Washington, D.C., 1978).

31. Rossman et al., "The Impact of the Mandatory Gun Law in Massachusetts," (Boston: Boston University School of Law, 1979), mimeo.

32. Ibid.

33. The exception is the 1968 federal law; see Zimring, "Firearms and Federal Law," and Wright et al., *Weapons, Crime and Violence in America* (Washington, D.C.: National Institute of Justice, 1981), pp. 501–46.

34. Norman B. Rushforth, A. B. Ford, C. S. Hirsh, N. M. Rushforth, and L. Adelson, "Violent Death in a Metropolitan County: Changing Patterns in Homicide (1958–74)," *New England Journal of Medicine* 297 (1977):531–38.

35. As used in this article, the terms *permissive licensing, restrictive licensing,* and *registration*

are defined following Newton and Zimring, *Firearms and Violence*, pp. 83–84. See also Franklin E. Zimring, "Getting Serious about Guns," *Nation* 214 (1972):457, 459–60.

36. Central storage of ownership data is possible even if records of purchase continue to be maintained by individual dealers. Duplicate forms could be forwarded to automatic data processing systems probably without any changes in the provisions of the Gun Control Act of 1968. See Zimring, "Firearms and Federal Law," pp. 151–54.

37. See Edward D. Jones III, "The District of Columbia's 'Firearms Control Regulations Act of 1975': The Toughest Handgun Control Law in the United States—Or Is It?" in *Annals of the American Academy of Political and Social Science* 455 (May 1981):138–49.

38. See Franklin E. Zimring, "Street Crime and New Guns, Some Implications for Firearms Control," *J. Criminal Justice* 4 (1976):95, 101–02.

39. See Zimring, "Firearms and Federal Law," p. 138. See also "The Politics of Ineffectiveness: Federal Firearms Legislation, 1919–38," *Annals of the American Academy of Political and Social Science* 455 (May 1981):48–62.

40. Newton and Zimring, *Firearms and Violence*, p. 62.

41. Ibid., p. 175; U.S. Department of Commerce, Bureau of the Census, *Current Population Reports*, Series P-20, no. 130 (Washington, D.C.: U.S. Government Printing Office, 1964).

42. U.S. Department of Commerce, Bureau of the Census, *Current Population Reports*, Series P-20, no. 376 (Washington, D.C.: U.S. Government Printing Office, 1982).

43. Newton and Zimring, *Firearms and Violence*, p. 175.

44. U.S. Department of Justice, Bureau of Justice Statistics, *Sourcebook of Criminal Justice Statistics, 1980* (Washington, D.C.: U.S. Government Printing Office, 1981), pp. 242, 249.

# PART II

# COLLECTIVE VIOLENCE

# 7

# Collective Violence:
# The Redress of Grievance
# and Public Policy

SANDRA J. BALL-ROKEACH AND JAMES F. SHORT, JR.

In remarks made to the National Advisory Commission on Civil Disorders, the eminent psychologist Dr. Kenneth Clark said:

> I read that report . . . of the 1919 riot in Chicago, and it is as if I were reading the report of the investigating committee on the Harlem riot of '35, the report of the investigating committee on the Harlem riot of '43, the report of the McCone Commission on the Watts riot.
>
> I must again in candor say to you members of this Commission—it is a kind of Alice in Wonderland—with the same analysis, the same recommendations, and the same inaction.

Clark's poignant remarks set the focus for our attempt to answer fundamental questions about the state of collective violence in America today. Did the major governmental commissions of the late 1960s—the Kerner, Violence, and Katzenbach commissions—merely do the same analyses and make the same recommendations, and were they followed by the same inaction? In order to address these questions, we must review the conclusions and recommendations of those commissions and assess their impact on public policy and on groups seeking to redress grievances via collective violence.

We will also ask whether the *phenomenon* of collective violence has changed since the events that gave rise to those commissions. Beyond questions of frequency and intensity, have the underlying causes of collective violence changed? It is, after all, the hope of those who have labored in research and policy analysis that the causes of collective violence will become sufficiently well understood to be effectively removed. We need to determine whether this hope has been realized in whole or in part. Can

**155**

we, for example, interpret the marked decline in the incidence of collective violence in the urban ghetto and on the college campus as a consequence of effective social policy?

## CONCLUSIONS AND RECOMMENDATIONS OF THE VIOLENCE, KERNER, AND CRIME COMMISSIONS

The National Commission on the Causes and Prevention of Violence (Violence Commission) was appointed by President Johnson in June 1968 following the assassinations of Martin Luther King and Senator Robert Kennedy. Its charge was broad, encompassing the many individual as well as collective acts of violence in American life. The Violence Commission's inquiry focused on collective violence associated with two phenomena: opposition to the Vietnam War, leading to violence on college campuses (Skolnick, *The Politics of Protest,* 1969; Orrick, *Shut it Down! A College in Crisis,* 1969), at the Democratic National Convention in Chicago (Walker, *Rights in Conflict,* 1968), and in response to the counterinaugural demonstration in Washington, D.C. (Sahid, *Rights in Concord,* 1969); and urban violence linked to racial inequality in Cleveland (Massotti, *Shoot-Out in Cleveland,* 1969) and Miami (Hector and Helliwell, *Miami Report,* 1969). The history of collective violence in America (Graham and Gurr, *History of Violence in America,* 1969) and the role of the mass media in collective violence (Baker and Ball, *Violence and the Media,* 1969) were also examined.

After noting that collective violence in this country is a relatively rare outcome of the exercise of the constitutional right of assembly to petition for redress of grievances, the commissioners put forth several conclusions about the causes of collective violence. President Johnson's suspicion at the time that collective violence was caused by an organized group of conspirators who held no allegiance to the democratic process was soundly rejected. To the contrary, the commissioners located the chief cause of both student and urban group violence in failures of the political system that either blocked legitimate expression of grievances or prevented decision makers from recognizing and effectively responding to legitimate grievances. Collective violence, then, was first and foremost a product of a breakdown in the democratic process that prevented rightful participation of groups in decisions affecting their lives. Violence as a response to threatened loss of status and position in life was also noted:

> Group violence occurs when expectations about rights and status are continually frustrated and when peaceful efforts to press these claims yield inadequate results. It also occurs when the claims of groups who feel disadvantaged are viewed as threats by other groups occupying a higher status in society. (p. 62)

The struggle to attain or to maintain political and economic rights and statuses was thus identified as the primary motive in the collective violence of both the poor, urban, ghetto black and those whites who fear racial equality for its threat to their rights and status, such as KKK members or representatives of traditional white power structures. In the case of largely middle-class college students and campus antiwar violence, the commissioners pointed to the additional motive of revolutionary ideology born of "cynicism about the system."

More proximate grievances giving rise to collective violence in the ghetto included deprivation in housing, employment, and educational opportunities. Finally, weak or inconsistent social control policies and practices were identified as important factors that could transform peaceful protest in the ghetto and on the campus into collective violence.

The recommendations of the Violence Commission pertaining to the prevention of collective violence were formulated to achieve three basic goals—"controlling disorder, keeping open the channels of protest, and correcting social injustices." Their recommendations to prevent and to control disorder were (1) increased federal funding of the criminal justice system, (2) creation of centralized criminal justice offices in metropolitan areas that incorporate citizen counterparts, (3) greatly increased police department planning and preparation for control of peaceful and violent assemblies, and (4) the creation of a national firearms policy. To guarantee open channels of protest, the commissioners recommended (1) that district court judges be empowered to grant injunctions against interference with the rights of freedom of speech, freedom of the press, peaceful assembly, and petition for redress of grievances, and (2) discouragement of trends that undermine the media's ability to provide an open marketplace of ideas, and encouragement of efforts to make of the media more efficacious channels for the expression of grievances by minority and other discontented groups, such as more interpretive reporting of social conflicts and hiring of minority persons. The final set of recommendations to correct social injustices included (1) political changes, such as draft reform, (2) institutional changes to improve decision makers' abilities to recognize and respond to grievances, such as providing legal services to the poor and the formation of community grievance agencies, and (3) fundamental reconstruction of urban life by way of housing, job, education, and income programs and the restructuring of local government.[1]

The Commission on Civil Disorders (Kerner Commission), formed one year earlier than the Violence Commission, also was appointed by President Johnson. This commission was charged specifically with the task of determining what had happened in the urban disorders of the 1960s in Detroit, Newark, and other cities, why they happened, and how such civil disorders could be prevented in the future. In the summer of 1967, at least 150 cities reported civil disorders, most of which occurred in the black ghettos of these cities. A mounting wave of "burn, baby, burn" swept the nation, leaving fear in its wake.

The Kerner Commission's hallmark analysis of twenty-four of the most destructive urban disorders produced a startling conclusion: the most basic cause of the disorders was that "our nation is moving toward two societies, one black, one white—separate and unequal" (p. 1). The term *institutionalized racism* captures the central diagnosis of the problem in the Kerner Commission report. Consistent with this diagnosis, the dominant motive attributed to rioters was to have their piece of the American pie—material and political resources that were being denied them by a white society ruled by the ideology and the practices of institutionalized racism. Among the specific grievances found in the twenty-three cities studied, the most intense were discriminatory and ineffective police practices, unemployment and underemployment, and inadequate housing. Other specific grievances included inadequacies in educational and recreational programs, ineffective police grievance mechanisms, disrespectful white attitudes, discriminatory administration of justice, inadequacy of federal and municipal services, and discriminatory consumer and credit practices. Thus, the general cause of civil disorders and the collective violence produced by them was identified as racism that ensures that nonwhites will be denied equal participation in American life and equal access especially to its material resources. Having thus spoken to the very fabric of American society, the commissioners put forth an equally monumental set of recommendations as to how civil disorders might be prevented from happening again.

Many of the recommendations were directed to problems at the local community level. They focused on (1) the creation or improvement of mechanisms for ghetto residents to communicate effectively their needs and grievances to appropriate government agencies and to ensure their participation in policy formation; (2) improvements in the criminal justice system to remove discriminatory practices and to better provide for the everyday security of ghetto residents and for effective control of ghetto disorders; and (3) increasing the quantity and quality of media coverage of ghetto life and the development of informed guidelines as to how the media might ameliorate, rather than exacerbate, crisis situations. The many recommendations for national action to create "a true union—a single society and a single American identity," were aimed at removing barriers to equal opportunity in jobs, education, and housing, designing efficacious means for ghetto residents to participate in the political process, and creating "a common ground" between whites and blacks for mutual respect and joint efforts to achieve both public order and social justice. Sounding what has since become a lonely clarion, the commission called for "the will to tax ourselves to the extent necessary to meet the[se] vital needs of the nation" (p. 23).

The Commission on Law Enforcement and Administration of Justice

(Katzenbach Commission), appointed in 1965, was the first of the 1960s commissions to work in an era when both crime and the law-and-order theme in American politics were on the rise. Of the three commissions, the Katzenbach Commission in *The Challenge of Crime in a Free Society* (1967) has the least to say about the phenomenon of collective violence. Its general theme concerning the causes and prevention of crime, however, is similar to the theoretical stance on the causes and prevention of disorder subsequently found in the reports of the Kerner and Violence commissions.

The common theme is that the roots of crime and disorder lie deep in the social fabric of American society, in its traditions, inequalities, and conflicts, and in ineffective governance. This common theme marked a substantial and significant departure from previous commission statements that emphasized psychological deficits and susceptibility to contagious processes in their accounts of the causes of collective violence and other disorders. Taken together, the Violence, Kerner, and Katzenbach reports articulate a fundamental shift in the political and policymaking spheres away from "psychological disorders" to "social disorders" as the primary causal nexus of both individual and collective violence. This common diagnostic theme carries over to the general thrust of the commissions' recommendations. Most pertinent to removing the causes and thus to the prevention of collective violence is the call for changes in the economic, educational, judicial, and political systems to deliver on the promise of a piece of the American pie for all her citizens, and specifically for equalizing opportunities for achievement of this goal. Making good on this promise, more than any other change, was said to have the greatest potential for removing the causes and thus preventing the emergence of collective violence to redress legitimate grievances.

## COLLECTIVE VIOLENCE IN THE DECADE OF THE SEVENTIES: CONTINUED GRIEVANCE, LITTLE REDRESS

For analysts of collective violence, the most glaring fact of the last decade is the rapid decline of urban disorders after 1968. The seventies were a decade of uneasy quiet when collective protest steadily declined on college campuses and riots virtually ceased in urban ghettos. It would be sheer sophistry to contend that these developments were due to the removal of the major social causes of collective violence identified by the Violence and Kerner commissions. So how can we explain the pattern of declining collective violence? In this section we seek to address, if not solve, this puzzle.

Civil rights gains, the end of the Vietnam War and its draft, and modest increases in the opportunity for student participation in university decision making removed some of the prime focal points of collective student protest. Affirmative-action programs led to significant increases in college enrollments of blacks, thus ameliorating this source of discontent. University administrations and faculty learned, often from experience, how to control and defuse potential conflicts on their campuses.

The several recessions and unemployment fears of this decade doubtless had a chilling effect. Quiet on the campus cannot, however, be attributed to the lack of issues. U.S. participation in El Salvador, nuclear power, draft registration, local and federal government dismantling of Great Society programs are only a few of the issues that might have activated student populations. It is, nonetheless, clear that the American college campus has not become the persistent political force that some had envisioned, but has instead returned to its historical (in this country) tenor of conventional quiescence.

The urban violence of the sixties led to considerably more damage to property and persons than did campus violence, and collective violence in the ghetto has been a more enduring aspect of American history. If the common thrusts of the Violence and Kerner commission reports provide a theory that can account for the high incidence of such urban violence in the 1960s *and* its markedly lower incidence in the 1970s, then substantial progress should be apparent in removing or ameliorating the causal conditions identified as responsible for the violence of the sixties. In the broadest sense, we might expect to find a substantial reduction in the institutionalized racism that had split America into two societies of advantaged whites and disadvantaged blacks. More specifically, we should observe steady improvements in the economic, political, familial, educational, and law enforcement conditions of the urban ghetto.

### Economic Conditions
Some progress has been made. Sociologist William Wilson, from the University of Chicago, notes that the number of blacks in managerial and professional jobs was 1.6 million in 1979, double the number in 1969.[2] However, total black unemployment in April 1982 was 18.4 percent, rising from 8.2 percent in 1970.[3] Overall increases in unemployment do not account for this rise as the comparable figures for whites are 4.5 percent and 8.4 percent, respectively.[4] Thus, the ratio of black to white unemployment rates has deteriorated from 1.8 in 1970 to 2.19 in April 1982.[5] The black unemployed are also more heavily concentrated in urban ghettos than are whites, with 60 percent of the black unemployed living in low-income areas of cities. Employment opportunities for low-income blacks have declined as cities have lost the goods-producing jobs that have been occupied by urban blacks in the past. From 1970 to 1976, for example, Chicago lost 92,000 jobs that were mostly in the goods-production area.[6] Nationally, the unemployment rate for all blue-collar workers is more than double that of

white-collar workers—13.7 versus 4.9 percent, respectively (April 1982).[7] Finally, there is the much publicized fact that the unemployment problem is most severe for black teenagers (sixteen to nineteen years old), standing at 48.1 percent in April 1982, twice the rate of white teenagers (20.8 percent).[8] That black poverty is still very much a feature of the urban ghetto is evidenced by the fact that 85.1 percent of all black families with yearly incomes under $4,000 in 1978 were families headed by women living in metropolitan areas.[9] Such concentration of poverty is not so evident for whites.

A significant change in the economic dynamics of poverty occurred in the decade between the early 1960s and 1970s: namely, blacks became more *like* whites with regard to the influence of parents' socioeconomic status. Whereas a 1962 study found that parents' socioeconomic status had little influence on the occupational status of blacks, in 1973 the occupational achievement of both blacks and whites was closely linked to that of their parents.[10] The significance of this change is that occupational discrimination based on race had become less important for the occupational achievement of blacks and their parental backgrounds more important. Viewed positively, young blacks from higher socioeconomic backgrounds were not as handicapped by their race in their own achievement as had been the case in the past. On the other hand, the young of both races had great difficulty in rising above their parents' status. The effect of this change is to freeze more blacks into lower economic status. Simply put, gains in reducing discrimination in the economic sector have been of little benefit to ghetto residents whose economic state today is worse, not better, than it was in the 1960s.

There is, moreover, disturbing evidence that for many in the United States poverty is a permanent condition and that for minorities the likelihood of permanent poverty is far greater than it is for the majority. Harvard sociologist Lee Rainwater, analyzing data from the University of Michigan's Panel Study of Income Dynamics, finds that over the 1967–76 decade he analyzed, 9.4 percent of the sample were "always poor" and an additional 7.1 percent were "near poor when not poor." Among young people, eighteen to twenty-four years old, "the likelihood of being poor or near poor was eight times greater for minority than for majority youth, and between the ages of twenty-five to fifty-four, the odds were seven times greater for minority people."[11]

## Political Conditions

Following passage of the Voting Rights Act of 1965, the number of blacks holding elective office in the United States increased rapidly, from 100 to 1,813 in 1980.[12] Unfortunately, these increases occurred during a period of increasing economic stress and the federal pullback from federal programs designed to aid cities under the Great Society and its War on Poverty. Goods-producing industry, the traditional economic and occupational base of many cities, was in many cases leaving the central city, thus weakening both the economic base of cities and occupational opportunities for ghetto residents. The dismantling of federal programs designed to aid cities has had consequences, not only with respect to services, jobs, and training opportunities for ghetto residents, but for employment of the black middle class as well. This, in turn, removes from the black community many government representatives who might be more sensitive than nonminority government employees to the needs of ghetto residents. In 1970, for example, 57 percent of black male college graduates and 72 percent of black female graduates were employed by government, many in agencies associated with Great Society programs.[13] The Community Service Administration abolished in 1981 is a case in point—of the nine hundred workers who lost their jobs, 60 percent were black.[14]

To the recent trend of transferring the problems of the urban ghetto onto local political leaders has been added an ever decreasing base of economic resources available to city officials. The repeated calls of the Violence and Kerner commissions for sensitive and effective local governance thus grew progressively less attainable from the early seventies to the present.

On the national level, some of the gains in black political participation, such as the presence of twenty-one blacks in the Ninety-eighth Congress and a rise in voter registration of blacks (e.g., in the South, from 29.3 percent in 1965 to 55.6 percent in 1980), have been threatened by reapportionment and by attempts to undercut the Voting Rights Act. Reapportionment is tied to the Voting Rights Act by a provision that bars dilution of minority representation in voting districts. Thus, the successful effort to extend the Voting Rights Act has payoffs not only in potential increases of voter registration but also in potential creation of new "black" seats in Congress, particularly in the South where population is increasing.

## Media
Many hoped that the trend toward concentration of media ownership might be countered by black ownership and operation of cable channels. That hope has not been realized as blacks have lost rights to approximately thirty cable franchises they had acquired in recent years because of insufficient financial resources. The total television station ownership picture is also poor with blacks owning only eight of the approximately one thousand stations nationally.[15] Commission recommendations on vastly increased hiring of blacks in the media have also gone unmet. There are, for example, no more than three black news directors and three black executive producers of news programs in the television stations of major cities and only one news director in a major market, KNXT in Los Angeles.[16] The only

exception to this somewhat dismal picture is the number of black-owned radio stations which increased from 50 in 1978 to 130 in 1981.[17] While black news and music radio stations may provide for more community identity, the full participation of blacks in mass-mediated politics requires increased access to local and national television.

## Familial Conditions

Sociologist Wilson's analysis notes that the urban family, especially the poor black family, changed for the worse in the decade of the seventies. In 1978, 53 percent of all black births were out of wedlock, and many of the infants were born to teenagers. From 1970 to 1979, the number of households headed by women increased 72.9 percent for blacks and 76.5 percent for Hispanics, compared to 42.1 percent for whites. The proportion of poor black families headed by a female was 74 percent in 1978. More than one-third of all black children under the age of six in 1978 were living in female-headed households with incomes below the poverty level. The median age of the black female head of household declined, going from 41.3 years in 1970 to 37.9 years in 1979. Finally, the number of black children less than eighteen years old in families receiving aid to families with dependent children went from 35 per thousand in 1960 to 113 per thousand in 1979.[18]

The fact of an astonishing number of female-headed households in the poor areas of cities is literal evidence of family dissolution in the sense that the both-parents-present nuclear family is becoming a rarity for poor urban blacks. The significance of the female-headed household is rarely detailed or theoretically specified. Presumably, the situation would be considered as serious (or more than serious) if most urban black poor families were headed by a male with no wife-mother present. Thus, this aspect of the dissolution of the black ghetto family is its single parentedness. The most commonly drawn implications of such dissolution focus on ineffective social control of the children. The declining age of the single female parent may result in less firm and effective control of children and in increased dependency on the welfare system. An implicit assumption of the Violence and Kerner reports is that a strong ghetto family is the best defense against uncontrolled violent expressions of grievance. Thus, weakening of the poor black ghetto family in the decade of the seventies can only be taken as a worsening condition insofar as collective violence is concerned.

## Law Enforcement Conditions

Affirmative action in police hiring became a reality in many cities during the 1970s. A 1969 survey of 254 U.S. cities found the percentage of minority police officers to be 5.1 percent, compared to the minority percentage in the total 1970 population of 16.7 percent in these cities. A 1981 survey of these same cities yielded figures of 11.6 percent minority officers and 27.6

percent minority population. These figures mask much variation, however. The top one-third high-affirmative-action cities in 1981 had increased minority representation on their police forces from an average of 2.6 percent in 1969 to 16.0 percent in 1981. In contrast, the percentage of minority police actually decreased during this period in the one-third low-affirmative-action cities, from 6.2 percent to 5.3 percent.[19] Both high- and low-affirmative-action cities had about the same minority percentage of total population (22.3 percent and 23.3 percent, respectively).

These figures tell us nothing of the process and the problems associated with integrating police forces or of failing to integrate them. Nor do they reflect changes and problems at other levels of the criminal (and juvenile) justice systems. Reports on the 1980 Miami riot, to be treated in greater detail below, dramatically illustrate the importance of conditions specific to that city at each level of the justice systems. Reports of both the Governor's Dade County Citizens' Committee and the U.S. Commission on Civil Rights point to problems throughout the juvenile justice system, in the state attorney's office, in jury selection and utilization, and in the Correction and Rehabilitation Department, as well as in the Miami Police Department and the Dade County Public Safety Department. The Civil Rights Commission concurred with the Kerner Commission that "racial violence in America almost invariably has occurred when an encounter between law enforcement officers and a member of the black community escalates to physical confrontation," noting that riots in Miami in 1969 "directly resulted from a harsh police crackdown, and the fatal beating of a black Miamian by local police officers led to the riots of 1980."[20] A series of such incidents during the two years preceding the riot "reinforced the black community's belief that a dual system of justice prevailed in Dade County—a system in which blacks received unequal treatment before the law."[21] The commission called for more blacks on the police force, particularly in supervisory positions, and for more black attorneys in the state attorney's office (where only 7 of 105 assistant attorney generals were black; i.e., 6.7 percent, compared to 16.4 percent of the Miami population in 1980 which was black).[22] Lack of adequate community review of police policies and practices and of procedures for receiving and handling complaints concerning public officials were also noted, as was the charge that some members of the state attorney's office "engage in the practice of excusing Black jurors from jury panels where the defendants are Black, solely because of the color of the [prospective] juror's skin."[23] The Miami reports, thus, document the unevenness observed across the nation with respect to implementation of affirmative-action programs in the criminal justice system.

No appraisal of law enforcement conditions during the period following the national commission reports would be complete without note of another development, namely the heavy influx of black—and in some states, Hispanic—inmates of the nation's prisons. How and why this occurred, and with what related developments and consequences, are the subject of later discussion. At this point it is sufficient, perhaps, to note that at the close of the 1970s many of the nation's prisons were filled beyond capacity as a result of the highest incarceration rates of any advanced society, "with the probable exception," as Elliott Currie notes, "of the Soviet Union and South Africa."

## ACCOUNTING FOR THE DECLINE IN COLLECTIVE VIOLENCE

Our analysis of economic, political, familial, and law enforcement conditions in the urban ghetto of the 1970s indicates that the ghetto poor were virtually untouched by the progress that has been made in reducing racial and ethnic discrimination in the economy, in politics, in the media, and in education. We thus face a puzzle of continued, even increasing, grievance and declining attempts to redress grievance through collective protest and violence. We must go beyond the Violence and Kerner commissions' analyses to solve this puzzle by looking to changes in social control, expectations, and economic structure that might account for the decline in collective violence.

### Social Control

Of all of the recommendations made by the Violence, Kerner, and Katzenbach reports, those concerning the beefing-up of the arsenal and size of law enforcement agencies received the most extensive financial and political support. None of these commissions envisioned reliance upon technological and strategic preparations that would "gulag" the ghetto by using fear to suppress collective protest. Nonetheless, a tantalizingly straightforward interpretation of the decline in the incidence of collective violence in the 1970s is that enormous federal and local expenditures on law enforcement have had the effect of increasing the *costs* of urban violence. Increased fear of reprisal for collective violence could be one possible factor in the declining incidence of collective violence in the 1970s. But the many indicators of increased crime and other problems in the ghettos suggest that social control per se has done little to alter the internal dynamics or the social fabric of ghetto life. Careful studies by urban ethnographers find that social control in ghetto communities occurs through relationships and institutions quite outside and often in opposition to conventional law enforcement agencies. It is doubtful, therefore, that these agencies can do little more than keep the lid on collective violence.

### Declining Expectations

A common premise in theories of collective violence is that rising expectations in the face of declining resources create the most volatile condition for the emergence of collective violence. We know that the resources of large northern cities have declined, but we do not know whether expectations have also declined, such that residents have become resigned to low-resource conditions. The most obvious change that might have brought about a decline in expectations is the progressive retreat of federal government policy with respect to problems of cities and minorities. The New Frontier–Great Society administrations of the sixties, which waged wars on poverty, were replaced by more conservative administrations that waged wars on crime, inflation, and taxes. As the hopes appealed to by federal government "wars" shifted from the hopes of the victims of racism and poverty to the hopes of the "silent," and "moral majorities," the expectations of the urban poor may have dropped, even as expectations of suburban America may have been raised.

### Economic Structure
Wilson has argued that the poor of the urban ghetto have become an underclass characterized by economic dependency caused by unemployability and community disorganization. At present, blacks predominate in the urban underclass, but Hispanics, who are increasingly migrating into the poor areas of large cities, are also represented along with a steady population of whites. The underclass pattern of life is marked by unstable families dependent on external social agencies for economic support, by high crime rates, and by an absence of negotiable occupational skills. As anachronisms from an industrial goods–production era, members of the underclass have no place to go in an information- and service-based economy.

While the development of an underclass was long in the making, the decade of the 1970s—a decade of ghetto deterioration and national retreat from ghetto problems—may have witnessed its crystallization. Recent evidence indicates that class identification is emerging as a more important dimension of group identity than race, particularly among those at the low end of the socioeconomic totem pole.[24] Moreover, those who subjectively identify with the "poor" or the "lower class" are more likely than their higher class counterparts to regard their class position as being a product of inequities in the policies and practices of government and other agencies. Thus, the highly controversial thesis that class is more important than race in understanding the dynamics of the urban ghetto receives some support insofar as the subjective identifications and perceptions of both poor whites and blacks are concerned.

Our interpretation of the economic, familial, political, law enforcement, and educational conditions of ghetto life in the 1970s is at least consistent with the underclass thesis. Most important in this regard is the increasing gap between haves and have-nots among urban blacks in most cities. To be sure, many have benefited from the antidiscriminatory policies called for by the Violence and Kerner commissions, but a majority have gone relatively untouched by such policies. Fragmentation into middle-class and underclass blacks is furthered by an exodus of middle-class blacks from the urban ghetto that significantly reduces their economic dependence upon the poor black community as clients for their services.

With regard to the question of why collective violence has declined in the urban ghetto of the 1970s, the underclass thesis provides at least two possible insights. One is that the urban ghetto population has become—objectively and subjectively—an underclass that, like other underclasses throughout history, exhibits a sort of political paralysis born of economic dependency and psychological despair. While the 1960s represented a time of collective action born of the hope of escape from deprivation for millions of ghetto residents, that hope remains unrealized. Indeed, for many, material and social conditions of ghetto life grew worse in the 1970s. The second and related insight is that the hope that spurs collective action is based on the perception that change is possible, that better conditions can be achieved through collective action. The political efficacy findings of studies of rioters in the 1960s is consistent with this view. It may be that the urban ghetto has lost much of the organizational infrastructure necessary to sustained collective protest, not only because of the exodus of the black middle class, but also because of the decline of the industrial city as a viable political and economic entity.

## Unique Social/Historical Circumstances
Commonwealth Award–winning sociologist-historian Charles Tilly emphasizes the importance of unique and local political, economic, and social conditions that combine to produce collective actions, including violence, by segments of a citizenry.[25] From this perspective, the identification of general causes, such as racial discrimination, necessarily fails to comprehend why collective violence occurs at a particular time and place. Variations in the history and structure of local governments and in police-community conflicts, and their convergence at particular points in time, heighten or lower the probability of collective violence and determine when and how collective action occurs.

This perspective sensitizes us to differences as well as similarities among communities that might provide a fuller understanding of why this and not that community experienced collective violence or why collective violence emerged at this and not that historical time. The Liberty City (Miami) riot of May 1980 provides a good case in point. This riot was not only the most extensive and destructive of the last decade but also stands out as an exception to the general pattern of decline in collective violence.

## THE LIBERTY CITY/MIAMI RIOT

Following a "not guilty" verdict in the trial of four Miami police officers accused of beating a black businessman to death, riots lasting several days broke out in the Liberty City slum a mile from downtown Miami. Fourteen people were killed, more than a million dollars of property damage was done, and more than three hundred arrests were made. The National Guard was called out and the area was declared a disaster area. A number of agencies investigated the causes of this highly destructive episode, including the White House Interagency Task Force on Civil Disturbances, the U.S. Commission on Civil Rights, and the Governor's Dade County Citizens' Committee.

### Why Did It Happen?

Our previous review of the state of economic, political, familial, and law enforcement conditions of the 1970s led us to conclude that the conditions of the urban ghetto nationally have gotten worse, not better, since the 1960s. Miami is no exception.[26] In the low-income areas of Dade County where a majority of the black population live, the unemployment rate was almost 18 percent in 1979, more than 32 percent of the residents lived in overcrowded housing, more than 85 percent of the residents rented, and the high school dropout rate among twenty- to twenty-four-year-olds was more than 38 percent. Owing to the at-large election procedure, black officeholders in local government were rare. Thus, black ghetto dwellers in Miami share with their black counterparts nationally a state of deprivation. The problem with such a generalization is that it does not tell us why collective violence is not epidemic in all the urban ghettos of America today and why the major collective-violence incident of recent years occurred in Miami. The recurrence of collective violence in Miami in January 1983 highlights the importance of this question. The 1983 incident has not, as yet, been thoroughly analyzed, but there are indications that it arose out of the same sorts of conditions, perhaps exacerbated since 1980.

Miami, in contrast to Detroit, Newark, and other cities, is a new city with a history of less than sixty years. Miami has been a boom and bust city, fluctuating with the fads and fashions of the tourist trade. Its most recent boom period began in the 1970s following a steady and massive in-migration of Cubans after Castro's rise to power combined with subsequent increases in tourism from Central and South America. In fact, while the decade of the sixties was a period of relative prosperity nationally, it was a period of decline for Dade County, and while the 1970s saw decline nationally, there was a period of growth and increasing prosperity in Dade County. Interestingly enough, Miami in the 1960s had only minor incidents of collective violence compared to that of many other cities. Despite Miami's economic ups and downs, the overall economic expansion of Dade

County from 1956 to 1977 greatly surpassed the national growth rate. The job market, for example, grew 133 percent compared to 60 percent nationally.

Differences between Miami and large northern cities in the social history of the black community and in the composition of the population are essential to understanding Miami's departure from national trends in the timing of collective violence. In the 1940s, a stable black community of interdependent middle- and lower-class blacks emerged in the Overtown area of Miami. It survived until the mid-1960s when it was physically and socially destroyed by "urban renewal." Thus, the fragmentation of the social fabric of the Miami black community is of recent origin. This source of decline in black Miamians' economic-political base came at approximately the same time as an equally potent source of decline, namely, the dramatic increase in the size of the Hispanic population, which went from 5.4 percent of the population of Dade County in 1960 to 41 percent in 1980. Two dominant consequences followed from the Hispanic influx. One was a reduction in political power of blacks who went from the second most numerous ethnic group to third, in 1980 constituting 16 percent of the population. Hispanics, who constitute just slightly less of the population than non-Hispanic whites, were better equipped than blacks with professional, business, and technical skills and thus were able to enter the market economy of Miami. It was the second wave of Hispanics arriving from the Mariel boat lift of 1980—some sixty to eighty thousand people—who were more like the majority of Miami blacks. The much larger first wave of Hispanics established their own residential and business areas, which included a far-reaching employment requirement that an employee must be able to speak both Spanish and English. This requirement effectively barred many blacks from employment in the more prosperous parts of the Miami economy.

The joint effects of reduced social integration in the black community and reduced political and economic efficacy, which occurred in the late 1960s and throughout the 1970s, must certainly have increased the probability of collective violence in the black ghetto—increased it because nonviolent political modalities for the expression of grievances became less viable and because economic opportunities to escape the ghetto declined. These circumstances combined with at least five highly visible instances of blacks being treated harshly and whites being treated softly by the criminal justice system—for example, trial decisions—and a long history of unsatisfactory relations between the black community and the police might provide a convincing argument for why Miami broke into collective violence in 1980. Again in 1983, the incident that precipitated collective violence involved the police, in this case, an Hispanic police officer shooting a young black man.

An additional argument made by a Miami mayor in 1980 is that there was a power vacuum in Miami caused by the nature of the white power structure. Maurice Ferre contended in his statements to the U.S. Commission on Civil Rights that it was impossible to gather together a dozen or so leaders to deal with the problems of the black ghetto because so many of the powerful parties in Miami were nonresident corporations. However, news accounts of Mayor Ferre's response to the events in early 1983 suggest that he, too, is becoming convinced that poor police–black community relations played an important part in collective violence in his city.

## Media Coverage

The primary problem in media coverage of collective-violence incidents identified by both the Violence and Kerner commissions was a failure to go beyond spectacular aspects of violence, such as fires, clubbings, or shootings, to address the substantive causes of the violence. Of all the national media, we would expect the *New York Times* to come closest to meeting the commissions' pleas for in-depth interpretive reporting. In the case of Liberty City, the organizing theme of the *New York Times*'s coverage was that violence between black residents and the police resulted from a widespread belief in the black community that there was a dual system of justice in Miami that denied justice to blacks. A secondary coverage theme related the disproportionately high black unemployment rate in Miami owing to the increased competition for jobs that resulted from massive migration of Hispanics into the Miami area. Also noted was the fact that the Hispanic population had grown to the point where it constituted approximately 35 percent of the Miami citizenry, such that the black population (16 percent) had experienced a political as well as a demographic decline.

More spectacular aspects of the Liberty City riot were, of course, also reported. The front-page headlines of May 19, 1980, provide an example: "14 DIE IN MIAMI RIOT; ARSON AND LOOTING PERSIST FOR 2D DAY—Toll of Injured Exceeds 200—Violence in Black Neighborhoods Follows Acquittal of 4 Whites Accused in Fatal Beating." This headline juxtaposed with the headline "ANGER LONG IN RISING AMONG MIAMI BLACKS, Leaders Cite Other Brutality Cases and the New Influx of Cubans," captures a fairly balanced attention to the spectacular and to the causal context of the riot in the *New York Times*'s coverage.

## Implications

There is basis for a credible argument that it was the unique combination of historical, political, and economic conditions experienced by blacks in the poor areas of Miami that led to collective violence in a time of little collective violence in most American cities. But there is another and more disquieting interpretation of what Miami signifies. That is the argument that the cause of the Liberty City–Miami riot was more fundamentally due to a transformation of the Miami black community into an underclass. David Whitman, senior research assistant at Harvard University's Kennedy School of Government, contends that the most important condition giving rise to the Miami riot was the fact that, while economic prosperity was being experienced by whites and many Hispanics, a large proportion of the city's blacks had been relegated to an underclass of unemployables with little hope of escaping the dependency wrought by their structural irrelevance.[27] What is disquieting about this interpretation, is that it forces a return to consideration of the similarities between Miami and other urban ghettos. It demands attention to a shared condition of poor blacks in American cities—their underclass status. As such, it is not only possible to treat the Liberty City/Miami riot as a delayed extension of the collective violence of the 1960s, but also to view it as a possible precursor to future collective violence in the black ghettos of America.

## PRISON GHETTOS: TIME BOMBS FOR THE FUTURE

The irony has often been remarked that blacks achieved political power in many U.S. cities only after those cities were locked into a spiral of poverty, deterioration, and declining resources. A second irony has received less recognition, though its potential for collective violence may be equal to the first. The second irony is that prisons may be the only major U.S. institution that is dominated internally by blacks. Exceptions occur in states and prisons in which the nation's second largest and most rapidly growing minority, Hispanics, dominate or contest with blacks for supremacy.

While prisons have long been characterized by segregation and discrimination, only in recent years have racial cleavages become perhaps the dominant feature of prison life. The recent history and the future of prisons and of collective violence in prisons and in the larger society are intimately and inevitably related to this development. Racial and ethnic relations in prison are, in turn, related to the prisoners' rights movement which began in the late 1950s as a result of the efforts of imprisoned Black Muslims. Jacobs notes that the Muslims demanded rights to practice their religion but that the political doctrines of black superiority and black nationalism were important as well. The success of religious-freedom litigation encouraged other prisoners to seek other rights such as protection against cruel and unusual punishment and adequate legal services. Many of these legal actions also were successful, and prisoners' rights became a social movement with broad support from national organizations such as the NAACP, the ACLU, and the prestigious American Bar Association.[28]

The prisoners' rights movement peaked during the mid-1970s, and it has declined since that time. The timing is important, as we suggest below. Jacobs concludes: "Federal funding for prisoner services has . . . become more difficult to obtain. . . . Increasingly, those government grants which are available prohibit civil rights suits and class actions. . . . The image of the prisoner as hero, revolutionary, and victim is disappearing. . . . Whether a viable prisoners' rights movement at the grass roots level can survive funding cutbacks, judicial retrenchment, and other social change is unclear."[29]

The success of the prisoners' rights movement and its effects on the daily lives of prisoners and on their political beliefs and activities are in dispute. Most, however, agree that tangible results have been obtained: religious freedoms, access to law books and other literature, recognition of jailhouse lawyers as well as access to more conventional legal services, decreased censorship of mail, and improvement in administrative procedures, including due process related to prison discipline. While he would undoubtedly agree with most of these points, Simon Dinitz, an astute and longtime observer of corrections, concludes that "the political process through which prisoners attempted to alter their daily reality" has failed. The spirit of prisoner solidarity was real but variable among prisons throughout the country. The reality, in Dinitz's view, ended abruptly at Attica in 1971. "After the shooting ceased in the Attica compound, the death toll stood at 32 inmates and 11 guards—all but three killed by the State forces who blew the wall and methodically ended the insurrection with a massive display of force."[30] The end of the abortive prisoner solidarity movement left prison populations without the charismatic inmate leaders who had led it and turned the prison back on itself.

The "absolute failure" of the movement, Dinitz notes, was signified by the riot at the New Mexico State Prison which began on February 2, 1980. In that riot, "unlike other riots in recent years, there was no carnival atmosphere, no leadership, no list of grievances, no organization, nothing. Only unspeakable brutality. In all these respects, New Mexico represents a turning point in U.S. prison history."[31]

Disagreement exists as to just how united prisoners were during the 1960s, as with regard to the success of the prisoners' rights movement. What did change clearly during the 1970s was the racial and ethnic composition of prisons. Christianson, writing on "Our Black Prisons," notes that "whereas the incarceration rate for whites increased from about 46.3 per 100,000 to about 65.1 from 1973 to 1979, the black incarceration rate rose from about 368 to 544.1 per 100,000 during that period." Furthermore, "in 1978 . . . black males accounted for only 5.4 percent of the general population. Yet a staggering 45.7 percent of the prisoners were black males."[32] Even this 8.5:1 ratio is small, however, compared to the roughly 25.1 ratio of the rate of incarceration of black males in their twenties, compared to the total U.S. population.[33] Divisions exist among black prisoners, to be sure, and among Hispanics, and these divisions are often the basis of internecine violence. But these divisions typically do not interfere with minority domination of prison social organization. Unlike the Kerner Commission's characterization of the nation as a whole ("moving toward two societies, one black, one white—separate and unequal"), prisons in this country have moved rapidly toward three societies, black, white, and Hispanic—separate, unequal, and often in violent confrontation.

In some states, the concentration of young black males in prison was aggravated by another factor: the imprisonment of large numbers of street gang members. The gangs proved to be better organized in prison than they had been on the street—and more willing to use violence than their predecessors. Violence in prisons—both one-on-one and collective—is, of course, not new. As Dinitz notes, "Interpersonal, one-on-one violence is endemic to prison life; group action precipitated chiefly by internal changes in prison structure and organization and by the intrusion of conflicts beyond the walls, is much more spectacular, deadly and destructive." Recent prison riots in other states have been similar to the New Mexico riot in that inmate solidarity has been conspicuously absent.[34]

It has often been remarked that prisons mirror the larger society of which they are a part. It is less often recognized that the relationship goes the other way in important respects. Dramatic cases of individuals who have come out of prisons to become political or religious leaders, such as Malcolm X or terrorist leaders of the Symbionese Liberation Army, are only the most obvious examples. The fact that the bulk of prisoners— particularly black and Hispanic prisoners—come to prison from the urban underclass and return to it is less dramatic but equally important. Moore and her associates describe the continuities of prison and barrio among Los Angeles Chicanos, demonstrating how "the illegal economy of the prisons contributed to the rise of a particularly vicious criminal organization—the Mexican Mafia."[35] Ianni notes the emergence, in the New York–New Jersey area, of black and Hispanic organized crime, with prison experience playing a critical role for recruitment to and legitimation of participants in a variety of criminal enterprises.[36] Given these interrelationships and the underclass origins of most prison inmates, we have come to view prison dynamics as potentially useful elements of analyses of collective violence in the urban ghetto.

## VIOLENCE FROM THE RIGHT

Due to a paucity of recent research, we can do little more than draw attention to another potential arena of collective violence—that from the extreme Right of the political spectrum. Conservative theorist Kevin Phillips writes of the "Balkanization of the national spirit" and the "politics of cultural despair" that followed the 1960s and 1970s, a period he (and others) have characterized as two decades of "erosion of American economic productivity, civic commitment and global determination." That period of "breakdown," he suggests, "has left a skittish populace beneath a patina of suburban affluence,"[37] which is likely to be politically unstable and perhaps volatile. While stopping short of predicting the occurrence of increased conflict among interest groups, Phillips points to the similarity of conditions that in the past have led to such conflict.

Media observers have pointed to more specific instances of fragmentation of conservative forces. For the most part, such journalistic analyses focus upon splits between ideological movements, such as the "moral majority" and NCPAC, and the present federal administration. Ideological rightist movements are apparently suffering the experience of unmet expectations, expectations that the present federal administration would institute a conservative economics on the one hand and a conservative morality on the other. Insofar as the failure to meet heightened expectations is a condition for the emergence of collective protest and violence, these developments may presage increased activity with the potential for collective violence among far-right groups. Very sketchy evidence may be found in recent protest and violence against abortion clinics. Failing to win a constitutional prohibition against abortions, splinter groups from the "prolife" movement are emerging. "The Army of God," for example, has employed unconventional means, including violence, to attain their ends.

The age-old problem of the waxing and waning Ku Klux Klan has also received heightened media attention. That attention derives largely from Klan protests and violence against Vietnamese immigrants and against what some claim is a rising incidence of violence against synagogues and Jews in general. Klan violence would seem less connected to fragmentation of the new Right than to historical dynamics of racism and working-class economic fears.

Whatever the reasons, as the violence associated with the counter-demonstration (against the Klan) held in Washington, D.C., in late November 1982 suggests, the potential for violence from extremist movements should not be underestimated.

## CONCLUSIONS AND RECOMMENDATIONS

Understanding collective violence requires both a general theoretical model and analysis of local conditions. Today, more than ever, however, local conditions are influenced by media reports, by the activities of participants in social movements, and in general by what is going on elsewhere. What *was* "going on elsewhere" at the close of the 1970s decade?

Throughout much of the United States, some progress was being made toward elimination of discrimination in employment, in schools, and in political enfranchisement. Many more black politicians were elected to office, and affirmative action worked for many, especially for the black middle class, which doubled between the mid-1960s and 1980. The promise of improvement was great, but progress left many untouched.

The black underclass was left behind by affirmative-action programs, and the structural features of the American economy and of urban areas provided little opportunity for movement out of its depressed condition. The gap between haves and have-nots increased, solidifying an urban underclass in which blacks are heavily overrepresented. The growth and solidifying of an urban underclass is, essentially, a structural process whereby changing demographic and economic conditions consign increasing numbers of citizens to permanent status as members of a class without realistic hope of movement out of their dependent status. Insofar as these citizens share racial or ethnic identity and are thrown together in residential ghettos and other segregated institutions (including prisons), the potential for racial or ethnic conflict, as well as class conflict, is enhanced. It was apparent, for example, that both racial discrimination and class conflict were involved in the Miami riot, the former (related to discriminatory law enforcement) as the trigger for the riot, the latter as perhaps the major underlying condition related to the riot.

The lull in collective violence following the decade of the 1960s should, thus, not be taken as evidence that the underlying problems of racism have been solved. Clearly this is not the case. The conditions that we have analyzed in the urban ghetto, prisons, and even the politicized Right of suburbia suggest that the conditions for collective violence in the future are in place.

Who can believe that the hopes generated in the 1960s and 1970s by political activism in America's urban ghettos and in its prisons will not be regenerated? Will we wait for this to happen and for incidents that will trigger more riot and destruction? If the urban underclass thesis is correct— as we believe it to be—the long-run prospect for collective violence against established institutions should not be taken lightly. Establishment of a permanent underclass runs counter to the American ideology of an egalitarian society and makes us more vulnerable to genuinely class-based violence on a scale not yet experienced in this country.

So, what can be done—what social policies flow from this analysis?

1. *Affirmative action must be continued and expanded.* Increasing minority proportions of police officers and other justice system personnel to approximate minority proportions in local populations remains a necessary, if insufficient, condition for avoiding the types of incidents that trigger episodes of collective violence. The benefits of affirmative action in this area go beyond protecting against violence-triggering incidents by increas-

ing occupational and income opportunities within the ghetto, reinforcing the goal of equal opportunity, and helping ameliorate strained relations between ghetto residents and institutions of the larger society.

Those affirmative-action programs in education and employment that have played an effective role in increasing the size of the black middle class must not be abandoned. To cut such financial backing as student aid and loan programs and to cut out the heart of affirmative action in employment by failure to enforce relevant laws is to abandon in midstream uncounted numbers of blacks who are struggling to achieve the promise of equality. Yet, for the majority of blacks who live in poverty in the urban ghetto, recent history has shown that established affirmative-action programs, even when duly enforced, are inadequate.

2. *Effective solutions to the problems of the urban underclass must be found.* In our judgment, perhaps the most pressing domestic problem facing the United States today is the existence and the growth of a structurally created urban underclass. Historical *and* contemporary forces of racism have determined the racial and ethnic composition of the urban underclass. The modern economy and the demographic and ecological structure of cities perpetuates it. If nothing else, enlightened self-interest requires the formulation and implementation of economic, educational, and social solutions that can break the cycle of generationally transmitted poverty. A nontotalitarian society that extols freedom and equality in the pursuit of material and social well-being is severely challenged by acute and permanent class cleavage.

*Education*: If education is to serve as a "bootstrap" for the underclass, we must begin a national commitment to revitalize public education. Even the disproportionately small numbers of black ghetto youth who receive a high school diploma have nowhere to go unless that education prepares them for jobs in an information- and service-based economy. Indeed, calls for training and retraining for such an economy are little more than Alice-in-Wonderland rhetoric unless they are accompanied by specific plans for financing an overhaul of public and community college educational systems. Colleges and universities seem to be making the transition to the new economy. But it is the educational system that is most essential to the needs of the underclass—public schools in large metropolitan poor areas—that are most anachronistic, anachronistic not by choice but because of declining resources in cities that are losing their economic bases as well as federal support for education and other social programs. To begin the massive overhaul required, we recommend that the Congress create a National Commission on Urban Education that would bring together educational leaders, ghetto leaders, and experts in the new economy. The tasks of this commission would include the design of both the substance and the funding of an educational system that can be effectively utilized by all young people—but with special focus on those who are presently in the underclass and those who may fall into it.

*Mediating Structures*: There is much strength to build upon in urban underclass communities, despite problems of poverty, discrimination, and ineffective political organization. Much of this strength is in social relationships which take place in families, among neighbors, and in voluntary associations. One of the functions of these institutions is mediation between individuals and bureaucracies, both private and public. Grass-roots organizations, with leaders indigenous to neighborhoods and communities often develop spontaneously in response to needs and problems. Many such organizations have the potential for political and economic organization and power, as well as for the accomplishment of broader social purposes. They should be encouraged to participate in—indeed to provide leadership for—programs of community regeneration and the strengthening of other indigenous institutions.

Some of the strength in underclass communities is found in the underground economy—much of it illegal—which flourishes in virtually every lower-class ethnic community. Illegal hustles and even large-scale economic enterprises probably can never be entirely eliminated, but they can be scaled down and the dependence of many citizens on them lessened. Hustling is "hard work," as Bettylou Valentine notes,[38] and programs that would train more citizens in skills relevant to the modern economy would improve the ability of many to survive and flourish without hustling or depending on illegal markets.

*Media: Policymakers and citizens need ongoing media coverage of the urban ghetto.* The media as a primary link between government and citizens have the unique opportunity and the responsibility of the Fourth Estate to play the constructive role of social analyst. The watchdog role could and should be expanded beyond investigative reporting of what our elected officials "are up to." Equally important to the long-term welfare of this nation is media articulation of what our society "is up to" in the sense of key economic and social dynamics that threaten domestic peace and societal stability. As we have seen in our analysis of *New York Times* coverage of the Miami riot, considerable progress has been made in media coverage, which goes beyond the spectacular to an analysis of the causes of collective violence. Our call is to go one step further to media coverage of the causes of emerging social conflicts, such as the explosive combination of continued racism, sexism, and emergence of an information and service economy that, together, produce an underclass locked in America's urban ghettos. Hiring and promotion of minorities into decision-making positions within media organizations should facilitate such coverage.

*Criminal and Juvenile Justice Systems*: The principle and the goal of rehabilitation must be reaffirmed, and humane discretion encouraged rather than curtailed. The suggestion from studies of rehabilitation programs that "nothing works"—too easily reached on the basis of both inadequate programs and inadequate research—and the well-documented abuses of the exercise of benevolently intended state power and of discretion should not blind us to the positive contributions of rehabilitative goals (and the negative consequence of their abandonment) and to the fact that discretion is a necessary factor in all human arrangements, that it will occur in justice systems despite efforts to prevent it. Focus should therefore be on increasing the justice and the humanitarianism of rehabilitative programs and on the exercise of discretion within them, on better trained and better informed officials, and on systems of accountability rather than on repudiation of rehabilitation and removal of discretion.

3. *Renewed attention must be given to so-called root causes of crime— many of which are the same as for collective violence, while others are closely linked.* Whether or not one agrees with the estimate that only 20 percent of the black disproportionality in prisons is due to discrimination, a very large percentage of this disproportionality certainly is due to the "underlying causes contributing to disproportionate involvement in crime by race." Every effort should be made to eliminate bias and discrimination based on race, ethnicity, or any other such categorical membership throughout the law enforcement process. But it is clear that the most significant impact on the racial mix in our prisons, and therefore on urban underclass communities, must come from addressing the factors in our society that generate the "life conditions that underlie the racially different involvement in crime" (particularly those associated with recidivism).[39] Both stronger research efforts and social policies aimed at root causes are necessary.

*Decision Makers: A national commitment on the part of political, economic, and social movement leaders is critical to the solution of problems associated with the continued existence in this country of racism, in both institutional and individual forms, and with the rise of an underclass. Without such a commitment, the transition from an industrial to a service economy is likely to generate more and greater inequalities among large segments of the citizenry.* The relevance of this recommendation to collective violence is clear. Collective violence is a product of social conflicts, which in turn reflect economic and social grievances. The lull in collective violence over the last decade is unlikely to continue unless action is taken against the origins of the most pressing social conflicts of our time—racism and a new economic order that renders huge segments of the population impotent. The alternative of relying on social control of dislocated masses is unacceptable on two counts—it will not work in the long run and it would necessitate increasingly repressive tactics.

Much is at stake in such choices. While the economic health of the nation is fundamental both to the creation and the redress of grievances associated with collective violence, balance should not be allowed to rest on conventional cost-effectiveness criteria. At issue are fundamental questions of value: of freedom and equality, as well as establishing justice and ensuring domestic tranquility.

## NOTES

1. The Report of the National Commission on the Causes and Prevention of Violence, *To Establish Justice, to Insure Domestic Tranquility* (Washington, D.C.: U.S. Government Printing Office, 1969).
2. William Julius Wilson, *The Declining Significance of Race: Blacks and Changing American Institutions,* 2d ed. (Chicago: University of Chicago Press, 1980).
3. Current Labor Statistics, "Household Data," *Monthly Labor Review,* June 1982.
4. Ibid.
5. Ibid.
6. William Julius Wilson, "The Urban Underclass in Advanced Industrial Society," paper presented at the Future of Our City Conference, University of Chicago, June 1982.
7. Current Labor Statistics, "Household Data."
8. Ibid.
9. Wilson, "The Urban Underclass in Advanced Industrial Society."
10. Richard B. Freeman, "Black Economic Progress since 1964," *Public Interest* 52 (Summer 1978).
11. Elizabeth Evanson, "The Dynamics of Poverty," *Focus* 5 (Summer 1981).
12. Vernon Jordan, Jr., and John E. Jacob, Introduction to *The State of Black America 1982,* ed. James D. Williams (New York: National Urban League, 1982).
13. Bernard E. Anderson, "Economic Patterns in Black America," in *State of Black America 1982.*
14. Jordan and Jacob, Introduction.
15. Pat Patterson, "Blacks and the Media in the 1980's," in *State of Black America 1982.*
16. Ibid.
17. Ibid.
18. Wilson, "The Urban Underclass in Advanced Industrial Society."
19. Nicholas P. Lovrich and Brent S. Steel, "Affirmative Action and Productivity in Law Enforcement Agencies," *Review of Public Personnel Administration,* forthcoming.
20. U.S. Civil Rights Commission, *Confronting Racial Isolation in Miami* (Washington, D.C.: U.S. Government Printing Office, 1982).
21. Ibid.
22. Other police-related issues include promotion and development policies with respect to minority officers, both of which have been the subject of litigation. Even the actions taken to give more racial balance to police forces sometimes create problems. In 1983, upon achieving an agreed upon level of minority police officers in response to a 1976 court action (*U.S. v. City of Miami et al.,* Civil Action #75-3096, U.S. District Court, Southern District of Florida, 1976), the city found itself with a large number of young and relatively inexperienced officers who had great difficulty policing a racially tense city.
23. *Report of Governor's Dade County Citizens' Committee* (1980). It has been proposed to change the basis of determining the available jury pool from voter registration to driver's licenses, which would increase the proportion of blacks in the pool. It should be noted, however, that by its very nature the adversary system encourages any tactic within the

law to represent one's client to the best of a lawyer's ability. Jury challenges have always been considered standard practice in American courts.

24. Mary R. Jackman and Robert W. Jackman, *Class Awareness in the United States* (Berkeley: University of California Press, in press).

25. Charles Tilly, *As Sociology Meets History* (New York: Academic Press, 1981).

26. We are grateful to Geoffrey Alpert for his advice concerning our interpretation of events in Miami.

27. David Whitman, "Behind the Miami Riot," *New York Times,* June 8, 1980, p. E19.

28. James B. Jacobs, "Race Relations and the Prisoner Subculture," in *Crime and Justice,* vol. 1, ed. Norval Morris and Michael Tonry (Chicago: University of Chicago Press, 1979).

29. James B. Jacobs, "The Prisoners' Rights Movement and Its Impacts," in *Crime and Justice,* vol. 2, ed. Norval Morris and Michael Tonry (Chicago: University of Chicago Press, 1980).

30. Simon Dinitz, "Are Safe and Humane Prisons Possible?" *Australian and New Zealand Journal of Criminology* 14 (March 1981).

31. Ibid.

32. Scott Christianson, "Our Black Prisons," *Crime and Delinquency,* July 1981.

33. Alfred Blumstein, "On the Racial Disproportionality of the United States' Prison Populations," *Journal of Criminal Law and Criminology* 73 (Fall 1982).

34. It is too early to know whether 1983's first prison riot, the relatively nonviolent event at the prison in Ossining, New York, represents a turning away from extreme violence. The memory of violence at Attica and the extreme brutality of more recent prison riots surely were in the minds of both officials and prisoners at Ossining. Factionalism among prisoners was clear, however, as evidenced by frequent changes in leaders and spokesmen.

35. Joan W. Moore, with Robert Garcia, Carlos Garcia, Luis Cerda, and Frank Valencia, *Homeboys* (Philadelphia: Temple University Press, 1978).

36. Francis A. J. Ianni, *Black Mafia: Ethnic Succession in Organized Crime* (New York: Simon & Schuster, 1974).

37. Kevin Phillips, *Post-Conservative America* (New York: Random House, 1982).

38. Bettylou Valentine, *Hustling and Other Hard Work* (New York: Free Press, 1978).

39. Alfred Blumstein and Elizabeth Graddy, "Prevalence and Recidivism in Index Arrests: A Feedback Model," *Law and Society Review* 16, no. 2 (1982).

# PART III

## POLITICAL VIOLENCE

# 8

# Terrorism and Public Policy: Domestic Impacts, International Threats

ROBERT H. KUPPERMAN

Terrorism is one aspect of political violence. Usually, terrorists belong to quasi-independent groups, which are at times manipulated by Libya and other rogue governments. These organizations create incidents intended to destabilize democratic governments and to perpetuate their ideological goals by exploiting the electronic and written media. There can be no sharp distinction between terrorism and related political violence. It is axiomatic that virtually all governments either commit or commission acts of violence in pursuit of political goals. Thus, for example, the Bulgarians and the Soviets have been accused of having arranged the assassination attempt against the pope and the Central Intelligence Agency is alleged to have sought the assassination of Fidel Castro. This chapter deals with subnational terrorism, not governmental terrorism.

International terrorism is a new class of violence, beyond the norms of common criminality, that exploits today's advanced technologies, especially jet transport and instant global communications. Regrettably, it is becoming established as a worldwide steady state phenomenon.

Although the United States has not so far been a primary target of attack, any optimism that this benign state of affairs will continue is misplaced. Terrorism has, among other things, become part of the arsenal of international warfare, recognized as a useful tool of low-intensity conflict. As a surrogate means of warfare, terrorism also becomes a tool of strategic importance. We must recognize the promotion of such violence from the level of a criminal act or political nuisance to a matter deserving serious national attention.

Hardly a day passes without a terrorist incident occurring somewhere in the world. It pervades the fabric of contemporary civilization. But the significance of the terror act has been raised exponentially by several different but interrelated factors. First, the tools available for destruction are suddenly much more lethal and much more frightening than ever before. Second, the media attention focused on terrorism is immediate, global, and usually undisciplined. Third, motives for terrorist attack today span a spectrum that includes, at the extremes, personal grudges and superpower ambitions of global hegemony—and there is little certainty as to which underlying motive may really be at play in any particular case.

These new and potential circumstances will require the close attention of both administrators and legislators. The most important questions raised are, first, how to ensure detailed and timely domestic intelligence without unduly infringing upon civil liberties, and second, how to avoid or control the public news of a terrorist crisis event without infringing upon the freedom of the press.

## THE THREAT TO AMERICA

Although the U.S. government has not so far been a primary target of international terrorists, both threats and actions have been directed at it from time to time. Take a recent year, like 1982. Puerto Rican Nationalists carried out killings on their island and a spectacular bombing on Wall Street in New York. Trials of IRA members on charges of arms smuggling were underway. Harassment of foreign national students on American campuses by both Libyan and Iranian groups continued. And domestic terrorists continued bombing of commercial facilities, particularly in California. In addition, of course, Americans and American facilities abroad continued to be prime targets for international terrorists. Finally, the Tylenol poisoning case, while not itself inspired by any terrorist group, was a fearsome reminder of the type of media-magnified "terror theater" that could all too easily occur here.

The first major terrorist action directly targeting the U.S. government occured in 1950 when two members of the Puerto Rican Nationalist party narrowly failed to assassinate President Truman during a shoot-out with the Secret Service and federal guards at Blair House where the president was in temporary residence.

In 1954, four other members of this same group struck again at the heart of the American government, this time firing from the gallery of the U.S. House of Representatives and wounding five members of Congress. Over the past eight years, after nearly two decades of relative inactivity, Puerto Rican Nationalist terror was revived under the auspices of the very small but violent Fuerzas Armadas de Liberación National (FALN), the ideological and organizational heirs of the earlier group. Between 1974 and 1977, law enforcement authorities estimate that the FALN was responsible for forty-nine bombings in the continental United States. The most serious of these took place in 1975 when a bomb in the Fraunces Tavern in the Wall Street district of New York City detonated during the lunch-hour rush, killing four persons and injuring fifty-five.

Domestic terrorist groups, such as the Weather Underground, Symbionese Liberation Army, and the Black Liberation Army, flourished in the so-called radical sixties and on into the seventies. All but forgotten today is the fact that these small nihilistic indigenous groups, which were technologically unsophisticated, without realistic political programs to mobilize popular support or even seriously threaten local, much less national power, succeeded in capturing the full attention of the American mass media, induced many officials to overreact against their exaggerated threat, and made authority—particularly local authority—appear largely impotent and foolish in the eyes of much of the general public.

Although the expressed fears of a "hot" summer in 1982—one of marked increase in domestic violence fueled by the declining economy—did not materialize, the potential existed. And it is a situation closely monitored by hostile foreign intelligence services, services that might under certain circumstances seek to exacerbate and exploit the situation by funding penetration, training, technical assistance, or mass media disinformation—all techniques that such major services as the Soviet KGB have proven adept at in Third World and West European states.

The number of terrorist incidents in the United States varies considerably from year to year as shown in table 1. The figures range from a high of 111 incidents in 1977 to a low of 29 in 1980. But there is no particular trend; it is simply a phenomenon that is present in this country.

The number of self-admitted incidents in 1981 was 42 (see table 2), with an additional 9 unclaimed but suspected terrorist acts not tabulated here. Typically, the major types of incidents involved 25 attempted explosive bombings (of which 17 were successful), 8 firebombings (7 successful), 4 takeovers, 2 shootings, and one incident each of armed robbery, arson, and assault. Fortunately, only 3 of the 42 incidents represented a direct threat to individuals—one person was killed and four injured. The principal tar-

**Table 1.** Number of Claimed Terrorist Incidents in the United States, 1977–1981

|      | No. of Incidents |
|------|------------------|
| 1977 | 111              |
| 1978 | 89               |
| 1979 | 52               |
| 1980 | 29               |
| 1981 | 42               |

*Source*: FBI.

**Table 2.** Claimed Terrorist Incidents by Group, Number, and Type of Incident, 1981

| Terrorist Group | Actual Bombings | Attempted Bombings | Actual Firebombings | Attempted Firebombings | Armed Robberies | Shootings | Takeovers | Arson | Assaults | Total Incidents | Persons Injured | Persons Killed |
|---|---|---|---|---|---|---|---|---|---|---|---|---|
| Armenian Groups: | | | | | | | | | | | | |
|   Armenian Secret Army for the Liberation of Armenia | 2 | | | | | | | | | 2 | | |
|   June 9 Organization | 2 | | | | | | | | | 2 | | |
|   Justice Commandos of Armenian Genocide | 1 | | | | | | | | | 1 | | |
|   October 3 | | 1 | | | | | | | | 1 | | |
| Croatian Groups: | | | | | | | | | | | | |
|   Croatian Freedom Fighters | 1 | | | | | | | | | 1 | | |
| Cuban Groups: | | | | | | | | | | | | |
|   Omega 7 | 3 | 1 | | | | | | | | 4 | | |
| Iranian Groups: | | | | | | | | | | | | |
|   Iranian Patriotic Army | | | 1 | | | | | | | 1 | | |
|   People's Mujaheddin Organization of Iran | | | | | | | 1 | | | 1 | 3 | |
| Jewish Groups: | | | | | | | | | | | | |
|   Jewish Defenders | | | 1 | | | | | | | 1 | | |
|   Jewish Defense League | 1 | 1 | 2 | 1 | | 1 | 1 | | | 7 | | |
| Libyan Groups: | | | | | | | | | | | | |
|   Libyan Groups in United States | | | | | | | 1 | | | 1 | | |
| Puerto Rican Groups: | | | | | | | | | | | | |
|   Armed Forces of Popular Assistance | | 1 | | | | | | | | 1 | | |
|   Berinquen People's Army—Macheteres | 4 | | | | 1 | | | | | 5 | | |
|   Star Group | 1 | | | | | | | | | 1 | | |
|   National Liberation Movement | | | | | | | 1 | | | 1 | 1 | |
|   People's Revolutionary Commandos | | | 3 | | | | | | | 3 | | |
|   Puerto Rican Armed Resistance | 1 | 4 | | | | | | | | 5 | | 1 |
| Other Domestic Groups: | | | | | | | | | | | | |
|   Communist Workers Party | 1 | | | | | | | | | 1 | | |
|   Revolutionary Communist Youth Brigade | | | | | | | | | 1 | 1 | | |
| Other Groups: | | | | | | | | | | | | |
|   Black Brigade | | | | | | | | 1 | | 1 | | |
|   Concerned Sierra Leone Nationals | | | | | | | 1 | | | 1 | | |
| Total | 17 | 8 | 7 | 1 | 1 | 2 | 4 | 1 | 1 | 42 | 4 | 1 |

*Source*: U.S. Senate, Committee on the Judiciary, 97th Cong., 2d sess., Hearing Before The Subcommittee on Security and Terrorism. . . . An Oversight on the Operations of the Federal Bureau of Investigation, February 4, 1982, p. 53.

gets were diplomatic and international (15 incidents), commercial establishments (5), public utilities (4), with transportation, postal, and recreational facilities each hit 3 times. The most active terrorist groups that year were Puerto Rican Nationalists (16 incidents), the Jewish Defense League (7), Armenian patriotic groups (6), the right-wing Cuban Omega Seven (4), Iranians (2), with 1 incident each contributed by Croatian, Libyan, and Sierra Leone National groups. The domestic American groups involved were the Jewish Defense League, the Jewish Defenders, the Communist Workers party, the Revolutionary Communist Youth Brigade, and the Black Brigade, each of which was responsible for a single incident (except the JDL which took responsibility for 7).

Perhaps the single most significant development in 1981–82 was the increasing threat of the Armenian nationalist terrorists, particularly through the Armenian Secret Army for Liberation of Armenia (ASALA). Although targeted against "Turkish" imperialism in some 170 major incidents so far, most of these incidents have been carried out outside Turkey, including now the United States.

This general pattern of international terrorist activity in the United States has continued into 1984.

## THE PERCEIVED THREAT AND THE VIOLENCE COMMISSION

The U.S. government and certain symbolically prominent American businesses together with their officials and officers at home and abroad have been targets of international as well as domestic terrorist groups. However, the frequency of incidents and levels of human and material cost have so far not approached those found elsewhere, particularly in Northern Ireland and England, Israel and throughout the Middle East, Italy, Germany, Spain, Turkey, and several countries of Latin America. For example, in the two years of 1977 and 1978, Italy experienced over 2,000 terrorist incidents, the United States only 200.

Given this historical and comparative perspective, it is not too surprising that few Americans shared the depth of concern of many foreign governments and societies about terrorism. Thus, while the various U.S. commissions on violence in the late 1960s did take terrorism—international as well as domestic—into account, this category was treated as only one among several dozens of others and with a much lower priority than most of them.

Attention was given to the problem of increasing the protection of U.S. presidents from assassination by the Violence Commission. Yet the recommendations of the commission have been only partially implemented—and insufficiently so to prevent the near success of the 1981 attempt on President Reagan by an amateur and ill-equipped assassin.

Since the time of the Violence Commission, there has been a dramatic increase in the frequency and level of terrorist incidents throughout the world. During the 1970s, transnational terrorism became a stark reality as the mass media transmitted, sometimes instantly, one horrifying spectacle after another. And as terrorist acts proliferated, controversy over terrorism heightened. Terrorism has become a rich topic for public debate, a subject of intense disagreement on the floor of the United Nations, and has demanded attention as a serious policy issue. Studied by academicians, weighed and reported by journalists, troublesome to governments, and feared especially by the largest corporations—terrorism has come of age.

The American public has become acutely aware of terrorism, not only through news sources but through movies, novels, and television specials. As early as 1977 a Harris survey revealed that "terrorism is viewed as a very serious world problem by 90% of the American people, and a very serious domestic problem by 60%." The survey went on to show that the American public favors extreme measures in dealing with terrorists—90 percent favoring the development of commando teams such as those used by the Israelis at Entebbe and West Germans at Mogadishu, 80 percent favoring airline service being cut off to and from countries that harbor terrorists, and more than half supporting the organization of a special world police force which would operate in any country of the world and which would investigate terrorist groups, arrest them, and put their leaders and members to death. Possibly these views were just a momentary overreaction or conceivably the seeds of hysteria, but the willingness to adopt a new vigilante justice is evident. Also, this public reaction to domestic and international terrorism is especially interesting, considering that the United States had been relatively free from terrorist assault at the time of that poll.

## THE U.S. RESPONSE

Not until 1981 did the U.S. government perceive the terrorist threat to be serious enough to warrant classification as a major component of American foreign policy. On January 27 of that year, only seven days after the release of the fifty-two American hostages who had been held 444 days in Iran in what U.S. authorities considered an act of government-encouraged terrorism, President Reagan spoke of swift and effective retribution in case of future incidents involving terrorism.

The next day, newly sworn-in Secretary of State Haig elaborated, declaring that "the greatest problem . . . in the human rights area today is . . . rampant international terrorism." Referring explicitly to the recently concluded hostage situation in Iran, the U.S. secretary of state put "terrorist governments" as well as conventional terrorist organizations on notice of a new and sterner U.S. policy, one not ruling out substantial "retaliatory action."

The United States currently maintains special military forces with counterterrorist capabilities. At the center of this counterterrorist program is a uniquely trained army unit of several hundred men called the Delta Team. Trained for preemptive action, this unit is capable of carrying out hostage rescue operations along the lines of the raid on Entebbe. Additionally, selected armed forces units are prepared to participate in counterterrorist operations, though not as a primary responsibility. These units include U.S. Army Ranger battalions geared for support of special counterterrorism units, the Navy Seals, at least one company of Marine Reconnaissance Forces, a Marine Amphibious unit, Marine Battalion landing teams, and Air Force Special Operation Forces together with military air-lift command units. All these specialized forces are capable of overseas operations, but would not conceivably be called into action except in the most serious international crisis.

One nonmilitary team that could be activated for a domestic crisis is the Nuclear Emergency Search Team (NEST) in the U.S. Department of Energy, operating independently of the military. NEST conducted the search for nuclear material following the Soviet satellite breakup over northern Canada in 1977. There is great concern that the terrorist arsenal will someday include weapons-grade fissile material through piracy of the commercial traffic in fissile materials. Some international measures have already been undertaken with U.S. participation. The United States and many other nations are signatories to the 1969 non-proliferation treaty. A Suppliers Conference has been meeting in London for quite some time to set security standards. The International Atomic Energy Agency (IAEA) in Vienna is an organization of more than 130 nations established to regulate the flow of nuclear materials. The U.S. Nuclear Regulatory Commission (NRC) has established stringent requirements concerning the security and transport of fissile materials. The U.S. internal standards for control of these materials are very high. In other countries, however, despite international standards established by IAEA and the Suppliers Conference, we can be less certain of the security of Plutonium-239 and Uranium-235. Prospective suppliers of nuclear fuels, plants, and components clearly need to specifically recognize the terrorist threat and be encouraged to enforce both the spirit and letter of their export licensing programs.

Another major area for U.S. involvement in international cooperation is that of conventional arms transfers. Arms sales conditions set by supplier states could include use of certification procedures to ensure that weapons are not subsequently sold to terrorists. Under such procedures, potential violators would face the threat of a cutoff of supplies if they diverted arms to third parties in violation of nontransfer agreements. Admittedly, enforcement of such agreements would not be easy, particularly given the big-business character of arms sales. A somewhat more promising area involves control of conventional explosives through a comprehensive tagging program.

During the last few years, the Bureau of Alcohol, Tobacco and Firearms in the U.S. Treasury Department has taken the lead in the development of explosive taggants. Put simply, taggants provide a means whereby concealed explosives would activate a detector. A successful program of detection would prevent the introduction of explosives into a given area for illegal use. Work is also being done on development of taggants for identification after the explosion has occurred. While important for event analysis and tracing of ownership, tagging for identification would not substantially deter the criminal use of explosives. Tagging for detection is a simpler process (if only because the taggant need not remain intact following detonation), and we are currently very close to realizing a program of this kind.

## TERRORISM AS THEATER AND THE ROLE OF THE MEDIA

When compared with the American homicide rate, the death toll from terrorism is indeed small. In the past decade terrorism has claimed only about a thousand lives worldwide. Yet it has become a major international issue. Why? Because terrorism is theater. The fourteen-month-long hostage crisis in Teheran is an example of such theatrics in the extreme.

Anxieties have become high, but the threshold for the spectacular assault has heightened as well. Americans, like Western Europeans, have insatiable appetites for the novel, the bizarre.

The role of the media in such incidents is pivotal. The media provide enormous political leverage to an act that, on its own, would simply be an example of criminal barbarism. The terrorist uses the media in a way democratic governments cannot. As a result, governments have often appeared inept—unable to defend themselves against a relatively small criminal element. Eventually, however, governments do learn to counteract the first-generation tools of terrorism, and both the media and public become inured to a given level of threatened or actual violence. At that point, terror, like a disease organism in the face of antibiotics, must mutate to survive both physically and in the public eye.

It may seem inconceivable that tactics of terror could be used successfully against a nation as powerful as the United States or indeed any industrial nation. No band of terrorists is a match for any metropolitan police force, much less the smallest standing army. None can command the resources of the tiniest nation. Yet terrorism has been characterized as a worldwide menace. The terror event enjoys an unparalleled power simply because of its media value.

Of all the reasons for terrorist success, the platform offered by the enthusiastic media is by far the most important. Terrorists have used the media as a springboard onto the world stage. As a result, the terrorist assault has come to resemble highly choreographed theater, with the Western media inadvertently emerging as an adversary of liberal democracies by working in de facto partnership with terrorists.

Both government and terrorists operate in the glare of the media spotlight. Without that attention, the outcome of the incident becomes relatively insignificant. The militants in Iran recognized this as an essential ingredient of success and acted accordingly. By encouraging regular media coverage, the terrorists made the torment of the hostages an integral part of American daily life for 444 days. The fifty-four hostages quickly became so well known that any action by the United States that could have jeopardized their lives would have engendered severe political penalties.

The media mold public perceptions about the success or failure of the terrorist operation, about official competence in the face of the threat, and about the prowess of the terrorist organization. For example, Israel's desperate decision to resist escalating terrorist demands and its attempt at a high-risk rescue at Entebbe were depicted by the media as a major triumph. The German counterterrorist rescue force at Mogadishu basked in the same affirmative limelight. By contrast, the American military experience in the Iranian desert was presented not simply as a justified attempt that failed, but as a debacle, a symbol of American command weakness and presidential bungling.

As a terror event unfolds, the media's involvement creates a peculiar synergy among the government, the public, and the terrorists. Each of the actors participates directly in the event, creating in effect a spectacle with a participatory audience. The problem for the terrorist comes when the level of violence loses its media sex appeal, when the next airline hijacking or "knee-capping" is no longer spellbinding news.

To maintain the media spotlight, terrorist organizations must heighten the threshold for the spectacular assault. Accepting the thesis that one of the terrorist's primary goals is governmental disruption and that there must be an aura of Broadway about the event, we can speculate about the next phase. Terrorists will be forced to change their methods, their tools, and their targets to stay ahead of government preparations and ensure front-page coverage.

Perhaps one of the clearest indications of the power of the mass media in America to generate widespread anxiety and concern among the general population and outright terror in a small portion of it, disrupting a major commercial business in the process, is the case of the 1982 Tylenol poisonings. Although the perpetrator was seemingly only an individual—a "crazy" or, perhaps, an extortionist—he or she gave America a profound lesson in "terrorism theater." Although only seven persons died from the cyanide substituted in only fifteen or so of the drugstore-shelf bottles, the incident highlighted the possibility of a much more widespread horror—through malicious imitators and/or by extension to other commonly used drugstore products. Precisely because this was a case of low-technology poisoning, it demonstrates the high vulnerability of each and every American to a similar action by organized and technologically more sophisticated terrorist groups. But would any terrorist group resort to such a tactic? The simple answer is yes, for it has already been done—and in America. This occurred only a few years ago when Palestinian terrorists poisoned a shipment to America of Israeli Jaffa oranges. Although only a handful of these oranges were found to be poisoned, the act seriously affected the Israeli orange industry. The only reason this incident did not become blown up into Tylenol-type proportions by the media was that the terrorists announced what they had done before the oranges had moved from the docks and warehouses to the food stores. Unlike the Tylenol killer, the Palestinian terrorists were at that time unwilling to adopt a policy that would involve killing Americans to gain the attention of the media.

## TERRORISM AS A STRATEGIC TOOL

The cause for concern is very real. America itself and American interests abroad are already direct targets of occasional actions. The future seems to promise more frequent and more serious acts. As the age of great power dominance is replaced by more open patterns of international relations, the traditional mechanisms of restraint are likely to become decreasingly effective. We should expect that the very diversity of actors on the world stage—each pursuing his own interests—will enhance the attractiveness of unconventional means of conflict. For the relatively weak, the high-level/ low-cost factor is essential because they cannot afford to compete militarily or economically. For the more powerful, the high-leverage/low-risk element is decisive since the costs of large-scale conventional or even nuclear confrontations are unacceptable.

International terrorism may become one of the dominant tools of unconventional warfare. Used as a strategic weapon, the vectored terrorist threat offers certain unique advantages in pursuit of foreign policy objectives. Although unimpressive in firepower, it is profound in leverage. Too, the initial uncertainty about the origin of attack often limits the full range of diplomatic and military response. And for the Soviet Union, its proxies, and certain radical national and subnational groups already on the terrorist scene, terrorism may offer an irresistibly low-cost/low-risk means of engaging America in low-intensity conflict.

The recent Libyan death threats against the U.S. president and the attacks against high-ranking NATO officials highlight the use of terrorism as a strategic instrument of policy influence as well as a tactical tool of social disruption. Whether or not a Libyan hit team actually existed is irrelevant; the threat itself forced the president to retreat into a "steel cocoon" and seemed to paralyze the American government. The dramatic and overplayed media coverage made the incident appear almost a self-inflicted act of terror with Colonel Kadaffi as the catalyst.

Incidents such as this and the kidnapping of General James Dozier raise the possibility of ever stronger leverage, an even broader scope for terrorist attacks. Increasingly, terrorism has become a strategic tactic, whether employed by neonihilistic or subnational groups or by nation-states.

These incidents also make clear that America is not immune to the terror event, either at home or abroad. If the usually random act of violence can paralyze a government, the strategically directed terrorist attack is potentially devastating. The United States appears unready to cope effectively with either tactically or strategically inspired terrorism, and that very unreadiness invites attack. In the immediate future, America can expect to join its European allies as a victim of major terrorist acts, playing the unwilling costar in a media event that undermines the government's credibility internationally and weakens it in the eyes of the domestic electorate. Unless the United States learns to deal at home and abroad with the phenomenology of terrorism in the longer term, it should expect to see its substantive strength sharply reduced as terrorism replaces conventional hostilities in the international allocation of power.

## TERRORISTS AS SURROGATES FOR HOSTILE FOREIGN GOVERNMENTS

The new class of "violence manipulators" we can expect to see grow in importance over the next few years includes: subnational terrorist groups, harbored willingly or unwillingly by various states, which seek to disrupt Western societies; Third World countries willing to exploit the tools of terrorism directly for their own ends; and larger powers, which desire to manipulate international events without running the risks of formal military confrontation.

Terrorist groups are known to receive substantial financial and military support from cooperative governments. There are, of course, many ways a government may support terrorist activities, ranging from the apparently passive provision of safe haven or use of air space to actively promoting and supporting terrorists with money, arms, or training. The list of nations that are now or have recently been involved in supporting terrorism includes Libya, Cuba, the Soviet Union, China, North Korea, Algeria, the People's Democratic Republic of Yemen (Aden), Tanzania, Congo, Zaire, Egypt, Syria, Iraq, and Lebanon.

Among the most active has been Libya, which supported and continues to support a wide range of nationalist groups of various ideologies. Much of this backing has been covert, but in the summer of 1972, Colonel Muammar Kaddafi, Libya's dictator, began openly to boast of his contributions to world terrorism. He added that he would be happy to supply weapons to American blacks, "unfurling in the United States the banner of the struggle against American racism."

With more secrecy, the training of terrorists has been occurring in Communist countries. In the late 1960s, Mexican guerrillas received training in North Korea and North Vietnam. In the early 1970s, African insurgents fighting the Portuguese were trained in the use of sophisticated weaponry, including ground-to-air missiles, by Soviet officers at bases within the Soviet Union.

Throughout the 1960s, the Soviets underwrote Cuban training programs in which Third World youths were given instruction in guerrilla methods. Similarly, in the 1970s, most of the Soviet support for terrorist groups was channeled through client states and other intermediaries. Since 1969, Moscow has been providing funds, weapons, and other assistance to Palestinian groups through a complex system of intermediaries. Much the same approach is used for the support of Western terrorists. There is no question that the Soviets view terrorism as dangerous primarily because of its uncontrollable nature, and their support for it outside the Middle East is highly selective, dictated by strategic considerations.

None of these actors operates wholly independently. The Soviet Union has provided funding and support for terrorist operations via Eastern Europe and its client nations like Libya or Cuba. With tacit Soviet approval, many groups have trained together in Cuba, Libya, Iraq, South Yemen, and Lebanon. Informal alliances among the members of different groups have often occurred. Palestinian and German terrorists operated together in the 1975 OPEC hostage incident and the Entebbe sky-jacking. It has been speculated that the Italian Red Brigades received cooperation from Germany's Red Army faction in the Dozier case. The PLO has provided aid and assistance to the Japanese Red Army (and were perhaps repaid in the Lod Massacre); the PLO, in turn, has received assistance from a number of Arab nations, such as Libya, which has supported groups as disparate as the Irish Provos and the right-wing Italian groups. This overlap in objective and method raises the specter of an international network for terrorism—a master conspiracy of disruption. Indeed, the Reagan administration declared early on that the Soviet Union was responsible for virtually all international terrorism, using it as a tool of surrogate warfare. Thus, a linkage between terrorism and the Soviet Union was made in 1980 in a CIA study and again in 1981 by Secretary of State Alexander M. Haig, Jr.

While there is incontrovertible evidence of Soviet support in training and equipment, the administration has not produced an actual "smoking gun"—direct control of terrorist's policy or actions. Terrorism, on the whole, is too complex an issue to be easily explained away as an example of Soviet interventionism. Even if the Soviet Union withdrew all patronage, terrorist activity would certainly continue, perhaps unabated. Terror has other independent patrons, currently the most prominent being Libya. Libya, for example, has become quite involved in Central America and Venezuela—having gained some influence with the media and with a number of ranking officials. This kind of link is of primary benefit to Libya in its quest for a leadership role in OPEC. Venezuela provides a natural platform for Libyan terrorism disguised as economic or political nationalism. While there might be tacit support from Moscow, there is little or no evidence that Libyan activities are planned or directed by the Soviets. The terror technique represents too useful a tool of low-intensity conflict to be discarded by any small group operating on its own behalf.

Moreover, subnational terrorist groups have matured into self-sustaining organisms; there is no organic need for a master conspiracy. Terrorist organizations are not mirror images of each other, even when there is a broad intersection of interest. Each group learns from the experience of others, its tactics evolving in response to governmental countermeasures and in the spotlight of media publicity. Hence, a loose confederacy of terrorist groups operates quite successfully without the limits that centralization would impose.

Contemporary terrorism offers its proponents few grand visions of a better world. Increasingly, it has become a strategic tactic, whether employed by neonihilistic subnational groups or by nation-states. As a result, the days in which terrorism was confined to isolated instances of social disruption are over. The destabilized international system provides the opportunity for profound disruption while the vulnerability of the West, in terms of its unprotected technical and democratic political infrastructure, offers a tempting avenue of attack not only for subnational terrorist groups but even for nations like Iran, Libya, or the Soviet Union that might choose to use them as "plausibly deniable" surrogate forces.

## CAN THE U.S. GOVERNMENT COPE WITH A SERIOUS ACT OF TERRORISM?

This nation (unlike others in the Western Alliance) has no internal consensus on how to respond to either acts of supercriminal violence or coercive political threats; has no common philosophical basis for accepting the high costs (in lives, materials, pride, and power) of occasional failure in dealing with terrorism; and has no internationally recognized commitment to firm, retributive deterrence of such violence.

Terrorism is manipulative; it seeks to turn an opponent's strengths against him. For example, it can exploit the technological, cultural, and legal infrastructure of a state against the state's own interests. This type of exploitation is particularly successful in cultures like the United States with its strong traditions of personal freedom and limitations on executive power; these cultures already endure a degree of disorder as the price of democracy and are less able than others to respond uncompromisingly to terrorist threats. By contrast, terrorism is relatively ineffective in totalitarian societies, because it is easily denied an environment for existence as a matter of state prerogative. To be effective in a totalitarian culture, terrorism must be raised to the level of full-scale revolution.

Unlike totalitarian states, democratic governments have had relatively few unequivocal successes in the face of terrorist activity. Embassies have been seized with impunity. Governments have been perceived to capitulate in the face of terrorist threats. Since 1972, terrorists have elevated the arts of assassination, hijacking, kidnapping, arson, and bombing into the public domain, paralyzing democratic nations and damaging the credibility of their governments. And, while America does not yet have the full degree of experience of terrorism that some other democratic societies have, the United States fully shares their vulnerabilities.

The seizure in 1979 of the American embassy in Teheran by a mob of uncertain allegiance paralyzed our nation for more than a year and probably altered American electoral history. America's paralysis was converted into ignominy when a rescue attempt failed before it was even under way. No atomic bomb could help. America failed diplomatically and militarily to deal in proportionate terms with the immoderate behavior of a rogue nation and with the terrorist tactics of subnational elements. The very high cost to America's leadership of the West has yet to be assessed.

A number of avenues for future attacks on the United States are open to the professional terrorist:

- Attacks on the infrastructure of metropolitan areas (systems such as the electric or gas networks, communications or computer facilities)
- Threats to thousands of people with agents of mass destruction (nuclear explosives, chemical or biological weapons)
- More subtle exploitation of contentious political issues (the antinuclear and environment movements)

Attacks on American society's infrastructure have already occurred. The New World Liberation Front has targeted Pacific Gas and Electric some seventy times albeit with minimal damage. A raid on an FALN safehouse prior to the 1980 Democratic National Convention turned up detailed plans of the power system of Madison Square Garden, implying a possible plot to black out the facility and disrupt the electoral process. To date, these terrorist attacks have been largely ineffective, but they raise the prospect of very large disruptive impacts being created with very few human and material resources.

As American society has grown dependent on technology for survival—with its technological infrastructure vertically stacked with little room for redundancy—its vulnerability to attack has become increasingly obvious. Certainly, electric generation and distribution systems, computer networks, nuclear installations, port facilities, water systems, and oil refineries provide leverageable targets. Too, certain responsible organizations have enough evidence to conclude that terrorist groups have been recruiting technical talent needed to correct past failures.

Biological and chemical agents, though readily attainable, have remained largely unused. Yet, in many respects, they represent the terrorist's easiest avenue into the mass destruction arena. In contrast to the concern over nuclear materials, the control and safeguard of chemical and biological agents has not been given adequate attention. It is far easier to culture anthrax than it is to steal or fabricate a nuclear device; and a biological attack is potentially more lethal than a nuclear explosion. A small nuclear device could kill a hundred thousand people if detonated in a dense population center. By contrast, an effectively delivered aerosol anthrax attack could rival the effects of a thermonuclear device. Indeed, biological weapons could become a "poor man's" bomb in an age of nuclear proliferation.

Although the penalties for using agents of mass destruction may be too high for industrialized and developing nations, extremely poor national and subnational groups may be less cautious. Even the possession of such weapons could be viewed as a quick and cheap route to political and coercive power by groups or countries with otherwise marginal political or military strength. It is important to recognize too, that a successful threat does not necessarily require the actual use of such weapons. The extortion potential will always be high where the capacity for mass destruction is present; hostage situations of the future could involve entire populations.

An equally plausible, albeit more subtle, means for terrorists to increase their leverage is the careful selection of highly symbolic targets within the international community. The level of violence remains the same, but the effect is expanded dramatically. The attack on General Dozier in Italy represents just such a new form of "cushion shot" terrorism. Dozier was not merely a high-ranking official whose kidnapping might seriously embarrass the American government; he was a symbol of the Western Alliance. His kidnapping was designed to provide the Red Brigades with power to influence, through the media, the outcome of issues of great political import: the structure of the Western Alliance and the decisions on theater force modernization.

By attacking Dozier, the Red Brigades placed themselves in a position to influence a range of targets—the military, the U.S. government, the Italian government, even the NATO alliance. Using the media as a springboard, the terrorists attempted a "cushion shot" to capitalize on the political strains in the alliance and the growing worldwide antinuclear movement. Had the terrorists chosen another day—not one in which events in Poland and the Golan Heights overshadowed their drama—the U.S. government as well as the entire alliance might have been even more seriously embarrassed.

## THE FEDERAL CRISIS MANAGEMENT SYSTEM

Authority for dealing with various aspects of a terrorist incident is dispersed over a number of U.S. government departments and jurisdictions in a manner that is well suited to handling day-to-day concerns but may impede efforts to deal with a crisis. To maintain public confidence that the government is reacting capably, it is important to avoid unnecessarily alarming emergency measures and to handle the crisis through channels—up to a point. At a certain level of public concern, on the other hand, handling things "through channels" may appear callous or stupid and the public will be more reassured that everything possible is being done if the White House is visibly involved. This is a very fine line to walk, and it is fraught with hazards for a president who is suddenly thrust into the midst of a developing situation.

To overcome this problem, it is appropriate that the primary organizational arrangements for dealing with terrorist incidents remain fixed along traditional law enforcement and diplomatic lines, but that a small group at the highest level of government, one having the confidence of the president, be given both the responsibility of monitoring emergent crises and the authority to coordinate and expedite federal actions when necessary. With such an arrangement, the president should be able to participate in management of a major threat in an informed way, to the degree desired, and with the amount of public visibility that seems appropriate. Following several reorganizations and dubious performance under successive administrations, this top-level group is now called the Special Situations Group (SSG). A committee of the National Security Council (NSC) and chaired by the vice-president, it is the senior crisis management echelon of the U.S. government. For expertise in managing terrorist crises, the SSG can now draw for expertise upon the NSC staff and, through it, on counterterrorism specialists in various government agencies.

A straightforward terrorist attack may pose impressive problems for the government's disaster-relief agencies and for those concerned with tracking down and prosecuting the criminals. A major attack would even warrant the sort of high-level coordination described above. A threat of national disruption, however, presents a much more complicated set of problems. The first of these is the credibility of the threat. This is an extremely delicate matter, especially in the case of chemical, biological, or nuclear threats. A reaction of uninformed panic could lead the government into hasty, foolish actions that would serve the terrorist's ends with no further need for action on his part. An overly phlegmatic reaction could result in tragedy if a valid threat is ignored. Rapid access to the requisite expert advice from appropriate scientists is crucial to making informed judgments of the credibility of exotic threats, but advice from behavioral scientists may also help to determine the credibility of particular threats. A high-level monitoring group such as a well-staffed SSG could serve to buffer the government from overreaction to negligible or unevaluated threats as well as to expedite response to a threat deemed valid.

The same organizational idea is the model for our national security apparatus. Preparations to manage the effects of a nationally disruptive terrorist act are part of civil emergency preparedness, a program that may exist in name only.

## IMPLICATIONS FOR POLICYMAKERS AND PROGRAM ADMINISTRATORS

Whether international terrorism is a form of warfare or not, responsible response begins with a public policy that recognizes the issue, places it in proper perspective among the hierarchy of standing problems on the national agenda, and provides useful operational guidance to those who will be dealing with specific future incidents. It should promise with chilling certainty to all who trespass against U.S. interests in this manner that eventual retribution will be exacted from actor and instigator alike. It should engage the confidence and common sense of the American people and not be regarded as just another governmental activity divorced from the real business of the country.

Ideally, the society attacked by terrorists reacts at three hierarchical levels. First, there is the immediate isolation and containment of the incident in an attempt to control its development. Second, there is the phase of domestic and international "damage control," or dealing with the derivative and delayed political, social, economic, security, and military implications, including reassurance of local governments that basic commitments will be upheld (after, say, the breakdown of a city's water system). Third, and probably least considered, is the phase of creating opportunity from adversity and consciously using the incident (in its fullest sense, including success or failure in containment and in dealing with its larger fallout implication) as an element to move forward basic national policy. The alternative, to try to encyst such events and then rely on the passage of time to remove them from the public consciousness, has two grave disadvantages: it invites new incidents, because the field is always fresh for public exploitation; and it inhibits inquiry into the root causes of this class of violence, which, if addressed as part of the political process, would be greatly weakened by routine and open review. By incorporating the ill fortune of terrorist acts into the rationale for forward flow of programs, policies, legislation, and individual activities, it would seem that the nation's vulnerability would decrease markedly.

Once a risk is recognized as likely and incorporated as such in the public consciousness, the kinetic energy of that risk in social terms is expended with little real effect. In short, a mature technological society can absorb the instabilities caused by occasional lack of success in managing the effects of terrorism; it is a matter of social perspective, of informed personal choice, and of educated expectancies backed up by a first-line defense of sound independent policy, quality and timely intelligence, rapid controlled resource allocation, and a straightforward mechanism for making difficult decisions quickly.

Having matters in hand, or at least appearing to have them so, implies advance preparation. Certainly, luck enters into the equation, but so do well-conceived organizational arrangements, ironed-out jurisdictional questions among local, state, and federal authorities, and planned uses of technology. Such contingency planning is basic if America is to meet the terrorist challenge. Its objective is not to prepare for specific crises but to develop general modes of operation and an awareness of available resources, to gain quick access to those resources, and to understand the logistics involved in using them. Gaming exercises, aimed at developing smooth working routines in crisis conditions, are a requisite of contingency planning. The creation of a professional U.S. "Red Team" of imaginative simulated terrorists would provide realistic training and testing opportunities at many levels of threat. Another area of exploration is to use technology to harden the target, to reduce the terrorist's capability for damage, and to deny him the leverage he seeks.

Exactly because the society itself is hostage in the largest scale terrorist extortions (e.g., those involving nuclear or biological materials, those attacking the life-support infrastructure of food, energy, and water), the society must embrace philosophically the quality of mature response that the threat warrants. A danger in the past has been a tendency to downplay the overall threat and to treat each conventional incident on its own theatrical merits; a graver danger of the future is the probability that unconventional incidents will have much greater impact than they perhaps warrant and will be allowed to resonate until they eventually fractionate some of our important stabilizing social and political structures.

## CONCLUSION

The United States must recognize the recent escalation of such violence from the level of a criminal act or political nuisance to a matter deserving serious international attention. More and more governments including the United States have become increasingly impatient with terrorist threats and acts. But if the United States cannot, out of indecision, or will not, out of ignorance, act now to meet future challenges, the costs in the decades to come could well be paid in the currency of national humiliation and social disintegration. Time is running out, but the question is for whom—the terrorist or the government?

To meet this challenge, government administrators and, perhaps, legislators will have to reconsider two very difficult points: first, how to assure detailed and timely intelligence about terrorist activities within the United States, and second, how to counter the terrorist theater that is so crucial to terrorist groups during an event. Finally, they must consider how to achieve both these governmental and public goals without infringing either civil rights or press freedom.

## BIBLIOGRAPHY

Alexander, Yonah, ed. *International Terrorism: National, Regional and Global Perspectives.* New York: Frederick Praeger, 1976.

Bell, J. Bowyer. "The Terrorist Threat." *Enterprise: The Journal of Executive Action,* August 1981, pp. 2–4.

———. *A Time of Terror: How Democratic Societies Respond to Revolutionary Violence.* New York: Basic Books, 1978.

———. *Transnational Terror.* Stanford, Calif., and Washington, D.C.: Hoover Institution and American Enterprise Institute, 1975.

Bell, J. Bowyer, and Ted Robert Gurr. "Terrorism and Revolution in America." In *Violence in America.* Edited by Hugh Davis Graham and Ted Robert Gurr. Rev. ed. Beverly Hills, Calif.: Sage Publications, 1979, pp. 329–47.

Burton, Anthony. *Urban Terrorism: Theory, Practice and Response.* New York: Free Press, 1975.

Carlton, David, and Carlo Schaerf, eds. *International Terrorism and World Security.* New York: John Wiley & Sons, Halsted Press, 1975.

Central Intelligence Agency. *Annotated Bibliography on Transnational and International Terrorism.* PR76–10073U. Washington, D.C., December 1976.

———, National Foreign Assessment Center. "Patterns of International Terrorism 1980." PA81–10634. Washington, D.C., 1981.

Clutterbuck, Richard. *Living with Terrorism.* New Rochelle, N.Y.: Arlington House, 1975.

Dobson, Christopher, and Ronald Payne. *The Carlos Complex: A Study in Terror.* New York: G. P. Putnam's Sons, 1977.

Finger, Seymour Maxwell, and Yonah Alexander, eds. *Terrorism: Interdisciplinary Perspectives.* New York: John Jay, 1977.

Fromkin, David. "The Strategy of Terrorism." *Foreign Affairs,* July 1975, pp. 683–98.

Hacker, Frederick J. *Crusaders, Criminals, and Crazies: Terror and Terrorism in Our Time.* New York: W. W. Norton, 1976.

Hyams, Edward. *Terrorists and Terrorism.* London: J. M. Dent, 1975.

Jenkins, Brian Michael. *Terrorism: Trends and Potentialities.* Santa Monica, Calif.: RAND Corp., 1977.

Kupperman, Robert H. *Facing Tomorrow's Terrorist Incident Today.* Report prepared for the Department of Justice. Washington, D.C.: U.S. Government Printing Office, October 1977.

———. "Terror, the Strategic Tool: Response and Control." *Annals of the American Academy of Political and Social Science,* September 1982, pp. 24–38.

Kupperman, Robert H., and Darrel M. Trent. *Terrorism: Threat, Reality, Response.* Stanford, Calif.: Hoover Institution Press, 1979.

Laqueur, Walter. *Terrorism.* Boston: Little, Brown & Co., 1977.

Moss, Robert. *Urban Guerrillas: The New Face of Political Violence.* London: Maurice Temple Smith, 1977.

Niezing, Johan, ed. *Urban Guerrilla: Studies on the Theory, Strategy and Practice of Political Violence in Modern Societies.* Rotterdam: University of Rotterdam Press, 1974.

Parry, Albert. *Terrorism: From Robespierre to Arafat.* New York: Vanguard, 1976.

Possony, Stefan T., and L. Francis Bouchey. *International Terrorism—The Communist Connection.* Washington, D.C.: American Council for World Freedom, 1978.

Sterling, Claire. *The Terror Network.* New York: Holt, Rinehart & Winston, 1981.

Stohl, Michael, ed. *The Politics of Terror: A Reader in Theory and Practice.* New York: Marcel Dekker, 1977.

U.S. Senate, Committee on the Judiciary, 97th Congress 2nd Session. *Hearing before the Subcommittee on Security . . . on Oversight on the Operations of the Federal Bureau of Investigation,* February 4, 1982.

# EPILOGUE

# Neighborhood, Family, and Employment: Toward a New Public Policy against Violence

LYNN A. CURTIS

*When in man's long history other great civiliza-*
*tions fell, it was less often from external assault*
*than from internal decay. . . . The greatness and*
*durability of most civilizations has been finally*
*determined by how they have responded to these*
*challenges from within. Ours will be no excep-*
*tion.*

*—Final Report,*
National Violence Commission, 1969

We asked Robert Kupperman to write the preceding chapter because terrorism has emerged so dramatically since the Violence Commission. But
this epilogue returns to the central theme of the volume—policy against
individual violence.

Since 1969, this nation's responses to individual violence have not exactly
suggested the kind of greatness that the Violence Commission had in mind.
As for the durability of our civilization, some have seen it expressed by
police hardware programs that may have rechanneled the expression of
grievance among the economically dispossessed from group protest to the
slower rioting of street crime.

But one also can detect a potentially more effective response to violence.
Since the Violence Commission, certain nonhardware programs have appeared to be successful in reducing crime and fear, even if more careful
evaluations of them still are needed. Together with some of the research
sponsored by the National Institute of Justice, these successes suggest the
foundation of a new national policy to reduce crime and fear. Such a policy
can do something about the causes of crime; it can work to prevent crime
in the way advocated by the original Violence Commission. But the policy

can avoid the vagueness of the Violence Commission's social reform proposals, refrain from merely throwing money at the problem, and replace a trickle-down process of diffuse change with more targeted direct action in specific geographic areas aimed at reducing specific crimes and fears.

In this concluding chapter, I am most concerned with suggesting innovative prevention programs and addressing the causes of crime because I am persuaded by Weiner and Wolfgang and by Currie that violent crime has increased significantly since 1969 (notwithstanding the reports that it may have held steady or declined in recent years), that levels of violent crime remain far higher in the United States than in most industrialized countries, and that high levels of fear also persist. Along with Currie, Lavrakas, and Gordon and Morris, I am convinced that the federal government's use of hardware and attempts at deterrence have been limited in effectiveness and inefficient in terms of their costs to the American taxpayer. I am persuaded by Comer and by Ball-Rokeach and Short that to address the causes of individual violence, which disproportionately involves poor minorities as both offenders and victims, is also to address the causes of group disorder. The common base of grievance also implies that a federal policy of reducing crime and fear through targeted, carefully evaluated economic and social programs needs to be part of a more inclusive policy of reducing the black and Hispanic underclass.

My objective in this chapter, then, is to identify such a policy, paying attention to themes suggested throughout this book, to innovations that are supported by scientific research, and to my own practical experience in running public- and private-sector programs—keeping in mind what seems to be politically feasible.

On the basis of these criteria, three words perhaps best suggest a future policy framework that can prevent individual and group violence in a cost-effective way: neighborhood, family, and employment. More specifically, I believe that we need to:

- Demonstrate and evaluate ways in which indigenous inner-city organizations can take the lead in reducing crime and fear—not only as an end in itself, but as a means of developing their neighborhoods economically and creating youth employment, especially among minorities;
- Demonstrate and evaluate how extended families and other personal networks can be a crucial source of support for minority youth in high crime areas; and
- Demonstrate and evaluate the linkage between the employment of minority youths and the reduction of crime committed by these youths

## THE HOUSE OF UMOJA AND EL CENTRO

Let me first illustrate how such policies already show signs of working successfully by summarizing a 1981 MacNeil-Lehrer Report on the House of Umoja Boy's Town in West Philadelphia.[1]

*Umoja* is a Swahili word that means "unity." The program begins with Sister Falaka Fattah, founder of Umoja, telling a reporter that young minority men are the cannon fodder of our society. Sister Falaka describes how, over ten years ago, she and her husband, David, opened the doors of their house on North Frazier Street to provide an alternative extended family for tough youth-gang members from broken homes.

The scene shifts to the president of the United States speaking before the National Alliance for Business. Describing Umoja's success in reducing recidivism, he is particularly impressed with the alternative-family support it provides. He almost appears to be criticizing skeptics who ask, "What agency do we create, what budget do we allocate, that will supply missing parental affection and restore to the child consistent discipline by a stable and loving family?"[2]

Back on Frazier Street, Sister Falaka is sitting at a table with several young men. She is leading the *Adella*—a Swahili word for "just" and "fair." It is a vehicle for character building, mediation, and self-government. Problems are raised and resolved. Today Sister Falaka shows her concern that James got fired from a construction job for talking back to the foreman. "If you were hanging on a rope by your mouth, and you just had to get in that last word, you'd be gone. Isn't that right?"

The young men listen to Sister Falaka because they respect her. That is because she listens to and respects them. *Respect* is a word these young men use over and over.

Robert MacNeil comments on the Swahili words and asks Sister Falaka whether she is Muslim. She is not. The words provide an African ethnic identity. The young men are encouraged to take pride in their ethnic origins—and build on them.

Such pride, the support of the extended family, the respect for Falaka and David Fattah, and the pressure of other young men at the house all come together. Some youths seem to become more willing to channel their interests into building a future for themselves. There are shots of these young men working for high school equivalency tests. Others are shown learning to rehabilitate row houses on Frazier Street. The remodeled houses, named for Martin Luther King and other black leaders, will be used for residences, services, and youth-operated businesses that will provide jobs and bring income into Umoja.

There is also an Umoja Security Institute. On the program, "Brother Rat," a former Umojan, describes to the Adella how he learned private security work through the institute. He now is a detective. "I didn't used to listen. But she [Falaka] turned me around. Now I got a good job, a wife, and a family. I feel real good about myself. And you can do the same thing."

The neighbhorhood shopping center is being patrolled by young men with Security Institute training. They wear Umoja uniforms, do not carry weapons, and serve as additional eyes and ears to protect the community. The street savvy of these young men is being tapped, not ignored or blocked (as was the case in many federal employment programs of the 1960s and 1970s). They know what suspicious behaviors to watch for, and they use that knowledge to prevent crime. Umoja has contracts with a nearby shopping mall, a 7-Eleven, and a Burger King to help keep crime and fear down. That also encourages businesses to stay in the neighborhood.

What do criminal justice leaders think of all this? On the program, a Philadelphia juvenile court judge says that community organizations like Umoja have made perhaps the biggest difference in reducing crime and gang violence in the city. A member of the Los Angeles Police Gang Unit adds that neighborhood groups are not the only answer but that they have an important role to play.

As for results, Sister Falaka cites a recent study by the Philadelphia Psychiatric Center that reported a 3 percent rearrest rate for Umojans compared to a rate of 70 to 90 percent for young people from conventional juvenile correction facilities.

Toward the end of the program, Sister Falaka is asked whether the Umoja system might be tried elsewhere. She answers that she is not unique. She believes that there are natural leaders in many communities across the nation. Their skill needs only to be tapped.

I do not want to place too much emphasis on Umoja. There are other examples of success—like the Center for Orientation and Services in Ponce, Puerto Rico, which has received national attention through Charles Silberman's *Criminal Violence, Criminal Justice*.[3] El Centro is run by a Catholic nun, Sister Isolina Ferre, whose brother is a former governor of Puerto Rico. Over the past decade, delinquency rates have been cut in half, despite a rapidly growing teenage population. Umoja and El Centro seem to get similar results, drawing on the strengths of their different cultures, black and Hispanic. Sisters Falaka and Isolina both create self-respect in youth, provide family-like support alternatives when there are broken families, motivate the young men to take action for the benefit of themselves and the community, and channel their energy from illegal to legal market activity.

### FAMILY

A practical question that emerges from the Umoja experience is whether the extended family it provides for young men who are involved in crime can be re-created in other communities.

Such extended families not only seem to work in places like Umoja but, in small ways, begin to reverse three hundred years of American history. In his chapter on black violence, James Comer points out that sixteenth-century West African extended families were systematically destroyed—even though later Irish, Italian, Jewish, and other immigrant groups were allowed to use their families, their social support networks, and their cultural traditions to remain intact. Comer traces our public-private policy after Emancipation, which shifted from the official breakup of black families and prohibition of social supports to various forms of neglect through denial of opportunity. This has not changed today for the black underclass. That is why establishing Umoja's form of extended family in other black communities would be a step in the right direction—to re-create kinship and social support. The work at El Centro shows such possibilities within a Hispanic culture. Similarly, in the South Bronx, mixed black and Hispanic extended families formed by Elizabeth Sturz's Argus Learning for Living Community have been successful in remotivating young people and teaching them to find and keep places in the legal labor market.[4]

Elliott Currie points out that the presidential commissions and existing research show the relation between family and crime to be a complex one. But, he says, "families that are burdened by the stresses of poor income, lack of responsive social networks, internal conflict and a tradition of parental violence are, not too surprisingly, less able to ensure the kind of supervision and guidance that, in families with better resources, reduce the risks of youth criminality and violence. This is not an area of really substantial disagreement in the serious criminological literature."

Beyond Umoja, the Argus community, and El Centro, Currie tells us about other family programs—like the Department of Health, Education and Welfare's Child and Family Resource Centers of the 1970s—the results of which suggested substantial enhancement of family functioning at very low cost. Although these programs were not explicitly designed to test how family supports can reduce crime, a General Accounting Office assessment predicted that they would reduce delinquency by improving early parent-child relations and school performance.[5] Future federal programs need to build on these centers and evaluate their crime-reducing impact. Variations on important related private-sector ventures, such as the Ford Foundation's Project Redirection, need to do the same.[6]

New departures are politically feasible if they can be made part of the national family policy advocated by Comer. We need to overturn the many existing federal policies that still fail to recognize the long history behind the weak black kinship institutions which the Violence and Kerner commissions observed. For example, Comer cautions that "traumatized families often overwhelm institutions and programs based on the notion that no previous trauma took place, that success as families and in the economic system is merely a matter of will and hard work. Housing programs that isolate the poor and then systematically remove the best organized and most effective families from the neighborhood or housing project through income limits are an example of such thinking."

## MINORITY YOUTH UNEMPLOYMENT

The National Urban League has estimated the unemployment rate during the 1970s among young urban minority men in high-crime groups to have been over 60 percent. The rate, the League says, has risen in the 1980s.[7] Much of this is structural—unemployment that persists despite business-cycle and seasonal fluctuations. Denied jobs directly through discriminating hiring behavior by employers and indirectly through inadequate educational opportunity, many young minority men have become victims of structural unemployment and have thus increasingly become part of the underclass. This is nothing more than the contemporary version of the denial of job opportunities experienced by blacks during earlier parts of our history.

Whether ex-offenders or not, many young blacks and Hispanics tend to be excluded from the legal primary labor market, where there are adequate wages and stable jobs. They tend to be limited to the legal secondary market, with low wages and unstable, dead-end jobs as dishwashers, busboys, hotel clean-up workers, and the like. Many previous federal job-training programs recruited primarily for this legal secondary market.

Yet these are only the *legal* job markets. The competition for the labor of a youth on the south side of Chicago includes offerings in a variety of illegal or quasi-legal job markets. To an intelligent young man in a Watts public housing project, whose education has been substandard and whose heroes include only some participants in the legal primary markets, it can be rational—that is, consistent with his values and experience[8]—to pick up one or more of the illegal options.

### The Vera Findings

Specifically, then, why might public- or private-sector employment not divert an underclass youth from committing crime—especially acquisitive crime and illegal market activity? The most sophisticated answers have come from research by the Vera Institute of Justice, funded by the U.S. Department of Justice.[9] If job training is directed to unrewarding dead-end work in the legal secondary labor market and if local work rules and hiring patterns make even these dead-end opportunities hard to find, competing illegal labor-market activities may be more attractive. Such illegal opportunities vary greatly from neighborhood to neighborhood, city to city, and time to time. Opportunity aside, common sense street-level decisions by young underclass men about pursuing legal opportunities, illegal ones, or some combination depend not only on the money involved. They also can depend on intrinsic satisfaction, what feels best given the values and expectations of the community and how one generates respect among peers. We know that a good number of minority youths earn more money and develop more self-respect from the skills involved in criminal pursuits, and from the autonomous work conditions of criminal business, than from available legal secondary labor-market jobs with low skill potential, limited scope, and arbitrary management.[10]

In addition, Vera found that broken family backgrounds tend to increase commitments to illegal options, whereas strong family supports and reliable kinship networks tend to increase legal market commitments. The impact of all these conditions on young men's decisions also varies with their age and stage in the life cycle. For example, marriage can provide some of the support to help a young man decide to work in the legal market.

There are clear and important policy implications to the Vera findings. We need to demonstrate and carefully evaluate programs that incorporate secure bridges between the secondary and primary legal labor markets; facilitate family, extended-family, and kinship network support; and build employment on interests and street skills that are intrinsically satisfying to the individual, but that previous public-sector programs often denied.

Vera has in fact begun some demonstrations in this direction. One is the Neighborhood Work Project.[11] Although it does not supply all the social supports of Umoja or the Argus Community, the Neighborhood Work Project provides employment that allows ex-offenders to bridge from dead-end secondary labor-market work to more permanent and rewarding primary labor-market work.

For many ex-offenders, lack of education, poor skills, and paucity of job experience, compounded by the stigma of prison, impede entrance into the primary job market. With no prospect of employment, many see a return to illegal market activity as the only available means of support. The Neighborhood Work Project provides another option: temporary, unskilled, part-time, legal employment in a structured work environment. No skills are required, only a willingness to work hard at strenuous physical labor.

The project also is modeled on the casual or day-labor market. The flexibility of this type of employment is appropriate for returning ex-offenders, many of whom have medical, governmental, or personal obligations that make a rigid five-day-a-week schedule difficult or impossible to manage. The project gives them a chance, without dependence on welfare, to get their bearings while they go about finding a permanent job.

Although evaluation of the project has not yet proceeded far enough to determine the ultimate crime-reduction impact, it has already been determined that the demand for recently released prisoners for legal market employment is considerable.

The crime-reducing impact of creating employment bridges for ex-offenders has already been demonstrated by studies done in the 1970s, which found that giving small temporary stipends, at about the level of unemployment insurance, to releasees readjusting to the community and searching for jobs significantly lowered rearrests for both violent and property crime.[12] Similarly, a Rand Corporation study of repeat offenders found that individuals who were "better employed" committed far fewer and less serious property and violent crimes than individuals who were in lower quality employment or unemployed.[13]

## Federal Programs

Most of the federal programs of the 1960s and 1970s failed to measure carefully the relationship between employment and crime, but some did. And some *were* successful at reducing crime by those employed. We need to build on these successes, just as we need to build on the implications of the work at Vera.

One good example was the supported work program, sponsored by several agencies, in which persons with special difficulty in the legal primary labor market were involved in a carefully supervised work program that encouraged self-support by gradually increasing their rewards and responsibilities. Although the effects were not always clear-cut across the populations involved, the Manpower Demonstration Research Corporation (MDRC) found significantly reduced crime within a sample of ex-addicts who had participated in the program.[14]

In the most thorough review of the 1970s public-sector employment and training programs, Robert Taggart concludes, "Comprehensive residential training (e.g., Job Corps) for the most disadvantaged youth pays off in earning gains . . . as well as in large reductions in crime and delinquency. . . . Every dollar spent on residential training yields at least $1.45 in social benefits, according to conservative estimates of the current values of benefits and costs and after accounting for the real rate of return on the same resources. . . . Naysayers who deny that labor market problems are real and serious, that social interventions can make a difference, or that the effectiveness of public problems can be improved will find little to support their preconceptions" in the information now available from evaluations of programs of the 1970s.[15]

The residential setting for the Job Corps is rural, but successful residential programs that incorporate training and employment, like Umoja and the Argus Community, are urban. They also include many of the family-like and other psychological features that research by the Vera Institute shows to be needed supports for training and jobs.

## Illegal Costs and Legal Benefits

Much of the past policy debate has centered around increasing the costs of illegal market employment versus increasing the benefits of legal market employment. Over the past two decades, the predominant policy has been to increase the costs of illegal market employment by following a strategy of deterrence. Often, little attention has been given to a deliberate, coordinated policy of simultaneously raising legal market benefits. Even when such attention has been given to benefits, some academics commonly add that it is nonetheless too difficult to use employment as a means of reducing minority-youth crime because the issues are too complex.[16]

This is nonsense. We now know from the experience of the Law Enforcement Assistance Administration (LEAA) and various academic studies that a policy of raising illegal market costs has not succeeded in reducing crime or fear. We also know, from the experience of groups like Umoja and the Argus Community, evaluations like that of Taggart and MDRC, and research like that of Vera and the Rand Corporation, that there do seem to be ways of increasing legal market benefits that work to reduce crime and fear.

This does not mean that we should reduce the costs of illegal market employment. But the time has come to begin spending our program, evaluation, and research dollars in the more promising direction of increasing legal market benefits. For too long, we have neglected coordinating a targeted, structural federal labor-market policy with a federal crime prevention policy.

## CRIME PREVENTION BY INNER-CITY NEIGHBORHOOD ORGANIZATIONS

Organizations like Umoja and El Centro illustrate the great potential for what today is called neighborhood or community-based crime prevention, as Lavrakas has shown. But there is much disagreement over what the term really means. The MacNeil-Lehrer broadcast described earlier helps put in perspective what is and is not needed.

### Addressing the Causes of Crime and Reducing Opportunities

A program like Umoja both addresses the causes of crime and reduces opportunities for crime. Causes are addressed by employing youth, empowering young men through participatory decision making, providing extended family support, and mediating disputes through mechanisms like the Adella. The youth patrols are ways of reducing opportunities for crime without necessarily addressing underlying causes. Other examples of opportunity reduction through other neighborhood organizations include block watches, escort services, and home security through hardware. Sometimes the causes of crime can be addressed while opportunities are reduced, as in the employment of youth on Umoja's security patrols.

The importance of *both* addressing the causes of crime *and* reducing opportunities for it in inner-city neighborhoods extends far beyond Umoja and El Centro. In San Francisco and other cities, Aaron Podolefsky and his colleagues found that lower socioeconomic ethnic communities tend to reject neighborhood-based crime prevention programs if they ignore the causes of crime and rely only on opportunity reduction.[17] Yet this practical experience and common sense feedback from the street are not sufficiently recognized by practitioners: it is most common today to pursue opportunity reduction alone.

Opportunity reduction *is* needed in the inner city—for example, to help reduce fear and to ensure that businesses will not move out. But opportunity reduction alone can, at best, displace crime to another location. If the displacement is to other parts of the inner city, what have we gained for a policy targeted at the underclass? If the displacement is to the suburbs, where much more economic and political power is present, the result probably will be a strong opportunity-reduction policy to displace crime back to the inner city. (Indeed, much of the popularity of opportunity reduction seems to be in middle-class suburbia—where, for example, block watches and patrols try, in effect, to displace crime out of the neighborhood.)

There may be political advantages to those who control a local game of displacement. But I do not believe that the people in the poorer communities surveyed by Podolefsky are being unreasonable in suggesting that we also pay some attention to why potential offenders choose to look for illegal opportunities or to commit violent acts in the first place.

Nor can we hope that organizing citizens around reducing opportunities for crime, cleaning up garbage, and maintaining order will necessarily lead to later activity that addresses the causes of crime. If neighborhood residents succeed in organizing themselves around relatively straightforward tasks, like starting block watches, keeping the streets clean, or displacing vagrants, then the organizers may gain confidence. This may increase their sense of control over their environment, and this in turn may lead to action like neighborhood-based employment and extended families, which proceeds beyond control and addresses the causes of crime. But such a progression is not inevitable. It is just as likely that the initial organization of citizens around the need to clean up garbage or throw out drunks will lead to other forms of order maintenance and target hardening that never ask why crime is being committed. Ultimately, a strategy of opportunity reduction alone in the inner city may only teach citizens to become better controllers—surrogate police who simply try to keep the lid on.

### Taking the Lead

Have police and police-type activities no role in the inner-city policy I am suggesting? I believe that the police have a strong role to play—but a supporting role, if and when a capable neighborhood organization is willing to take the lead. At Umoja and El Centro, the community organization runs crime prevention activities, and the police play a backup role as deemed appropriate—not the other way around.

By contrast, in many places, crime prevention is viewed as something that is controlled by the police, who ask citizens for help. Such crime prevention invariably is of the opportunity-reduction variety (like block watches, hardware, and property identification). It rarely addresses the causes of crime, as the police are first to point out. At times, police crime prevention units perform an efficient job in guiding citizens to opportunity reduction. At other times, the units come closer to public relations vehicles.

In inner-city areas, citizens must take the lead in prevention because the police forces have been institutionalized to *react* to crime after it has been committed, not to *prevent* it from happening. As Paul Lavrakas points out:

> Too many of our "supposed" crime prevention experts and policymakers may well be expert about the workings of criminal justice system agencies, but do not appear to recognize the implication of acknowledging the limitations of these agencies in our democratic society. Until we change the emphasis of our public policies away from viewing the police, courts, and prisons as the *primary mechanisms* for reducing crime, I believe that we will continue to experience the tragic levels of victimization with which our citizens now live. These criminal justice agencies are our means of *reacting to crime*—but they should not be expected to prevent it by themselves.

With crime and fear rates so high, police have their hands full merely in reacting to crime. In spite of all the LEAA hardware and command-and-control strategies, police today still make arrests in only about 25 percent of the robberies reported to them and 15 percent of the burglaries. Partly because citizens often believe that police cannot do much, only about half of all crimes committed are even reported to police.[18]

A reason for encouraging crime prevention by indigenous neighborhood groups is that people are motivated to action if they have a stake in what is happening and if they can control their own turf—even if they make some mistakes in learning what to do. In American cities, most police do not live in the neighborhoods they patrol and therefore do not necessarily have a deep personal stake in the community. They are outsiders—professionals, like social workers, who come in to do a job and, however dedicated, leave for home at the end of their working day. By comparison, in Japan, police are assigned to small geographic areas where they live with their families, try to become integrated into neighborhood life, make door-to-door visits with their wives, are known as neighbors to most people there, and consequently receive much more cooperation from citizens—for example, in reporting crime—than do American police.[19] Reforms in this direction would be welcome in the United States, although I believe that they will be slow in coming.

It also makes sense that, if neighborhood organizations take the lead in crime prevention, they should be funded directly by grant makers rather than filtering the money through the criminal justice system.

Some police departments may resist playing only a supporting role; many other departments will be responsive. The record already shows that successful inner-city organizations can make the work of police much easier and more efficient. For example, key to El Centro's success are advocates, young people who work directly with youth in trouble with the law and often mediate between them and the criminal justice system. The police were at first wary of the advocates. Today, they concede that a call to an advocate can cut down on police work and often head off a personal problem with a potentially delinquent youth.[20]

More generally, if citizens believe that they themselves are the initiators rather than the recipients of "help" from outside professionals, and if those professionals—here the police—make themselves available for advice when needed, then the potential exists for more cooperation by citizens with police. This can result in more citizen reporting of crime, more tips on suspects, and improved police apprehension rates. Note that the means are not capital-intensive hardware and command-control policies imposed on the community by police but labor-intensive citizen self-help supported by a police force.

Of course, in inner-city communities where citizens and neighborhood groups are insufficiently organized to take the lead, we need to welcome whatever the police can do while we facilitate the development of community organizations.

## Using Crime Prevention as a Means to Economic Development

At Umoja and El Centro, crime prevention is not an end in itself. It is used as a means to make the community secure and encourage economic development, housing rehabilitation, the retention of old businesses, and the attraction of new ones. This, in turn, encourages employment, including work for the minority youth who commit so much of the crime.

I believe that this is a crucial precedent for the future. If we are to integrate neighborhood-based crime prevention in the inner city with a program to reduce the underclass, such prevention needs to be part of the economic development process, not conceptualized as an arm of the criminal justice system. This Charles Silberman recognized when he called El Centro "the best example of community regeneration I found anywhere in the United States."[21] Conceived as part of the development process, neighborhood crime prevention is more naturally made available to the grassroots constituencies that must make the program work, block by block. The jobs and sense of ownership that can be generated by development help address the causes of crime. There also are more opportunities to finance crime prevention—as, for example, when developers and neighborhood organizations set aside a portion of their property-management funds for security. By contrast, crime prevention as an adjunct of the criminal justice system is more vulnerable to the politics of the local police chief, his relationship with the mayor, and their attitudes toward citizen grass-roots leadership. Funding for programs is more dependent on outside grants limited to criminal justice and does not benefit as much from linkages to the economic development process.

## Working toward Financial Self-Sufficiency

The federal programs begun in the 1970s at LEAA, the Department of Housing and Urban Development (HUD), and ACTION have been closed down without adequate evaluations, along with many of the anticrime efforts of the neighborhood organizations they funded. By contrast, organizations that have survived over the years, like Umoja and El Centro, have taken at least the first steps toward financial self-sufficiency. They are by no means independent of various forms of public- and private-sector support. But they also are forming reciprocal arrangements with local businesses. Remember that the Umoja security patrols work under contract with local businesses and that the rehabilitated row houses are being turned into minority business—light trucking, printing, a restaurant. At El Centro, young people with cameras donated by a corporation take pictures that are used each year to produce a calendar sold around the world.

These are self-sufficient ways that help keep Umoja and El Centro afloat. To avoid the failures of the past, future national crime prevention programs must understand that creating financial self-sufficiency is as important as addressing the causes of crime and reducing opportunities for crime. Otherwise, new local programs again will go out of business. Local crime prevention programs can promote financial self-sufficiency if they are run by neighborhood organizations that have a sound financial-management system in place, a supportive board, a well-defined constituency, and a good track record in economic development, housing rehabilitation, and youth employment. Such stable, multipurpose organizations already have diversified sources of income, which can be useful in financially sustaining crime prevention designed as a security support for the other activities. In addition, a multipurpose organization can foster community interest and hence financial support. This is not always possible for a single-purpose neighborhood anticrime organization, which can lose interest and financial support after a wave of crime and fear subsides.

## A National Plan

To have any significant impact on crime and fear, neighborhood-based crime prevention and the employment and family programs that can be integrated with it need a policy that is national and coordinated in scope for both the private and public sectors.

In the private sector, the Eisenhower Foundation, as the re-creation of the Violence Commission, already is funding and facilitating neighborhood-based self-help among inner-city organizations across the country in the ways I have indicated. An attempt is being made to address the causes of crime while also reducing the opportunities for crime, to use crime prevention as a means of economic development, to create at least partial financial self-sufficiency, to directly fund inner-city organizations in order to ensure their leadership role, to allow programs to "bubble up" on the basis of local circumstances rather than "trickle down" from dictates in Washington, to provide unobtrusive technical assistance when needed, and—for the first time in a national program of this kind—to carefully evaluate what works and what does not through impact and process measures. In England, much the same kind of innovation is being undertaken by the private-sector National Association for the Care and Resettlement of Offenders,[22] and we are hoping to gain perspective through ongoing comparisons of our results.

Parallel to the work of the Eisenhower Foundation, the Local Initiatives Support Corporation (LISC) and developer James Rouse's Enterprise Foundation are facilitating neighborhood economic development and housing rehabilitation across the country. In some cities, LISC, the Enterprise Foundation, and the Eisenhower Foundation are making grants and loans or providing technical assistance to the same neighborhood organizations.

This is a modest but hopeful beginning for creating a national perspective in the private sector that integrates crime prevention into the economic development process. But the need is too great and resources today are too limited for the private sector to cover more than a part. Even with some progress toward self-sufficiency, Umoja and El Centro continue to need much public-sector support. And even if there were sufficient private-sector monies, it is better to have a public- and private-sector mix of resources in order to avoid the undue influence of any one funding source. In the 1980s, there is much potential for such a mix, especially for using public-sector challenge grants to leverage private-sector matches.

To ensure the link between economic development and crime prevention, it might help to give the national public-sector lead to a development agency rather than to a criminal justice agency. For example, the late Monsignor Geno Baroni's Office of Neighborhood Development at HUD was evaluated as successful by the Urban Institute.[23] There is bipartisan support in Congress for a new program, and it could take the public-sector lead for the kind of effort I have been describing.

Although initial bureaucratic resistance can be expected to the notion of a developmental rather than a criminal justice setting, there is a precedent. In the late 1970s, the crime prevention program that the author administered at HUD was accepted to the extent that the Justice Department, the Labor Department, and the Department of Health and Human Services transferred discretionary monies to HUD for youth-employment, victim/

witness, juvenile-delinquency-prevention, and drug-abuse-prevention components. Within HUD, career civil servants at first conceived the effort as a security target-hardening program but later came to refer to it as an anticrime program and embraced the importance of resident initiatives and employment to get at the causes of crime.

Whatever the federal institutional focus for development and prevention, attention should be paid to Jeff Faux's comment that "national economic policy remains the only significant organized human activity in America where planning is considered irrational."[24] Without entering the debates over urban banks, industrial policy, or the mobility of capital in the hands of those who have no stake in a community, I can foresee the benefits of planning the crime prevention underpinning of public outlays that develop the inner city and its underclass.

On the basis of past federal experience, it appears that public-sector support for neighborhood organizations needs to reduce red tape and that it could operate through private-sector mediating institutions. I am not calling for contracting out government to the profit-making private sector; there have been too many instances of appalling inefficiency and abuse.[25] But nonprofit mechanisms through which public support could be channeled hold promise, I believe, for streamlining bureaucracy, creating close relationships to local neighborhood organizations, and avoiding excessive costs to the taxpayer.

The most basic need is to improve the managerial competence of existing neighborhood organizations capable of integrating development and prevention. Private-sector national groups like the Support Center, the Center for Community Change, the Public/Private Ventures Training Institute, the Enterprise Foundation, and LISC have done or are doing such training, but the public sector needs to become reinvolved. We also need to expand the number of solid neighborhood organizations in the future, especially in inner-city areas. LISC estimates that there are now over two hundred well-established neighborhood organizations in the country. We need perhaps one thousand such organizations in the next ten years and three times that number by the year 2000. The political trick will be to empower such institutions without threatening those who want to continue the dependency on outsiders that Comer has documented as characteristic of our policy toward the underclass.

## THE AGENCIES OF CONTROL

Most volumes on policy against crime end with a phrase like, "Of course, the criminal justice system cannot do the job alone." The tone of this book has been more the opposite—that we should not downgrade the Violence Commission's concern for law and order, even though future national priorities need to be redirected to more promising strategies. The commission shared Lavrakas's caution that, as an instrument of response, not prevention, the criminal justice system must be made more efficient.

Others have thoroughly debated the criminal justice reforms that make most sense for the rest of the century.[26] My interest here is merely to touch upon some of the criminal justice policies that fit the recommendations of the original commission and the themes of this update.

There is little disagreement on the appropriateness of an improved law-enforcement strategy when it comes to political assassination and terrorism. The typical presidential assassin is not a member of a disenfranchised minority but an idiosyncratic loner who needs to be controlled. The original recommendations of the Violence Commission still need to be carried out. A democracy must debate the issues underlying a terrorist attack but cannot be blackmailed by the planned violence of trained professionals. That is why Kupperman's tough policies are in order.

The Violence Commission joined the Katzenbach Commission in seeking improved treatment of victims by the criminal justice system—especially through comprehensive crisis and treatment centers for victims, financial victim-compensation programs, and efforts to assist witnesses (who often are also victims) in testifying. Inner-city minorities are disproportionately victims, as well as offenders, in individual violence. The bipartisan federal interest in improving the treatment of victims that began in the 1970s and has expanded in the 1980s would do well to focus on inner-city populations, where the view often is held that the system of justice also has been disproportionately victimizing them. As an added potential benefit, inner-city victims who believe that they are better treated by the system may be more motivated to participate in citizen-based self-help crime prevention.

Although technology often may be the appropriate way to improve the functioning of the justice system, people-oriented programs can be just as efficient—and can serve to employ inner-city minorities. Increased employment of minority police in minority communities can improve community trust, citizen reporting, and therefore police apprehension rates. It also can redress symptoms of the more underlying issues of race that often serve to trigger group disorder, as has been evident in the Liberty City, Miami, riots of the 1980s. Computerized systems now track cases and identify repeat offenders, but the overburdened courts can be relieved as well through training and employing inner-city youths as paraprofessionals to assist prosecutors, public defenders, victims, and witnesses. By successfully bridging between prison and permanent jobs that become the key to a stable life, programs like Vera's Neighborhood Work Project can allow for more efficient use of prison space for those who must be incarcerated.

As the first major publication to report on the cohort studies showing that a very small proportion of violent repeat offenders commits most vio-

lent crime,[27] the Violence Commission final report began the modern debate on who in fact must be incarcerated. The findings on repeat offenders,
plus the acknowledged limitations of deterrence as a national policy, have
led many to advocate the currently fashionable policy of selective
incapacitation[28] for identifying repeaters as early as possible and keeping
them locked up (for periods of time that are still being debated).

In fact, some controversies on criminal justice policy can be minimized
and efficiency can be improved by following the implications that flow from
a strategy of selective incapacitation. Police and prosecutor resources can
be directed toward career criminals and violent juveniles. Judges can set
aside outmoded notions of deterrence and simply keep high-risk offenders
off the streets. Prison officials and parole authorities need not waste time
with emotional and ideological arguments over constructing more prisons
versus abandoning them; rather, high-risk offenders can be imprisoned and
lower risk offenders diverted to other settings.[29]

I believe that society must be protected and that incapacitation, when
applied with considered judgment rather than wholesale abandon, can be
one imperfect means. But national policy must never lose sight of the limitations to incapacitation.

The most obvious concern is the possibility of unjustly sentencing an
offender to a prison term on the basis of a false prediction of his future
criminality. After a relatively brief time, most high-risk youth leave high-
risk, low-return street crime for less dangerous criminal opportunities and
for places in the legal labor market.[30] Selective incapacitation for long periods interrupts the process. As a result, unless we keep high-risk youths
in prison till they are old men (a policy advocated by some), it is possible
that, upon release, they will continue in high-risk crime. They will have
been stockpiled in a prison system that reinforces the underclass and
teaches violence.

Umoja, El Centro, and other groups are successfully dealing with these
same young repeaters in carefully coordinated and managed community
programs. Even with their intensity, such programs cost less than imprisonment (which is more per year than room, board, and tuition at Yale).
Recidivism rates, at least at successful operations like Umoja and El Centro, are far lower than for offenders released from prison. As Elliott Currie
observes:

> Perhaps, surprisingly, some of the same evidence often presented to support an
> anticrime strategy that relies heavily on "incapacitation" *also* supports (indeed
> more convincingly) an intensified search for more effective programs of inter-
> vention *outside* the correctional system.

Why have policymakers and researchers chosen to look mainly at the criminal justice system when using the findings that relatively few offenders commit most violent acts?

We ought to keep in mind, as well, that the criminal justice system has already had considerable success in incapacitating repeaters, so the margin for improvement is not wide. Also, the weakest part of the system is police apprehension, so that improving selective incapacitation depends considerably on improving arrest rates at the front end—which has proved very difficult to do.

Ultimately, selective incapacitation is limited because it conveniently dodges the issue of underlying causes and the fact that the overwhelmingly white-controlled criminal justice system is creating an even more predominantly black and Hispanic prison population. Even if false predictions were not an issue, the possibility exists that the incapacitated repeaters will simply be replaced by a fresh cohort of offenders generated by the unchanged fabric of our society, economy, and policy.

## CONCLUSION

The Bureau of the Census reports that perhaps one-third of all households in the United States are touched by major crime in a given year.[31] Because crime affects so many of us, it is a personal, gut-level issue. As Elliott Currie implies, the reason for taking one policy position on violence rather than another often seems to have less to do with theory, logic, or scientific evidence than with the political and social agendas tapped by those visceral feelings.

Even with the experience and empirical findings that support it, the potential of neighborhood, family, and employment as a national policy of crime prevention integrated with a policy to reduce the underclass will be resisted by those who are unable or unwilling to move beyond preconceptions and face the limitations of deterrence and incapacitation. Those who say that the relationship between unemployment and crime is too complex to unite structural labor-market policy and crime prevention policy cannot be paying attention to Taggart's study of federal programs and the Vera and Rand studies funded by the federal government. Those who say that they have never seen the causes of crime and that we cannot create effective extended-family programs have not seen the Argus Community, the House of Umoja, and the evaluations of the U.S. General Accounting Office. Those who believe that police, rather than community organizations, must control neighborhood-based crime prevention appear uninformed of El Centro's good relations with the police and of the cost-effective benefits that Charles Silberman suggests can accrue from integrating community regeneration, economic development, and crime prevention.

I believe that Robert Kennedy, whose assassination led to the formation of the Violence Commission, would have shared endorsement by conservatives of Umoja. The advocate who sought "community action" and sponsored "mobilization for youth" in the 1960s came from a different philosophic position than the observer who today wants people to "pull themselves up by their bootstraps." Yet it is clear that certain political common ground is present—and must be utilized. Political feasibility is no small point when it comes to creating change in our inner cities and recognizing the continuing American dilemma of the underclass. We can recall the words of the Violence Commission. There may yet be hope that we can respond, in a civilized and durable way, to the often overwhelming challenges from within.

## NOTES

1. "The MacNeil-Lehrer Report," Public Broadcasting System, December 8, 1981.
2. James Q. Wilson quoted in Elliott Currie, "Fighting Crime," *Working Papers,* May-June 1982(a), p. 31.
3. Charles E. Silberman, *Criminal Violence, Criminal Justice* (New York: Random House, 1978).
4. Jane Howard, "Youth of the South Bronx," *New York Times Book Review,* January 30, 1984, p. 15.
5. Currie, "Fighting Crime," *Working Papers,* July-August 1982(b), p. 23.
6. Ford Foundation, *Annual Report, 1981* (New York: Ford Foundation, 1982).
7. National Urban League, *State of Black America, 1984* (New York: National Urban League, 1984).
8. A great deal of research and policy action is based on misperceptions and inaccurate definitions by mainstream outsiders of what *rational* means in the inner city. In *Dangerous Currents* (New York: Random House, 1983), Lester C. Thurow justifiably criticizes the use of the term in econometric modeling and forecasting on the basis of a definition derived from the nineteenth-century white middle-class notion of economic rationality set forth in the utilitarian economics of Jeremy Bentham.

   Using this definition, Edward C. Banfield, in *The Unheavenly City* (Boston: Little, Brown & Co., 1970), noted deploringly that inner-city minorities could not "defer gratification" (for example, by saving money) but instead seemed wedded to "immediate gratification" (like spending or mugging). In *Behind Ghetto Walls* (Chicago: Aldine, 1970), Lee Rainwater responded that immediate gratification is a very rational goal when, as often is the case in the underclass, the choice is between immediate gratification and no gratification at all. Similarly, a large proportion of robbery is committed by young poor minority men. The most common victims are other young poor minority men, who tend to have the least money and are the most likely to fight back with lethal weapons. To an outsider, it therefore might appear "irrational" to try to rob such young men. But this might be rational behavior, for example, to a young man who seeks the approval of peers in order to gain admittance to a gang.

   Unless researchers and policymakers take more care to understand how their values and experience differ from those of the inner city, federal actions regarding the underclass and crime will continue to be misdirected, to the detriment, of course, of the disadvantaged.
9. James W. Thompson, et al. *Employment and Crime* (Washington, D.C.: National Institute of Justice, October 1981).

10. One evaluation of a federal employment program found that many verbally skillful, enterprising, and intelligent minority youths dropped out of job training because they experienced more personal self-esteem and often derived more economic rewards from work in illegal markets than from the legal secondary markets offered by the federal government. See Nathan Caplan, "Competency among Hard-to-Employ Youths," *Institute for Social Research Newsletter* (Ann Arbor, Mich.: Institute for Social Research, June 1973).

11. See Thompson, *Employment and Crime.*

12. Currie, "Fighting Crime," 1982(b), p. 22.

13. As Ann Witte has suggested, empirical studies that do not show a relationship between unemployment and crime usually do not measure for "economic viability"—good jobs with decent wages. See Currie, "Fighting Crime," 1982(b), p. 21.

14. Currie, "Fighting Crime," 1982(b), p. 18.

15. Robert Taggart, *A Fisherman's Guide: An Assessment of Training and Remediation Strategies* (Kalamazoo, Mich.: Upjohn Institute, 1981).

16. See, for example, James Q. Wilson, *Thinking about Crime* (New York: Basic Books, 1975). For a critique, see Lynn A. Curtis, "The New Criminology," *Society,* March-April 1977, p. 8.

17. Aaron Podolefsky, "Community Response to Crime Prevention: The Mission District," *Journal of Community Action* 1, no. 5:43–49.

18. See, for example, Lynn A. Curtis, *Criminal Violence* (Lexington, Mass.: Lexington Books, 1973).

19. William Clifford, *Crime Control in Japan* (Lexington, Mass.: Lexington Books, 1976).

20. Silberman, *Criminal Violence,* p. 439.

21. Ibid., p. 434.

22. National Association for the Care and Resettlement of Offenders (NACRO), *Annual Report, 1982–1983* (London: NACRO, 1983).

23. Neil S. Mayer and Sue A. Marshall, with Jennifer L. Blake, *Neighborhood Organizations and Community Development* (Washington, D.C.: Urban Institute, 1983).

24. Jeff Faux, "Who Plans?" *Working Papers,* November-December 1982, p. 13.

25. Robert Kuttner, "Going Private," *New Republic,* May 30, 1983, p. 29.

26. See, for example, Silberman, *Criminal Violence.*

27. The study was later published as Marvin E. Wolfgang et al., *Delinquency in a Birth Cohort* (Chicago: University of Chicago Press, 1972).

28. See, for example, Peter W. Greenwood, with Allan Abrahamse, *Selective Incapacitation* (Santa Monica: Rand Corporation, 1982).

29. See Kenneth R. Feinberg, ed., Foreword to *Violent Crime in America* (Washington, D.C.: National Policy Exchange, 1983).

30. Michael E. Smith and James W. Thompson, "Employment, Youth and Violent Crime" in Feinberg, *Violent Crime.*

31. U.S. Department of Justice, *Sourcebook of Criminal Justice Statistics—1982* (Washington, D.C.: U.S. Government Printing Office, 1983).

# APPENDIX

**Table 1.** City Survey Data, 1974: Direction of Crime Trends in the United States (Percentage Distribution for Population Aged 16 and Over)

| City | Increased | Same | Decreased | Total[a] |
|---|---|---|---|---|
| Boston | 80.8 | 11.5 | 2.0 | 94.3 |
| Houston | 75.7 | 16.0 | 3.6 | 95.3 |
| Miami | 69.7 | 15.9 | 5.3 | 90.9 |
| Minneapolis | 72.5 | 3.5 | 18.6 | 94.6 |
| San Francisco | 74.9 | 14.1 | 3.4 | 92.4 |
| Washington, D.C. | 59.8 | 22.1 | 8.0 | 89.9 |

Source: Adapted from U.S. Department of Justice, National Criminal Justice Information and Statistics Service, *Boston: Public Attitudes about Crime,* table 1, p. 14; *Houston: Public Attitudes about Crime,* table 1, p. 14; *Miami: Public Attitudes about Crime,* table 1, p. 14; *Minneapolis: Public Attitudes about Crime,* table 1, p. 16; *San Francisco: Public Attitudes about Crime,* table 1, p. 16; *Washington, D.C.: Public Attitudes about Crime,* table 1, p. 16.

[a]Percentages do not total to 100.0 because in some cases responses were "Not available" or the respondent answered "Don't know."

**Table 2.** Present Attitudes toward Personal Safety on the Streets Compared to a Year Ago: United States, 1969, 1970, 1973, 1975, 1977, 1978, 1981[a] (Percentage Distribution)

| Year | Increased | Same | Decreased | Total[b] |
|---|---|---|---|---|
| 1969 | 46.0 | 43.0 | 4.0 | 93.0 |
| 1970 | 62.0 | 30.0 | 3.0 | 95.0 |
| 1973 | 48.0 | 40.0 | 7.0 | 95.0 |
| 1975 | 70.0 | 24.0 | 3.0 | 97.0 |
| 1977 | 58.0 | 33.0 | 6.0 | 97.0 |
| 1978 | 46.0 | 42.0 | 7.0 | 95.0 |
| 1981 | 68.0 | 27.0 | 4.0 | 99.0 |

Source: Adapted from U.S. Department of Justice, Bureau of Justice Statistics, *Sourcebook of Criminal Justice Statistics, 1981,* figure 2.1, p. 178.

[a]This table was constructed from responses to the following question: "In the past year do you feel the crime rate in your area has been increasing, decreasing, or has it remained the same as it was before?"

[b]Percentages do not total to 100.0 because some respondents answered "Not sure."

**Table 3.** Respondents Reporting Fear of Walking Alone at Night: United States, 1967, 1972, 1975, 1979, 1981[a] (Percentage Distribution)

| Year | Yes | No | Total |
|------|------|------|-------|
| 1967 | 31.0 | 69.0 | 100.0 |
| 1972 | 42.0 | 58.0 | 100.0 |
| 1975 | 45.0 | 55.0 | 100.0 |
| 1979 | 42.0 | 58.0 | 100.0 |
| 1981 | 45.0 | 55.0 | 100.0 |

Source: Adapted from U.S. Department of Justice, Bureau of Justice Statistics, *Sourcebook of Criminal Justice Statistics, 1981*, figure 2.4, p. 181.
[a]This table was constructed from responses to the following question: "Is there any area right around here—that is, within a mile—where you would be afraid to walk alone at night?"

**Table 4.** Violent and Property Index Crimes: United States, 1969 to 1982

| Year | Violent Index Crimes[a] % (N) | Property Index Crimes[b] % (N) | Total Index Crimes % (N) |
|------|------|------|------|
| 1969 | 8.9 (661,870) | 91.1 (6,749,000) | 100.0 (7,410,900) |
| 1970 | 9.1 (738,820) | 90.9 (7,359,200) | 100.0 (8,098,000) |
| 1971 | 9.5 (816,500) | 90.5 (7,771,700) | 100.0 (8,588,200) |
| 1972 | 10.1 (834,900) | 89.9 (7,413,900) | 100.0 (8,248,800) |
| 1973 | 10.0 (875,910) | 90.0 (7,842,200) | 100.0 (8,718,100) |
| 1974 | 9.5 (974,720) | 90.5 (9,278,700) | 100.0 (10,253,400) |
| 1975 | 9.1 (1,026,280) | 90.9 (10,230,300) | 100.0 (11,256,600) |
| 1976 | 8.7 (986,580) | 91.3 (10,318,200) | 100.0 (11,304,800) |
| 1977 | 9.2 (1,009,500) | 90.8 (9,926,300) | 100.0 (10,935,800) |
| 1978 | 9.5 (1,061,830) | 90.5 (10,079,500) | 100.0 (11,141,300) |
| 1979 | 9.7 (1,178,540) | 90.3 (10,974,200) | 100.0 (12,152,700) |
| 1980 | 9.8 (1,308,900) | 90.2 (11,986,500) | 100.0 (13,295,400) |
| 1981 | 10.0 (1,321,900) | 90.0 (11,968,400) | 100.0 (13,290,300) |
| 1982 | 10.0 (1,285,710) | 90.0 (11,571,500) | 100.0 (12,857,210) |

Source: Adapted from U.S. Department of Justice, Federal Bureau of Investigation, *Uniform Crime Reports for the United States, 1978* and *1982: 1978*, table 2, p. 39; *1982*, table 2, p. 43.
[a]Includes murder and nonnegligent manslaughter, forcible rape, robbery, and aggravated assault.
[b]Includes burglary, larceny-theft, and motor-vehicle theft. In 1979, arson was added to the list of property index crimes.

**Table 5.** Violent Personal Crimes and Nonviolent Personal Crimes, Household Crimes, and Commercial Crimes: United States, 1973 to 1980

| Year | Violent: Personal Crimes[a] % (N) | Nonviolent: Personal and Household Sectors[b] % (N) | All Crimes[c] % (N) |
|------|------|------|------|
| 1973 | 8.8 | 91.2 | 100.0 |
|      | (2,960,900) | (30,514,200) | (33,475,100) |
| 1974 | 8.5 | 91.5 | 100.0 |
|      | (3,031,000) | (32,473,000) | (35,504,000) |
| 1975 | 7.9 | 92.1 | 100.0 |
|      | (2,862,000) | (33,237,000) | (36,099,000) |
| 1976 | 8.1 | 91.9 | 100.0 |
|      | (2,956,000) | (33,718,000) | (36,674,000) |
| 1977 | 8.0 | 92.0 | 100.0 |
|      | (2,976,000) | (34,414,000) | (37,389,000) |
| 1978 | 7.8 | 92.2 | 100.0 |
|      | (2,917,000) | (34,471,000) | (37,388,000) |
| 1979 | 8.1 | 91.9 | 100.0 |
|      | (3,077,000) | (35,090,000) | (38,167,000) |
| 1980 | 8.3 | 91.7 | 100.0 |
|      | (3,008,000) | (33,355,000) | (36,363,000) |

Source: Adapted from U.S. Department of Justice, National Criminal Justice Information and Statistics Service, *Criminal Victimization in the United States, 1973,* table 1, p. 67; *Criminal Victimization in the United States, 1975,* table 1, p. 17; *Criminal Victimization in the United States, 1976,* table 1, p. 22; *Criminal Victimization in the United States, 1977,* table 1, p. 20; U.S. Department of Justice, Bureau of Justice Statistics, *Criminal Victimization in the United States, 1978,* table 1, p. 18; *Criminal Victimization in the United States, 1979,* table 1, p. 22; *Criminal Victimization in the United States, 1980,* table 1, p. 22.

[a]Includes rape, personal-sector robbery, and aggravated assault. This category excludes single assault in order to make it more comparable to the *UCR* violent index crimes. As we have noted in the text, this category of violent personal crimes does not include criminal homicide, whereas it is included among the *UCR* violent index crimes. Also, this category does not include commercial-sector robbery because the NCS discontinued collecting commercial-sector data in 1977.

[b]Includes personal-sector theft and household-sector burglary, larceny- and motor-vehicle theft.

[c]Includes personal-sector victimizations and household-sector incidents. A victimization is person-based, whereas an incident is event-based. Each victim in an event is counted in personal-sector victimizations, whereas for household-sector incidents each event is counted one time regardless of the number of persons victimized.

**Table 6.** Index Crimes: United States, 1969 to 1982 (Offense Rate per 100,000 Population)

| Year | Total Violent Index Crimes | Murder and Nonnegligent Manslaughter | Forcible Rape | Robbery | Aggravated Assault | Total Property Index Crimes | Burglary | Larceny-Theft | Motor-Vehicle Theft |
|---|---|---|---|---|---|---|---|---|---|
| | Violent Index Crimes | | | | | Property Index Crimes | | | |
| 1969 | 328.7 | 7.3 | 18.5 | 148.4 | 154.5 | 3351.3 | 984.1 | 1930.9 | 436.2 |
| 1970 | 363.5 | 7.9 | 18.7 | 172.1 | 164.8 | 3621.0 | 1084.9 | 2079.3 | 456.8 |
| 1971 | 396.0 | 8.6 | 20.5 | 188.0 | 178.8 | 3768.8 | 1163.5 | 2145.5 | 459.8 |
| 1972 | 401.0 | 9.0 | 22.5 | 180.7 | 188.8 | 3560.4 | 1140.8 | 1993.6 | 426.1 |
| 1973 | 417.4 | 9.4 | 24.5 | 183.1 | 200.5 | 3737.0 | 1222.5 | 2071.9 | 442.6 |
| 1974 | 461.1 | 9.8 | 26.2 | 209.3 | 215.8 | 4389.3 | 1437.7 | 2489.5 | 462.2 |
| 1975 | 481.5 | 9.6 | 26.3 | 218.2 | 227.4 | 4800.2 | 1525.9 | 2804.8 | 469.4 |
| 1976 | 459.6 | 8.7 | 26.4 | 195.8 | 228.7 | 4806.8 | 1439.4 | 2921.3 | 446.1 |
| 1977 | 466.6 | 8.8 | 29.1 | 187.1 | 241.5 | 4588.4 | 1410.9 | 2729.9 | 447.6 |
| 1978 | 486.9 | 9.0 | 30.8 | 191.3 | 255.9 | 4622.4 | 1423.7 | 2743.9 | 454.7 |
| 1979 | 535.5 | 9.7 | 34.5 | 212.1 | 279.1 | 4986.0 | 1499.1 | 2988.4 | 498.5 |
| 1980 | 580.8 | 10.2 | 36.4 | 243.5 | 290.6 | 5319.1 | 1668.2 | 3156.3 | 494.6 |
| 1981 | 576.9 | 9.8 | 35.6 | 250.6 | 280.9 | 5223.0 | 1632.1 | 3122.3 | 468.7 |
| 1982 | 555.3 | 9.1 | 33.6 | 231.9 | 280.8 | 4997.8 | 1475.2 | 3069.8 | 452.8 |
| Percentage Change, 1969 to 1982 | (+68.9) | (+24.7) | (+81.6) | (+56.3) | (+81.8) | (+49.1) | (+49.9) | (+59.0) | (+3.8) |

Source: Adapted from U.S. Department of Justice, Federal Bureau of Investigation, *Uniform Crime Reports for the United States, 1978 and 1982: 1978*, table 2, p. 39; *1982*, table 2, p. 43.

**Table 7.** Victimization by Violent Personal Crimes: United States, 1973 to 1980 (Rate per 100,000 Population Aged 12 and Over)

| Year | Total Violent Personal Victimization | Rape | Personal-Sector Robbery | Aggravated Assault |
|---|---|---|---|---|
| 1973 | 1800.0 | 100.0 | 700.0 | 1000.0 |
| 1974 | 1840.0 | 100.0 | 710.0 | 1030.0 |
| 1975 | 1710.0 | 90.0 | 670.0 | 950.0 |
| 1976 | 1720.0 | 80.0 | 650.0 | 990.0 |
| 1977 | 1710.0 | 90.0 | 620.0 | 1000.0 |
| 1978 | 1660.0 | 100.0 | 590.0 | 970.0 |
| 1979 | 1730.0 | 110.0 | 630.0 | 990.0 |
| 1980 | 1660.0 | 90.0 | 650.0 | 920.0 |
| Percentage Change, 1973 to 1980 | (−7.8) | (−10.0) | (−7.1) | (−8.0) |

Source: Adapted from U.S. Department of Justice, National Criminal Justice Information and Statistics Service, *Criminal Victimization in the United States, 1973,* table 1, p. 67; *Criminal Victimization in the United States, 1974,* table 1, p. 17; *Criminal Victimization in the United States, 1975,* table 1, p. 17; *Criminal Victimization in the United States, 1976,* table 1, p. 22; *Criminal Victimization in the United States, 1977,* table 1, p. 20; U.S. Department of Justice, Bureau of Justice Statistics, *Criminal Victimization in the United States, 1978,* table 1, p. 18; *Criminal Victimization in the United States, 1979,* table 1, p. 22; *Criminal Victimization in the United States, 1980,* table 1, p. 22.

**Table 8.** Rate Comparisons Between the *UCR*[a] and the NCS[b]: Rape, Robbery, and Aggravated Assault (Rate per 100,000: Total Population, *UCR*; Population Aged 12 and Over, NCS)

| Year | Rape | | Robbery | | Aggravated Assault | |
|---|---|---|---|---|---|---|
| | *UCR* | NCS | *UCR* | NCS[c] | *UCR* | NCS |
| 1973 | 24.5 | 100.0 | 183.1 | 700.0 | 200.5 | 1000.0 |
| 1974 | 26.2 | 100.0 | 209.3 | 710.0 | 215.8 | 1030.0 |
| 1975 | 26.3 | 90.0 | 218.2 | 670.0 | 227.4 | 950.0 |
| 1976 | 26.4 | 80.0 | 195.8 | 650.0 | 228.7 | 990.0 |
| 1977 | 29.1 | 90.0 | 187.1 | 620.0 | 241.5 | 1000.0 |
| 1978 | 30.8 | 100.0 | 191.3 | 590.0 | 255.9 | 970.0 |
| 1979 | 34.5 | 110.0 | 212.1 | 630.0 | 279.1 | 990.0 |
| 1980 | 36.4 | 90.0 | 243.5 | 650.0 | 290.6 | 920.0 |
| Percentage Change, 1973 to 1980 | (+48.6) | (−10.0) | (+33.0) | (−7.1) | (+44.9) | (−8.0) |

[a]These rates were obtained from table 6.
[b]These rates were obtained from table 7.
[c]NCS rates include only personal-sector robbery.

**Table 9.** Violent Index Crimes by City and Rural Areas: United States, 1969 to 1982 (Offense Rate per 100,000 Population)

| Year | Total Violent Index Crimes | | Murder and Nonnegligent Manslaughter | | Forcible Rape | | Robbery | | Aggravated Assault | |
|---|---|---|---|---|---|---|---|---|---|---|
| | City[a] | Rural[b] | City | Rural | City | Rural | City | Rural | City | Rural |
| 1969 | 434.9 | 102.9 | 8.5 | 4.9 | 21.0 | 10.6 | 219.2 | 13.4 | 186.2 | 73.9 |
| 1970 | 501.2 | 101.9 | 9.3 | 5.5 | 22.4 | 9.5 | 264.4 | 13.3 | 205.1 | 73.6 |
| 1971 | 538.6 | 115.7 | 10.3 | 5.9 | 24.5 | 10.7 | 284.1 | 14.5 | 219.7 | 84.6 |
| 1972 | 538.3 | 128.2 | 10.7 | 6.2 | 27.3 | 10.9 | 271.7 | 16.1 | 228.7 | 94.9 |
| 1973 | 552.4 | 134.0 | 11.1 | 6.5 | 29.7 | 11.9 | 270.2 | 16.7 | 241.4 | 98.9 |
| 1974 | 602.9 | 161.6 | 11.4 | 7.8 | 31.5 | 13.1 | 303.3 | 22.7 | 256.7 | 118.0 |
| 1975 | 628.2 | 176.8 | 11.1 | 8.4 | 31.7 | 13.2 | 315.9 | 24.9 | 269.4 | 130.4 |
| 1976 | 580.2 | 174.2 | 9.9 | 7.5 | 30.8 | 13.3 | 275.9 | 20.7 | 263.7 | 132.6 |
| 1977 | 584.8 | 175.5 | 10.2 | 7.9 | 34.2 | 14.4 | 262.4 | 20.8 | 278.1 | 132.4 |
| 1978 | 602.4 | 185.4 | 10.1 | 7.9 | 36.0 | 14.9 | 262.9 | 21.4 | 293.4 | 141.2 |
| 1979 | 668.3 | 194.0 | 11.2 | 7.6 | 40.7 | 15.6 | 293.6 | 22.8 | 322.8 | 148.1 |
| 1980 | 745.9 | 185.9 | 11.8 | 7.4 | 43.1 | 16.0 | 341.5 | 23.0 | 349.6 | 139.5 |
| 1981 | 752.1 | 179.4 | 11.4 | 7.0 | 42.5 | 15.7 | 357.7 | 22.1 | 340.4 | 134.6 |
| 1982 | 722.6 | 184.2 | 10.8 | 6.8 | 40.3 | 15.4 | 334.8 | 20.4 | 336.7 | 141.6 |
| Percentage Change, 1969 to 1982 | (+66.2) | (+79.0) | (+27.1) | (+38.8) | (+91.9) | (+45.3) | (+52.7) | (+52.2) | (+80.8) | (+91.6) |

Source: Adapted from U.S. Department of Justice, Federal Bureau of Investigation, *Uniform Crime Reports for the United States, 1969–1982: 1969,* table 9, pp. 94–95; *1970,* table 9, pp. 104–05; *1971,* table 9, pp. 100–01; *1972,* table 10, pp. 102–03; *1973,* table 10, pp. 104–05; *1974,* table 14, pp. 160–61; *1975,* table 14, pp. 160–61; *1976,* table 14, pp. 153–54; *1977,* table 14, pp. 153–54; *1978,* table 14, pp. 168–69; *1979,* table 14, pp. 170–71; *1980,* table 14, pp. 173–74; *1981,* table 13, pp. 144–45; *1982,* table 13, pp. 149–50.

[a]Refers to "Total Cities" in the *UCR* source tables.

[b]Refers to "Rural Areas" in the *UCR, 1969–1979* source tables and to "Rural Counties" in the *UCR, 1980–1982* source tables.

**Table 10.** Violent Personal Crimes: Type of Locality or Residence of Victims: United States, 1973 to 1980 (Victimization Rate per 100,000 Resident Population Aged 12 and Over)

| | Rape | | | | Personal-Sector Robbery | | | | Aggravated Assault | | | |
|---|---|---|---|---|---|---|---|---|---|---|---|---|
| | Metropolitan | | | | Metropolitan | | | | Metropolitan | | | |
| Year | Central City | Outside Central City | Nonmetro-politan | Total | Central City | Outside Central City | Nonmetro-politan | Total | Central City | Outside Central City | Nonmetro-politan | Total |
| 1973 | 150.0 | 110.0 | 100.0 | 100.0 | 1240.0 | 570.0 | 300.0 | 700.0 | 1310.0 | 990.0 | 800.0 | 1000.0 |
| 1974 | 150.0 | 90.0 | 60.0 | 100.0 | 1250.0 | 610.0 | 320.0 | 710.0 | 1420.0 | 1020.0 | 670.0 | 1030.0 |
| 1975 | 140.0 | 70.0 | 80.0 | 90.0 | 1240.0 | 560.0 | 280.0 | 670.0 | 1280.0 | 920.0 | 690.0 | 950.0 |
| 1976 | 130.0 | 80.0 | 50.0 | 80.0 | 1230.0 | 510.0 | 260.0 | 650.0 | 1270.0 | 980.0 | 720.0 | 990.0 |
| 1977 | 120.0 | 90.0 | 60.0 | 90.0 | 1190.0 | 490.0 | 260.0 | 620.0 | 1310.0 | 980.0 | 730.0 | 1000.0 |
| 1978 | 160.0 | 90.0 | 50.0 | 100.0 | 990.0 | 600.0 | 220.0 | 590.0 | 1410.0 | 840.0 | 740.0 | 970.0 |
| 1979 | 140.0 | 110.0 | 80.0 | 110.0 | 1170.0 | 560.0 | 220.0 | 630.0 | 1330.0 | 980.0 | 710.0 | 990.0 |
| 1980 | 130.0 | 90.0 | 70.0 | 90.0 | 1310.0 | 510.0 | 260.0 | 650.0 | 1200.0 | 890.0 | 720.0 | 920.0 |
| Percentage Change, 1973 to 1980 | (−13.3) | (−18.2) | (−30.0) | (−10.0) | (+5.6) | (−10.5) | (−13.3) | (−7.1) | (−8.4) | (−10.1) | (−10.0) | (−8.0) |

Source: Adapted from U.S. Department of Justice, National Criminal Justice Information and Statistics Service, *Criminal Victimization in the United States, 1973,* table 25, p. 80; *Criminal Victimization in the United States, 1974,* table 25, p. 32; *Criminal Victimization in the United States, 1975,* table 29, p. 36; *Criminal Victimization in the United States, 1976,* table 18, p. 34; *Criminal Victimization in the United States, 1977,* table 19, p. 31; U.S. Department of Justice, Bureau of Justice Statistics, *Criminal Victimization in the United States, 1978,* table 19, p. 32; *Criminal Victimization in the United States, 1979,* table 19, p. 36; *Criminal Victimization in the United States, 1980,* table 19, pp. 34–35.

**Table 11.** Total Violent Index Crimes by City Population: United States, 1969 to 1982 (Offense Rate per 100,000 Population)

| Year | 250,000 and over | 100,000 to 249,999 | 50,000 to 99,999 | 25,000 to 49,999 | 10,000 to 24,999 | Under 10,000 |
|---|---|---|---|---|---|---|
| 1969 | 859.7 | 358.5 | 231.8 | 173.9 | 135.7 | 108.6 |
| 1970 | 980.4 | 450.3 | 273.5 | 214.4 | 159.2 | 141.4 |
| 1971 | 1047.5 | 503.3 | 299.8 | 242.8 | 187.6 | 170.8 |
| 1972 | 998.6 | 502.3 | 322.5 | 267.3 | 199.8 | 203.8 |
| 1973 | 1003.4 | 545.0 | 371.5 | 295.2 | 220.7 | 199.0 |
| 1974 | 1107.9 | 600.0 | 405.8 | 330.6 | 249.7 | 217.8 |
| 1975 | 1158.9 | 631.6 | 450.7 | 343.0 | 267.8 | 231.5 |
| 1976 | 1095.4 | 572.7 | 415.9 | 337.9 | 254.1 | 215.5 |
| 1977 | 1070.4 | 599.6 | 444.0 | 341.8 | 264.5 | 230.1 |
| 1978 | 1120.8 | 626.9 | 486.1 | 364.2 | 275.5 | 244.9 |
| 1979 | 1237.8 | 701.5 | 525.5 | 420.1 | 315.3 | 278.6 |
| 1980 | 1414.2 | 812.4 | 602.5 | 454.6 | 352.1 | 297.5 |
| 1981 | 1440.9 | 826.4 | 583.7 | 451.9 | 342.3 | 291.0 |
| 1982 | 1353.9 | 778.6 | 560.8 | 431.3 | 320.3 | 284.1 |
| Percentage Change, 1969 to 1982 | (+57.5) | (+117.2) | (+141.9) | (+148.0) | (+136.0) | (+161.6) |

Source: Adapted from U.S. Department of Justice, Federal Bureau of Investigation, *Uniform Crime Reports for the United States, 1969–1982*: *1969,* table 9, pp. 94–95; *1970,* table 9, pp. 104–05; *1971,* table 9, pp. 100–101; *1972,* table 10, pp. 102–03; *1973,* table 10, pp. 104–05; *1974,* table 14, pp. 160–61; *1975,* table 14, pp. 160–61; *1976,* table 14, pp. 153–54; *1977,* table 14, pp. 153–54; *1978,* table 14, pp. 168–69; *1979,* table 14, pp. 170–71; *1980,* table 14, pp. 173–74; *1981,* table 13, pp. 144–45; *1982,* table 13, pp. 149–50.

**Table 12.** Total Violent Index Crimes by Region: United States, 1969 to 1982 (Offense Rate per 100,000 Population)

| Year | United States | Northeast | North Central | South | West |
|------|--------------|-----------|---------------|-------|------|
| 1969 | 324.4 | 330.4 | 293.3 | 326.2 | 363.9 |
| 1970 | 360.0 | 385.3 | 323.2 | 362.2 | 380.0 |
| 1971 | 392.7 | 454.9 | 330.1 | 386.9 | 417.3 |
| 1972 | 397.7 | 449.8 | 334.6 | 391.4 | 438.0 |
| 1973 | 414.3 | 453.8 | 353.3 | 411.8 | 461.4 |
| 1974 | 458.8 | 495.7 | 409.5 | 447.0 | 507.2 |
| 1975 | 481.5 | 535.4 | 416.8 | 460.8 | 547.1 |
| 1976 | 459.6 | 523.6 | 381.7 | 429.3 | 548.3 |
| 1977 | 466.6 | 510.3 | 373.5 | 451.8 | 575.8 |
| 1978 | 486.9 | 528.6 | 378.3 | 478.7 | 608.3 |
| 1979 | 535.5 | 590.1 | 409.4 | 528.9 | 660.7 |
| 1980 | 580.8 | 660.2 | 433.5 | 568.7 | 712.5 |
| 1981 | 576.9 | 685.1 | 417.5 | 564.1 | 690.9 |
| 1982 | 555.3 | 638.8 | 401.2 | 562.4 | 653.0 |
| Percentage Change, 1969 to 1982 | (+71.2) | (+93.3) | (+36.8) | (+72.4) | (+79.4) |

Source: Adapted from U.S. Department of Justice, Federal Bureau of Investigation, *Uniform Crime Reports for the United States, 1969–1982: 1969,* table 3, pp. 58–63; *1970,* table 3, pp. 66–71; *1971,* table 3, pp. 62–67; *1972,* table 3, pp. 62–67; *1973,* table 3, pp. 60–65; *1974,* table 3, pp. 56–61; *1975,* table 3, pp. 50–55; *1976,* table 3, pp. 38–43; *1977,* table 3, pp. 38–43; *1978,* table 3, pp. 40–45; *1979,* table 3, pp. 42–47; *1980,* table 3, pp. 42–47; *1981,* table 3, pp. 40–45; *1982,* table 3, pp. 44–49.

**Table 13.** Percentage Distribution of Arrests for Violent Index Crimes by Sex: United States, 1969 to 1982

| Year | Total Violent Index Crimes Male % (N) | Female % (N) | Murder and Non-negligent Manslaughter Male % (N) | Female % (N) | Forcible Rape Male % (N) | Female % (N) | Robbery Male % (N) | Female % (N) | Aggravated Assault Male % (N) | Female % (N) |
|---|---|---|---|---|---|---|---|---|---|---|
| 1969 | 90.4 (195,350) | 9.6 (20,844) | 84.8 (9,763) | 15.2 (1,746) | 100.0 (14,428) | 0.0 (0) | 93.8 (71,757) | 6.2 (4,776) | 87.4 (99,402) | 12.6 (14,322) |
| 1970 | 90.4 (218,665) | 9.6 (23,240) | 84.6 (10,857) | 15.4 (1,979) | 100.0 (15,411) | 0.0 (0) | 93.9 (82,340) | 6.1 (5,347) | 87.4 (110,057) | 12.6 (15,914) |
| 1971 | 90.0 (245,788) | 10.0 (27,421) | 83.7 (12,184) | 16.3 (2,365) | 100.0 (16,582) | 0.0 (0) | 93.7 (95,293) | 6.3 (6,435) | 86.7 (121,729) | 13.3 (18,621) |
| 1972 | 90.0 (269,268) | 10.0 (29,953) | 84.6 (12,727) | 15.4 (2,322) | 100.0 (19,374) | 0.0 (0) | 93.5 (102,117) | 6.5 (7,100) | 86.8 (135,050) | 13.2 (20,531) |
| 1973 | 89.8 (260,800) | 10.2 (29,582) | 84.9 (12,223) | 15.1 (2,176) | 100.0 (19,198) | 0.0 (0) | 93.2 (94,998) | 6.8 (6,896) | 86.8 (134,381) | 13.2 (20,510) |
| 1974 | 89.8 (264,481) | 10.2 (30,136) | 85.4 (11,800) | 14.6 (2,018) | 100.0 (17,804) | 0.0 (0) | 93.2 (101,098) | 6.8 (7,383) | 86.6 (133,779) | 13.4 (20,735) |
| 1975 | 89.7 (332,133) | 10.3 (38,320) | 84.4 (13,912) | 15.6 (2,573) | 99.0 (21,748) | 1.0 (215) | 93.0 (120,650) | 7.0 (9,138) | 86.9 (175,823) | 13.1 (26,394) |
| 1976 | 89.5 (303,433) | 10.5 (35,416) | 85.1 (12,011) | 14.9 (2,102) | 99.1 (21,488) | 0.9 (199) | 92.9 (102,456) | 7.1 (7,840) | 86.9 (167,478) | 13.1 (25,275) |
| 1977 | 89.6 (346,510) | 10.4 (40,296) | 85.5 (14,670) | 14.5 (2,493) | 98.9 (25,518) | 1.1 (282) | 92.6 (113,399) | 7.4 (9,115) | 87.2 (192,923) | 12.8 (28,406) |
| 1978 | 89.8 (400,697) | 10.2 (45,425) | 85.9 (16,103) | 14.1 (2,652) | 99.1 (28,013) | 0.9 (244) | 92.6 (131,563) | 7.0 (9,918) | 87.3 (225,018) | 12.7 (32,611) |
| 1979 | 89.8 (390,566) | 10.2 (44,212) | 86.3 (15,761) | 13.7 (2,503) | 99.2 (28,945) | 0.8 (219) | 92.6 (121,107) | 7.4 (9,646) | 87.6 (224,753) | 12.4 (31,844) |
| 1980 | 90.0 (401,589) | 10.0 (44,784) | 87.2 (16,354) | 12.8 (2,391) | 99.1 (29,161) | 0.9 (270) | 92.8 (129,412) | 7.2 (10,064) | 87.6 (226,662) | 12.4 (32,059) |
| 1981 | 89.9 (417,757) | 10.1 (47,069) | 87.3 (17,846) | 12.7 (2,586) | 99.1 (29,772) | 0.9 (278) | 92.8 (136,816) | 7.2 (10,580) | 87.4 (233,323) | 12.6 (33,625) |
| 1982 | 89.6 (397,644) | 10.4 (46,216) | 86.7 (16,052) | 13.3 (2,459) | 99.1 (28,070) | 0.9 (262) | 92.7 (128,047) | 7.3 (10,071) | 87.1 (225,475) | 12.9 (33,424) |

Source: Adapted from U.S. Department of Justice, Federal Bureau of Investigation, *Uniform Crime Reports for the United States, 1969–1982: 1969*, table 29, p. 116; *1970*, table 30, p. 129; *1971*, table 31, p. 125; *1972*, table 34, p. 129; *1973*, table 32, p. 131; *1974*, table 36, p. 189; *1975*, table 38, p. 191; *1976*, table 34, p. 184; *1977*, table 34, p. 183; *1978*, table 34, p. 197; *1979*, table 34, p. 199; *1980*, table 34, p. 203; *1981*, table 35, p. 178; *1982*, table 35, p. 183.

Total Violent Index Crimes ... Murder & ...

| Year | Under Age 15 % | (N) | Ages 15 to 17 % | (N) | Ages 18 to 24 % | (N) | Age 25 and Over % | (N) | Under Age 15 % | (N) | Ages 15 to 17 % | (N) | Ages 18 to 24 % | (N) | Age 25 and Over % | (N) | Under Age 15 % | (N) | Ages 15 to 17 % | (N) | Ages 18 to 24 % | (N) | Age 25 and Over % | (N) | Under Age 15 % | (N) | Ages 15 to 17 % | (N) | Ages 18 to 24 % | (N) | Age 25 and Over % | (N) | Under Age 15 % | (N) | Ages 15 to 17 % | (N) | Ages 18 to 24 % | (N) | Age 25 and Over % | (N) |
|---|---|---|---|---|---|---|---|---|---|---|---|---|---|---|---|---|---|---|---|---|---|---|---|---|---|---|---|---|---|---|---|---|---|---|---|---|---|---|---|---|
| 1969 | 7.3 | (15,739) | 15.1 | (32,457) | 36.2 | (78,285) | 41.5 | (89,699) | 0.1 | (157) | 8.0 | (926) | 32.7 | (3,767) | 57.9 | (6,654) | 3.8 | (541) | 16.4 | (2,391) | 45.0 | (6,489) | 34.9 | (5,034) | 11.8 | (9,022) | 21.6 | (16,577) | 43.3 | (33,175) | 23.2 | (17,757) | 5.3 | (6,019) | 11.1 | (12,593) | 30.6 | (34,854) | 53.0 | (60,254) |
| 1970 | 7.1 | (17,283) | 15.4 | (37,313) | 36.0 | (86,939) | 41.5 | (100,319) | 1.5 | (187) | 9.0 | (1,159) | 33.0 | (4,229) | 56.5 | (7,265) | 4.1 | (634) | 16.7 | (2,571) | 43.7 | (6,735) | 35.5 | (5,471) | 11.1 | (9,695) | 22.4 | (19,594) | 43.6 | (38,221) | 23.0 | (20,177) | 5.4 | (6,767) | 11.1 | (13,989) | 30.0 | (37,754) | 53.5 | (67,461) |
| 1971 | 7.2 | (19,539) | 15.6 | (42,763) | 36.5 | (99,642) | 40.7 | (111,205) | 1.3 | (190) | 8.9 | (1,300) | 33.9 | (4,927) | 55.9 | (8,132) | 4.0 | (667) | 16.6 | (2,757) | 43.4 | (7,209) | 36.0 | (5,945) | 10.4 | (10,534) | 21.8 | (22,221) | 44.7 | (45,443) | 23.1 | (23,500) | 5.8 | (8,148) | 11.8 | (16,485) | 30.0 | (42,063) | 52.4 | (73,628) |
| 1972 | 7.2 | (21,520) | 15.4 | (46,035) | 36.0 | (107,627) | 41.4 | (123,860) | 1.5 | (221) | 9.4 | (1,413) | 32.8 | (4,944) | 56.5 | (8,461) | 4.2 | (818) | 15.6 | (3,024) | 42.8 | (8,293) | 37.4 | (7,231) | 10.4 | (11,387) | 21.5 | (23,436) | 44.0 | (48,077) | 24.1 | (26,279) | 5.8 | (9,094) | 11.7 | (18,162) | 29.8 | (46,313) | 52.6 | (81,889) |
| 1973 | 7.0 | (20,244) | 15.7 | (45,669) | 35.7 | (103,643) | 41.5 | (120,613) | 1.5 | (216) | 8.9 | (1,281) | 34.2 | (4,929) | 55.4 | (7,973) | 4.2 | (813) | 15.4 | (2,959) | 41.0 | (7,861) | 39.4 | (7,549) | 10.8 | (11,015) | 22.9 | (23,359) | 42.6 | (43,399) | 23.7 | (24,077) | 5.3 | (8,200) | 11.7 | (18,070) | 30.6 | (47,454) | 52.4 | (81,014) |
| 1974 | 6.4 | (18,904) | 16.2 | (47,595) | 37.1 | (109,316) | 40.2 | (118,566) | 1.5 | (206) | 8.6 | (1,193) | 34.9 | (4,826) | 55.0 | (7,584) | 4.3 | (771) | 15.1 | (2,684) | 40.7 | (7,250) | 39.9 | (7,086) | 9.2 | (9,984) | 23.4 | (25,361) | 44.3 | (48,074) | 23.1 | (25,002) | 5.1 | (7,943) | 11.9 | (18,357) | 31.8 | (49,166) | 51.2 | (78,894) |
| 1975 | 6.5 | (24,166) | 16.5 | (61,252) | 36.4 | (134,956) | 40.4 | (149,854) | 1.1 | (184) | 8.4 | (1,389) | 35.3 | (5,823) | 55.2 | (9,082) | 4.0 | (867) | 13.6 | (2,996) | 40.4 | (8,880) | 42.0 | (9,213) | 9.6 | (12,515) | 24.6 | (31,955) | 42.8 | (55,483) | 22.9 | (29,768) | 5.2 | (10,600) | 12.3 | (24,912) | 32.0 | (64,770) | 50.4 | (101,791) |
| 1976 | 6.1 | (20,813) | 15.9 | (53,902) | 35.8 | (121,038) | 42.2 | (142,913) | 1.4 | (190) | 7.9 | (1,112) | 33.4 | (4,711) | 57.4 | (8,055) | 4.2 | (915) | 13.0 | (2,830) | 39.9 | (8,658) | 42.8 | (9,275) | 9.2 | (10,156) | 24.3 | (26,834) | 42.5 | (46,866) | 24.0 | (26,395) | 5.0 | (9,552) | 12.0 | (23,126) | 31.5 | (60,803) | 51.5 | (94,839) |
| 1977 | 5.7 | (21,997) | 15.4 | (59,371) | 35.4 | (140,328) | 44.1 | (164,953) | 1.2 | (215) | 8.5 | (1,455) | 33.8 | (5,792) | 56.5 | (9,652) | 4.2 | (1,081) | 12.3 | (3,176) | 39.8 | (10,278) | 43.7 | (11,253) | 8.4 | (10,309) | 23.6 | (28,950) | 42.4 | (51,890) | 25.6 | (31,324) | 4.7 | (10,392) | 11.6 | (25,790) | 32.7 | (72,368) | 50.9 | (112,684) |
| 1978 | 5.8 | (25,940) | 15.6 | (69,653) | 36.1 | (160,952) | 42.5 | (189,357) | 1.3 | (244) | 8.0 | (1,491) | 34.1 | (6,401) | 56.7 | (10,609) | 3.9 | (1,102) | 12.1 | (3,415) | 37.8 | (10,694) | 46.2 | (13,034) | 9.2 | (13,086) | 24.7 | (35,002) | 42.9 | (58,605) | 24.6 | (34,747) | 4.5 | (11,508) | 11.6 | (29,745) | 33.1 | (85,232) | 50.9 | (130,987) |
| 1979 | 5.2 | (22,597) | 14.9 | (64,778) | 37.3 | (162,246) | 42.5 | (184,817) | 1.1 | (206) | 8.2 | (1,501) | 34.9 | (6,366) | 55.7 | (8,063) | 3.7 | (1,081) | 12.2 | (3,570) | 39.8 | (11,619) | 43.4 | (12,878) | 8.1 | (10,622) | 23.4 | (30,535) | 42.9 | (56,091) | 25.6 | (33,446) | 4.2 | (10,688) | 11.4 | (29,172) | 34.4 | (88,350) | 49.9 | (128,132) |
| 1980 | 4.8 | (21,181) | 14.6 | (65,039) | 37.3 | (166,596) | 43.4 | (193,557) | 1.1 | (200) | 8.2 | (1,542) | 35.4 | (6,636) | 44.7 | (10,376) | 3.6 | (1,052) | 11.2 | (3,294) | 39.2 | (11,529) | 46.0 | (13,556) | 7.1 | (9,941) | 23.0 | (32,056) | 42.9 | (59,873) | 27.8 | (37,606) | 3.9 | (9,988) | 10.9 | (28,147) | 34.2 | (88,558) | 51.1 | (132,028) |
| 1981 | 4.8 | (22,106) | 13.7 | (63,747) | 36.3 | (168,728) | 45.2 | (210,245) | 1.0 | (205) | 8.1 | (1,653) | 34.1 | (6,971) | 56.8 | (11,603) | 4.0 | (1,193) | 10.8 | (3,256) | 37.1 | (11,144) | 48.1 | (14,457) | 7.0 | (10,250) | 21.7 | (31,964) | 42.5 | (62,593) | 28.9 | (42,589) | 3.9 | (10,458) | 10.1 | (26,874) | 33.0 | (88,020) | 53.0 | (141,596) |
| 1982 | 4.5 | (19,894) | 12.7 | (56,469) | 36.2 | (160,777) | 46.6 | (206,720) | 1.0 | (183) | 7.5 | (1,396) | 34.4 | (6,370) | 57.1 | (10,562) | 4.0 | (1,134) | 10.7 | (3,025) | 37.4 | (10,581) | 48.0 | (13,592) | 6.6 | (9,114) | 19.8 | (27,366) | 42.9 | (59,273) | 30.7 | (42,965) | 3.7 | (9,463) | 9.5 | (24,682) | 32.7 | (84,553) | 54.2 | (140,201) |

Source: Adapted from U.S. Department of Justice, Federal Bureau of Investigation, *Uniform Crime Reports for the United States, 1969–1982: 1969*, table 27, pp. 113–14; *1970*, table 28, pp. 126–27; *1971*, table 29, pp. 122–23; *1972*, table 29, pp. 126–27; *1973*, table 30, pp. 128–29; *1974*, table 34, pp. 186–87; *1975*, table 36, pp. 188–89; *1976*, table 32, table 28, pp. 126–27; *1977*, table 32, pp. 180–81; *1978*, table 32, pp. 181–82; *1979*, table 32, pp. 194–95; *1980*, table 32, pp. 196–97; *1981*, table 31, pp. 200–201; *1982*, table 31, pp. 176–77.

**Table 14.** Arrests for Violent Index Crimes by Sex: United States, 1969 to 1981 (Rate per 100,000 Sex-Specific Population)[a]

| Year | Total Violent Index Crimes Male | Female | Murder and Non-negligent Manslaughter Male | Female | Forcible Rape Male | Female | Robbery Male | Female | Aggravated Assault Male | Female |
|---|---|---|---|---|---|---|---|---|---|---|
| 1969 | 276.6 | 28.5 | 13.8 | 2.4 | 20.4 | 0.0 | 101.6 | 6.5 | 140.8 | 19.6 |
| 1970 | 296.2 | 29.9 | 14.7 | 2.5 | 20.9 | 0.0 | 111.5 | 6.9 | 149.1 | 20.5 |
| 1971 | 324.7 | 34.4 | 16.1 | 3.0 | 21.9 | 0.0 | 125.9 | 8.1 | 160.8 | 23.4 |
| 1972 | 344.7 | 36.4 | 16.3 | 2.8 | 24.8 | 0.0 | 130.7 | 8.6 | 172.9 | 24.9 |
| 1973 | 345.5 | 37.2 | 16.2 | 2.7 | 25.4 | 0.0 | 125.8 | 8.7 | 178.0 | 25.8 |
| 1974 | 405.0 | 43.8 | 18.1 | 2.9 | 27.3 | 0.0 | 154.8 | 10.7 | 204.9 | 30.1 |
| 1975 | 380.6 | 41.7 | 15.9 | 2.8 | 24.9 | 0.2 | 138.2 | 9.9 | 201.5 | 28.7 |
| 1976 | 355.0 | 39.3 | 14.0 | 2.3 | 25.1 | 0.2 | 119.9 | 8.7 | 196.0 | 28.1 |
| 1977 | 359.4 | 39.5 | 15.2 | 2.4 | 26.5 | 0.3 | 117.6 | 8.9 | 200.1 | 27.8 |
| 1978 | 398.2 | 42.7 | 16.0 | 2.5 | 27.8 | 0.2 | 130.7 | 9.3 | 223.6 | 30.6 |
| 1979 | 392.7 | 42.0 | 15.8 | 2.4 | 29.1 | 0.2 | 121.8 | 9.2 | 226.0 | 30.3 |
| 1980 | 396.9 | 41.8 | 16.2 | 2.2 | 28.8 | 0.2 | 127.9 | 9.4 | 224.0 | 30.0 |
| 1981 | 401.0 | 42.7 | 17.1 | 2.3 | 28.6 | 0.2 | 131.3 | 9.6 | 224.0 | 30.5 |
| Percentage Change, 1969 to 1981 | (+45.0) | (+49.8) | (+23.9) | (-4.2) | (+40.2) | (-) | (+29.2) | (+47.7) | (+59.1) | (+55.6) |

[a]The computations presented in this table were derived as follows: (1) The percentages of the population that were male and female in each year were calculated from estimates of the resident population of the United States. See U.S. Bureau of the Census, Current Population Reports. *Estimates of the Population of the United States by Age, Race, and Sex, July 1, 1969-Th ...*

**Table 15.** Percentage Distribution of Arrests for Violent Index Crimes by Age: United States, 1969 to 1982

Murder and Nonnegligent

**Table 16.** Arrests for Violent Crimes by Age: United States, 1970 to 1981 (Rates per 100,000 Age-Specific Population)[a]

| | Total Violent Index Crimes | | | | Murder and Nonnegligent Manslaughter | | | | Forcible Rape | | | | Robbery | | | | Aggravated Assault | | | |
|---|---|---|---|---|---|---|---|---|---|---|---|---|---|---|---|---|---|---|---|---|
| Year | Under Age 15 | Ages 15 to 17 | Ages 18 to 24 | Age 25 and Over | Under Age 15 | Ages 15 to 17 | Ages 18 to 24 | Age 25 and Over | Under Age 15 | Ages 15 to 17 | Ages 18 to 24 | Age 25 and Over | Under Age 15 | Ages 15 to 17 | Ages 18 to 24 | Age 25 and Over | Under Age 15 | Ages 15 to 17 | Ages 18 to 24 | Age 25 and Over |
| 1970 | 40.1 | 424.3 | 486.0 | 121.7 | 0.4 | 13.2 | 23.6 | 8.8 | 1.5 | 29.2 | 37.6 | 6.6 | 22.5 | 222.8 | 213.6 | 24.5 | 15.7 | 159.1 | 211.0 | 81.8 |
| 1971 | 45.0 | 474.3 | 525.4 | 132.5 | 0.4 | 14.4 | 26.0 | 9.7 | 1.5 | 30.6 | 38.0 | 7.1 | 24.3 | 246.5 | 239.6 | 28.0 | 18.8 | 182.8 | 221.8 | 87.7 |
| 1972 | 49.1 | 486.4 | 545.5 | 141.9 | 0.5 | 14.9 | 25.0 | 9.7 | 1.9 | 32.0 | 42.0 | 8.3 | 26.0 | 247.5 | 243.7 | 30.1 | 20.8 | 191.9 | 234.7 | 93.8 |
| 1973 | 49.1 | 491.1 | 539.3 | 141.5 | 0.5 | 13.8 | 25.6 | 9.4 | 2.0 | 31.8 | 40.9 | 8.9 | 26.7 | 251.2 | 225.8 | 28.3 | 19.9 | 194.3 | 246.9 | 95.0 |
| 1974 | 54.4 | 591.6 | 647.0 | 159.3 | 0.6 | 14.8 | 28.6 | 10.2 | 2.2 | 33.4 | 42.9 | 9.5 | 28.7 | 315.2 | 284.6 | 33.7 | 22.9 | 228.2 | 291.0 | 106.0 |
| 1975 | 53.5 | 579.4 | 583.8 | 149.6 | 0.4 | 13.1 | 25.2 | 9.1 | 1.9 | 28.3 | 38.4 | 9.2 | 27.7 | 302.2 | 240.0 | 29.7 | 23.5 | 235.6 | 280.2 | 101.6 |
| 1976 | 48.4 | 520.6 | 530.5 | 144.1 | 0.4 | 10.7 | 20.6 | 8.1 | 2.1 | 27.3 | 37.9 | 9.4 | 23.6 | 259.2 | 205.4 | 26.6 | 22.2 | 223.3 | 266.5 | 95.6 |
| 1977 | 46.3 | 515.9 | 535.8 | 145.9 | 0.4 | 12.6 | 22.1 | 8.6 | 2.3 | 27.6 | 39.2 | 10.0 | 21.7 | 251.6 | 198.1 | 27.7 | 21.9 | 224.1 | 276.3 | 99.6 |
| 1978 | 53.5 | 580.0 | 589.0 | 158.8 | 0.5 | 12.4 | 23.4 | 8.9 | 2.3 | 28.4 | 39.1 | 10.9 | 27.0 | 291.4 | 214.4 | 29.2 | 23.8 | 247.7 | 311.8 | 109.8 |
| 1979 | 48.2 | 565.3 | 596.2 | 155.2 | 0.4 | 13.1 | 23.4 | 6.8 | 2.3 | 31.2 | 42.7 | 10.8 | 22.7 | 266.5 | 206.1 | 28.1 | 22.8 | 254.6 | 324.6 | 107.6 |
| 1980 | 45.0 | 578.5 | 606.2 | 158.4 | 0.4 | 13.7 | 24.1 | 8.5 | 2.2 | 29.3 | 42.0 | 11.1 | 21.1 | 285.1 | 217.9 | 30.8 | 21.2 | 250.4 | 322.2 | 108.0 |
| 1981 | 46.2 | 571.9 | 593.3 | 165.4 | 0.4 | 14.8 | 24.6 | 9.1 | 2.5 | 29.2 | 39.4 | 11.4 | 21.4 | 286.7 | 221.2 | 33.5 | 21.9 | 241.1 | 311.1 | 111.4 |
| Percentage Change, 1970 to 1981 | (+15.2) | (+34.8) | (+22.7) | (+35.9) | (0.0) | (+12.1) | (+5.6) | (+3.4) | (+66.7) | (0.0) | (+4.8) | (+72.7) | (−4.9) | (+28.7) | (+3.6) | (+36.7) | (+39.5) | (+51.5) | (+47.4) | (+36.2) |

[a]The computations presented in this table were derived as follows: (1) The percentage of the population in each age group was calculated from estimates of the resident population of the United States. See U.S. Bureau of the Census, Current Population Reports, *Estimates of the United States by Age, Race and Sex: July 1, 1969* (Washington, D.C.: U.S. Government Printing Office, 1969), table 2, p. 2; *Preliminary Estimates of the Population of the United States by Age, Sex, and Race: 1970 to 1981* (Washington, D.C.: U.S. Government Printing Office, 1982), table 2, pp. 26–43. (2) The percentage of the resident population in each age group in a year was multiplied by the "estimated population" covered by the *UCR* reporting agencies for the corresponding year as listed at the head of the *UCR* table, "Total Arrests, Distribution by Age," producing the number of persons in each age group in the "estimated population." This computation assumes that the distribution by age in the resident population of the United States in a given year is the same as that in the "estimated population" covered by the *UCR* reporting agencies for that same year. The *UCR* data on "estimated population" were obtained from U.S. Department of Justice, Federal Bureau of Investigation, *Uniform Crime Reports for the United States, 1969–1981* (Washington, D.C.: U.S. Government Printing Office, 1970–82): *1969*, pp. 113–14; *1970*, pp. 126–27; *1971*, pp. 122–23; *1972*, pp. 126–27; *1973*, pp. 128–29; *1974*, pp. 186–87; *1975*, pp. 188–89; *1976*, pp. 181–82; *1977*, pp. 180–81; *1978*, pp. 194–95; *1979*, pp. 196–97; *1980*, pp. 200–201; *1981*, pp. 171–72. (3) The number of arrests in each age group for a given year was divided by the number of persons in that age group as calculated from the "estimated population" for that year (see step 2), producing the age-specific arrest rate. The number of arrests within each age group in a year was obtained from the same table that provided the data on the "estimated population" covered by the *UCR* reporting agencies (see step 2). (4) The age-specific arrest rates calculated in step 3 were multiplied by 100,000 for purposes of standardization.

It also should be noted that census data were not available for 1969 in age groupings that allowed us to compute rates for this table.

**Table 17.** Percentage Distribution of Arrests for Violent Index Crimes by Race: United States, 1969 to 1982

| Year | Total Violent Index Crimes | | | Murder and Nonnegligent Manslaughter | | | Forcible Rape | | | Robbery | | | Aggravated Assault | | |
|---|---|---|---|---|---|---|---|---|---|---|---|---|---|---|---|
| | White % (N) | Black % (N) | Other[a] % (N) | White % (N) | Black % (N) | Other % (N) | White % (N) | Black % (N) | Other % (N) | White % (N) | Black % (N) | Other % (N) | White % (N) | Black % (N) | Other % (N) |
| 1969 | 42.5 (80,720) | 55.7 (105,781) | 1.8 (3,556) | 35.9 (3,743) | 61.9 (6,444) | 2.2 (225) | 47.8 (6,407) | 50.2 (6,726) | 2.0 (265) | 32.4 (21,127) | 65.8 (42,980) | 1.8 (1,171) | 49.0 (49,443) | 49.2 (49,631) | 1.8 (1,895) |
| 1970 | 44.7 (96,100) | 53.3 (114,602) | 2.0 (4,201) | 38.0 (4,503) | 59.9 (7,097) | 2.1 (247) | 50.4 (7,260) | 47.9 (6,900) | 1.7 (259) | 33.3 (24,770) | 64.8 (48,282) | 1.9 (1,432) | 52.2 (59,567) | 45.8 (52,323) | 2.0 (2,263) |
| 1971 | 43.1 (103,128) | 54.8 (131,245) | 2.1 (5,006) | 35.5 (4,716) | 62.2 (8,276) | 2.3 (310) | 47.8 (7,386) | 50.3 (7,781) | 1.9 (301) | 31.6 (26,524) | 66.4 (55,745) | 2.0 (1,667) | 50.9 (64,502) | 46.9 (59,443) | 2.2 (2,728) |
| 1972 | 44.3 (115,021) | 53.7 (139,630) | 2.0 (5,186) | 37.3 (5,145) | 60.5 (8,347) | 2.2 (314) | 48.7 (8,684) | 49.2 (8,776) | 2.1 (364) | 31.6 (28,236) | 66.7 (59,612) | 1.7 (1,591) | 52.6 (72,956) | 45.3 (62,890) | 2.1 (2,917) |
| 1973 | 47.1 (118,541) | 51.3 (129,000) | 1.6 (3,930) | 40.6 (5,236) | 57.9 (7,478) | 1.5 (199) | 51.4 (8,832) | 46.7 (8,022) | 1.9 (324) | 35.4 (29,688) | 63.4 (53,206) | 1.2 (1,059) | 54.4 (74,785) | 43.9 (60,294) | 1.7 (2,348) |
| 1974 | 47.5 (119,175) | 49.9 (125,202) | 2.6 (6,438) | 39.3 (4,897) | 57.1 (7,122) | 3.6 (445) | 49.1 (7,665) | 48.0 (7,482) | 2.9 (453) | 35.2 (31,477) | 62.3 (55,728) | 2.5 (2,210) | 56.4 (75,136) | 41.2 (54,870) | 2.4 (3,330) |
| 1975 | 50.8 (165,819) | 47.1 (153,534) | 2.1 (6,819) | 43.4 (6,581) | 54.4 (8,257) | 2.2 (335) | 52.3 (10,414) | 45.4 (9,050) | 2.3 (416) | 39.5 (43,598) | 58.8 (64,867) | 1.7 (1,946) | 58.2 (105,226) | 39.5 (71,360) | 2.3 (4,082) |
| 1976 | 50.4 (149,336) | 47.5 (140,697) | 2.1 (6,002) | 45.0 (5,792) | 53.5 (6,886) | 2.5 (197) | 51.2 (10,124) | 46.6 (9,218) | 2.2 (449) | 38.9 (35,228) | 59.2 (53,681) | 1.9 (1,709) | 56.8 (98,192) | 41.0 (30,912) | 2.2 (3,647) |
| 1977 | 52.2 (201,074) | 45.7 (176,125) | 2.1 (8,285) | 45.9 (7,866) | 51.0 (8,731) | 3.1 (525) | 50.4 (12,932) | 47.3 (12,156) | 2.3 (593) | 40.8 (49,864) | 57.0 (69,606) | 2.2 (2,646) | 59.1 (130,412) | 38.8 (85,632) | 2.1 (4,521) |
| 1978 | 50.3 (223,809) | 46.2 (205,780) | 3.5 (15,396) | 46.5 (8,703) | 49.4 (9,243) | 4.1 (752) | 48.4 (13,623) | 48.3 (13,588) | 3.3 (944) | 37.7 (53,276) | 58.7 (82,819) | 3.6 (5,039) | 57.7 (148,207) | 39.0 (100,130) | 3.3 (8,661) |
| 1979 | 53.7 (232,936) | 44.1 (191,462) | 2.2 (9,480) | 49.4 (9,010) | 47.7 (8,693) | 2.9 (535) | 50.2 (14,578) | 47.7 (13,870) | 2.1 (620) | 41.0 (53,527) | 56.9 (74,275) | 2.1 (2,783) | 60.9 (155,821) | 37.0 (94,624) | 2.1 (5,542) |
| 1980 | 54.4 (242,672) | 44.1 (196,810) | 1.5 (6,456) | 50.6 (9,480) | 47.9 (8,968) | 1.5 (281) | 50.8 (14,925) | 47.7 (14,036) | 1.5 (444) | 41.1 (57,308) | 57.7 (80,494) | 1.2 (1,619) | 62.3 (160,959) | 36.1 (93,312) | 1.6 (4,112) |
| 1981 | 53.0 (246,154) | 45.7 (212,373) | 1.3 (6,181) | 49.6 (10,129) | 49.0 (9,998) | 1.4 (277) | 50.2 (15,077) | 48.2 (14,457) | 1.6 (487) | 38.9 (57,448) | 60.0 (88,524) | 1.1 (1,547) | 61.3 (163,500) | 37.3 (99,394) | 1.4 (3,870) |
| 1982 | 51.9 (229,253) | 46.7 (206,529) | 1.4 (6,041) | 48.8 (9,008) | 49.7 (9,174) | 1.5 (293) | 48.7 (13,730) | 49.7 (13,991) | 1.6 (458) | 38.2 (52,480) | 60.7 (83,522) | 1.1 (1,560) | 59.8 (154,035) | 38.8 (99,842) | 1.4 (3,730) |

Source: Adapted from U.S. Department of Justice, Federal Bureau of Investigation, *Uniform Crime Reports for the United States, 1969–1982: 1969*, table 31, pp. 118–19; *1970*, table 32, pp. 131–33; *1971*, table 33, pp. 127–29; *1972*, table 72, pp. 131–33; *1973*, table 34, pp. 133–35; *1974*, table 38, pp. 191–93; *1975*, table 39, pp. 192–94; *1976*, table 35, pp. 185–87; *1977*, table 77, pp. 184–86; *1978*, table 35, pp. 200–202; *1979*, table 35, pp. 198–200; *1980*, table 35, pp. 204–06; *1981*, table 36, pp. 179–81; *1982*, table 36, pp. 184–86.

[a] Includes Indian, Chinese, Japanese, and All Others (including unknown races) for the years 1969 to 1979. For the years 1980 to 1982, the category includes American Indian, Alaskan Native, Asian, or Pacific Islander.

**Table 18.** Violent Personal Crimes: Percentage Distribution of Perceived Race of Offender for Single-Offender Victimizations: United States, 1973 to 1980

| Year | Rape | | | | Personal-Sector Robbery | | | | Aggravated Assault | | | |
|---|---|---|---|---|---|---|---|---|---|---|---|---|
| | White | Black | Other | Total[a] | White | Black | Other | Total | White | Black | Other | Total |
| 1973 | 52.0 | 43.0 | 3.0[b] | 99.9 | 42.0 | 51.0 | 5.0 | 98.0 | 67.0 | 30.0 | 3.0 | 100.0 |
| 1974 | 62.6 | 33.6 | 1.9[b] | 98.1 | 40.4 | 49.9 | 5.9 | 96.2 | 67.6 | 25.5 | 4.6 | 97.7 |
| 1975 | 67.5 | 24.8 | 5.6[b] | 97.9 | 40.9 | 50.6 | 4.7 | 96.2 | 63.7 | 31.7 | 2.8 | 98.2 |
| 1976 | 54.4 | 44.7 | 0.0[b] | 99.1 | 45.4 | 49.0 | 2.9 | 97.3 | 66.0 | 28.0 | 4.2 | 98.2 |
| 1977 | 60.8 | 28.1 | 7.9[b] | 96.8 | 46.8 | 47.1 | 3.4 | 97.3 | 70.8 | 24.7 | 2.9 | 98.4 |
| 1978 | 52.6 | 40.9 | 5.1[b] | 98.6 | 56.5 | 34.6 | 5.8 | 96.9 | 68.8 | 25.8 | 4.2 | 98.8 |
| 1979 | 61.8 | 30.0 | 6.1[b] | 97.9 | 47.9 | 46.0 | 3.3 | 97.2 | 69.6 | 26.8 | 2.1 | 98.5 |
| 1980 | 65.5 | 26.5 | 5.0[b] | 97.0 | 44.2 | 50.4 | 4.7 | 99.3 | 71.0 | 22.0 | 5.0 | 98.0 |

Source: Adapted from U.S. Department of Justice, National Criminal Justice Information and Statistics Service. *Criminal Victimization in the United States, 1973*, table 35, p. 85; *Criminal Victimization in the United States, 1974*, table 35, p. 38; *Criminal Victimization in the United States, 1975*, table 39, p. 41; *Criminal Victimization in the United States, 1976*, table 40, p. 47; *Criminal Victimization in the United States, 1977*, table 41, p. 42; U.S. Department of Justice, Bureau of Justice Statistics, *Criminal Victimization in the United States, 1978*, table 41, p. 44; *Criminal Victimization in the United States, 1979*, table 41, p. 48; *Criminal Victimization in the United States, 1980*, table 41, p. 48.

[a]Percentage may not total to 100.0 because for some victimizations the perceived race of the offender was "not known or not available."

[b]Estimate is based on too few cases to be reliable statistically.

**Table 19.** Violent Personal Crimes: Percentage Distribution of Perceived Race of Offenders for Multiple-Offender Victimizations: United States, 1973 to 1980

| Year | Rape | | | | | Personal-Sector Robbery | | | | | Aggravated Assault | | | | |
|---|---|---|---|---|---|---|---|---|---|---|---|---|---|---|---|
| | All White | All Black | All Other Races | Mixed Races | Total[a] | All White | All Black | All Other Races | Mixed Races | Total | All White | All Black | All Other Races | Mixed Races | Total |
| 1973 | 45.0 | 29.0 | 7.0 | 16.0 | 97.0 | 23.0 | 63.0 | 4.0 | 6.0 | 96.0 | 51.0 | 35.0 | 4.0 | 6.0 | 96.0 |
| 1974 | 39.4 | 48.5 | 0.0 | 12.0 | 99.9 | 31.0 | 57.3 | 3.2 | 6.9 | 98.4 | 63.7 | 26.0 | 3.8 | 5.2 | 98.7 |
| 1975 | 41.7 | 36.7 | 10.6[b] | 7.5[b] | 96.5 | 27.4 | 61.0 | 3.0 | 7.0 | 98.4 | 57.3 | 26.5 | 6.2 | 7.7 | 97.7 |
| 1976 | 62.8 | 23.7[b] | 0.0[b] | 13.5[b] | 100.0 | 28.9 | 56.7 | 3.5 | 7.9 | 97.0 | 66.8 | 23.3 | 5.9 | 3.1 | 99.1 |
| 1977 | 70.8 | 17.1[b] | 3.9[b] | 8.1[b] | 99.9 | 35.7 | 48.4 | 5.6 | 6.1 | 95.8 | 60.7 | 20.9 | 5.2 | 9.8 | 96.6 |
| 1978 | 35.2 | 36.5 | 3.2[b] | 25.2[b] | 100.1 | 34.4 | 51.3 | 3.4 | 7.0 | 96.1 | 66.5 | 17.5 | 4.1 | 10.6 | 98.7 |
| 1979 | 53.3 | 41.8[b] | 0.0[b] | 4.8[b] | 99.9 | 29.1 | 53.3 | 5.3[b] | 10.0 | 97.7 | 65.1 | 18.9 | 4.4 | 7.6 | 96.0 |
| 1980 | 47.7[b] | 40.7[b] | 5.6[b] | 6.1[b] | 100.1 | 28.8 | 53.8 | 4.5 | 9.8 | 96.9 | 66.1 | 20.2 | 3.7 | 7.0 | 97.0 |

Source: Adapted from U.S. Department of Justice, National Criminal Justice Information and Statistical Service, *Criminal Victimization in the United States, 1973*, table 39, p. 87; *Criminal Victimization in the United States, 1974*, table 39, p. 41; *Criminal Victimization in the United States, 1975*, table 43, p. 44; *Criminal Victimization in the United States, 1976*, table 45, p. 50; *Criminal Victimization in the United States, 1977*, table 46, p. 45; U.S. Department of Justice, Bureau of Justice Statistics, *Criminal Victimization in the United States, 1978*, table 46, p. 46; *Criminal Victimization in the United States, 1979*, table 46, p. 50; *Criminal Victimization in the United States, 1980*, table 46, p. 50.

[a] Percentages may not total to 100.0 because for some victimizations the perceived race of the offenders was "not known or not available."

[b] Estimate is based on too few cases to be reliable statistically.

**Table 20.** Arrests for Violent Index Crimes by Race: United States, 1969 to 1981 (Rate per 100,000 Race-Specific Population)[a]

| Year | Total Violent Index Crimes | | Murder and Nonnegligent Manslaughter | | Forcible Rape | | Robbery | | Aggravated Assault | |
|---|---|---|---|---|---|---|---|---|---|---|
| | White | Black | White | Black | White | Black | White | Black | White | Black |
| 1969 | 69.2 | 710.0 | 3.2 | 43.4 | 5.5 | 45.1 | 18.1 | 288.5 | 42.4 | 333.1 |
| 1970 | 77.0 | 724.6 | 3.6 | 44.9 | 5.8 | 43.6 | 19.8 | 305.3 | 47.7 | 330.8 |
| 1971 | 80.4 | 799.5 | 3.7 | 50.4 | 5.8 | 47.4 | 20.7 | 339.6 | 50.3 | 362.1 |
| 1972 | 87.3 | 818.7 | 3.9 | 48.9 | 6.6 | 51.4 | 21.4 | 349.5 | 55.4 | 368.8 |
| 1973 | 93.8 | 787.5 | 4.1 | 45.6 | 7.0 | 49.0 | 23.5 | 324.8 | 59.2 | 368.1 |
| 1974 | 110.0 | 883.2 | 4.5 | 50.2 | 7.1 | 52.8 | 29.1 | 393.1 | 69.4 | 387.0 |
| 1975 | 112.6 | 787.9 | 4.5 | 42.4 | 7.1 | 46.4 | 29.6 | 332.9 | 71.4 | 366.2 |
| 1976 | 99.3 | 705.2 | 3.8 | 34.5 | 6.7 | 46.2 | 23.4 | 269.1 | 65.3 | 355.4 |
| 1977 | 117.8 | 770.7 | 4.6 | 38.2 | 7.6 | 53.2 | 29.2 | 304.6 | 76.4 | 374.7 |
| 1978 | 125.4 | 851.3 | 4.9 | 38.2 | 7.6 | 56.2 | 29.8 | 342.6 | 83.0 | 414.2 |
| 1979 | 132.1 | 800.7 | 5.1 | 36.4 | 8.3 | 58.0 | 30.5 | 310.6 | 88.4 | 395.7 |
| 1980 | 135.7 | 802.2 | 5.3 | 36.6 | 8.3 | 57.2 | 32.0 | 328.1 | 90.0 | 380.4 |
| 1981 | 134.2 | 841.9 | 5.5 | 39.6 | 8.2 | 57.3 | 31.3 | 350.9 | 89.1 | 394.0 |
| Percentage Change, 1969 to 1981 | (+93.9) | (+18.6) | (+71.9) | (−8.8) | (+49.1) | (+27.0) | (+72.9) | (+21.6) | (+110.4) | (+18.3) |

[a]The computations presented in this table were derived as follows: (1) The percentage of the population falling into each racial group in each year was calculated from estimates of the resident population of the United States. See U.S. Bureau of the Census, Current Population Reports, *Estimates of the Population of the United States by Age, Race and Sex: July 1, 1969*, table 2, p. 2; *Preliminary Estimates of the Population of the United States by Age, Sex, and Race: 1970 to 1981*, table 2, pp. 26–43. (2) The percentage of the resident population falling into each racial group in a year was multiplied by the "estimated population" covered by the UCR reporting agencies for the corresponding year as listed at the head of the UCR table, "Total Arrests, Distribution by Race," producing the number of persons in each racial group in the "estimated population." This computation assumes that the distribution by race in the resident population of the United States in a given year is the same as that in the "estimated population" covered by the UCR reporting agencies for that same year. The UCR data on "estimated population" were obtained from U.S. Department of Justice, Federal Bureau of Investigation, *Uniform Crime Reports for the United States, 1969–81* (Washington, D.C.: U.S. Government Printing Office, 1970–82): *1969*, pp. 118–19; *1970*, pp. 131–33; *1971*, pp. 127–29; *1972*, pp. 131–33; *1973*, pp. 133–35; *1974*, pp. 191–93; *1975*, pp. 192–94; *1976*, pp. 185–87; *1977*, pp. 184–86; *1978*, pp. 198–200; *1979*, pp. 200–202; *1980*, pp. 204–06; *1981*, pp. 179–81. (3) The number of arrests in each racial group for a given year was divided by the number of persons in that racial group as calculated from the "estimated population" for that year (see step 2), producing the race-specific arrest rate. The number of arrests in each racial group in a year was obtained from the same table that provided the data on the "estimated population" covered by the UCR reporting agencies (see step 2). (4) The race-specific arrest rates calculated in step 3 were multiplied by 100,000 for purposes of standardization.

**Table 21.** Sex of Victims of Violent Personal Crimes: United States, 1973 to 1980 (Victimization Rate per 100,000 Population Aged 12 and Over)

| Year | Total Violent Personal Victimizations[a] | | Rape | | Personal-Sector Robbery | | Aggravated Assault | |
|---|---|---|---|---|---|---|---|---|
| | Male | Female | Male | Female | Male | Female | Male | Female |
| 1973 | 2600.0 | 1200.0 | <50.0[b] | 200.0 | 1000.0 | 400.0 | 1600.0 | 600.0 |
| 1974 | 2640.0 | 1130.0 | 10.0[b] | 180.0 | 1030.0 | 430.0 | 1600.0 | 520.0 |
| 1975 | 2400.0 | 1110.0 | 10.0[b] | 170.0 | 980.0 | 400.0 | 1410.0 | 540.0 |
| 1976 | 2370.0 | 1110.0 | 20.0 | 140.0 | 910.0 | 400.0 | 1440.0 | 570.0 |
| 1977 | 2440.0 | 1050.0 | 20.0 | 160.0 | 870.0 | 400.0 | 1550.0 | 490.0 |
| 1978 | 2320.0 | 1050.0 | 20.0 | 170.0 | 830.0 | 370.0 | 1470.0 | 510.0 |
| 1979 | 2390.0 | 1110.0 | 20.0 | 180.0 | 880.0 | 400.0 | 1490.0 | 530.0 |
| 1980 | 2330.0 | 1060.0 | 30.0 | 160.0 | 900.0 | 420.0 | 1400.0 | 480.0 |
| Percentage Change, 1973 to 1980 | (−10.4) | (−11.7) | (−) | (−20.0) | (−10.0) | (+5.0) | (−12.5) | (−20.0) |

Source: Adapted from U.S. Department of Justice, National Criminal Justice Information and Statistics Service, *Criminal Victimization in the United States, 1973,* table 3, p. 68; *Criminal Victimization in the United States, 1974,* table 3, p. 19; *Criminal Victimization in the United States, 1975,* table 3, p. 19; *Criminal Victimization in the United States, 1976,* table 3, p. 24; *Criminal Victimization in the United States, 1977,* table 3, p. 22; U.S. Department of Justice, Bureau of Justice Statistics, *Criminal Victimization in the United States, 1978,* table 3, p. 20; *Criminal Victimization in the United States, 1979,* table 3, p. 24; *Criminal Victimization in the United States, 1980,* table 3, p. 23.

[a]The rates are the sum for each sex across victimization categories. The sum excludes rates that are simply reported by the NCS to be below the cut-off point of 50 but for which no precise figure is given. These rates are designated by "<50.0."

[b]Estimate is based on too few cases to be reliable statistically.

**Table 22.** Race of Victims of Violent Personal Crimes: United States, 1973 to 1980 (Victimization Rate per 100,000 Population Aged 12 and Over)

| Year | Total Violent Personal Victimizations | | | Rape | | | Personal-Sector Robbery | | | Aggravated Assault | | |
|---|---|---|---|---|---|---|---|---|---|---|---|---|
| | White | Black | Other | White | Black | Other | White | Black | Other | White | Black | Other |
| 1973 | 1700.0 | 3400.0 | 1400.0 | 100.0 | 200.0 | 100.0[a] | 600.0 | 1400.0 | 1000.0 | 1000.0 | 1800.0 | 300.0[a] |
| 1974 | 1690.0 | 3010.0 | 2140.0 | 80.0 | 210.0 | 220.0[a] | 620.0 | 1500.0 | 660.0 | 990.0 | 1300.0 | 1260.0 |
| 1975 | 1560.0 | 2960.0 | 2230.0 | 90.0 | 120.0 | 90.0[a] | 580.0 | 1410.0 | 690.0 | 890.0 | 1430.0 | 1450.0 |
| 1976 | 1540.0 | 3110.0 | 1880.0 | 70.0 | 190.0 | 0.0[a] | 550.0 | 1360.0 | 930.0 | 920.0 | 1560.0 | 950.0 |
| 1977 | 1590.0 | 2790.0 | 920.0 | 90.0 | 100.0 | 70.0[a] | 540.0 | 1300.0 | 410.0 | 960.0 | 1390.0 | 440.0 |
| 1978 | 1530.0 | 2680.0 | 1060.0 | 80.0 | 210.0 | 0.0[a] | 520.0 | 1140.0 | 480.0 | 930.0 | 1330.0 | 580.0 |
| 1979 | 1600.0 | 2700.0 | 1930.0 | 100.0 | 160.0 | 50.0[a] | 550.0 | 1250.0 | 560.0 | 950.0 | 1290.0 | 1320.0 |
| 1980 | 1530.0 | 2730.0 | 1780.0 | 90.0 | 110.0 | 100.0[a] | 570.0 | 1390.0 | 240.0[a] | 870.0 | 1230.0 | 1440.0 |
| Percentage Change, 1973 to 1980 | (−10.0) | (−19.7) | (+27.1) | (−10.0) | (−45.0) | (—) | (−5.0) | (−1.0) | (−76.0) | (−13.0) | (−31.7) | (—) |

Source: Adapted from U.S. Department of Justice, National Criminal Justice Information and Statistics Service, *Criminal Victimization in the United States, 1973*, table 6, p. 70; *Criminal Victimization in the United States, 1974*, table 6, p. 21; *Criminal Victimization in the United States, 1975*, table 6, p. 21; *Criminal Victimization in the United States, 1976*, table 6, p. 26; *Criminal Victimization in the United States, 1977*, table 6, p. 24; U.S. Department of Justice, Bureau of Justice Statistics, *Criminal Victimization in the United States, 1978*, table 6, p. 22; *Criminal Victimization in the United States, 1979*, table 6, p. 26; *Criminal Victimization in the United States, 1980*, table 6, p. 25.

[a] Estimate is based on too few cases to be reliable statistically.

**Table 23.** Victim-Offender Relationship by Type of Violent Personal Crime: United States, 1973 to 1980 (Rate per 100,000 Population Aged 12 and Over)

| Year | Total Violent Personal Victimizations[a] | | Rape | | Personal-Sector Robbery | | Aggravated Assault | |
|---|---|---|---|---|---|---|---|---|
| | Stranger | Nonstranger | Stranger | Nonstranger | Stranger | Nonstranger | Stranger | Nonstranger |
| 1973 | 1300.0 | 550.0 | 100.0 | <50.0 | 600.0 | 100.0 | 600.0 | 400.0 |
| 1974 | 1350.0 | 470.0 | 70.0 | 30.0 | 610.0 | 110.0 | 670.0 | 360.0 |
| 1975 | 1250.0 | 460.0 | 60.0 | 30.0 | 570.0 | 100.0 | 620.0 | 330.0 |
| 1976 | 1210.0 | 520.0 | 60.0 | 30.0 | 530.0 | 120.0 | 620.0 | 370.0 |
| 1977 | 1180.0 | 530.0 | 60.0 | 30.0 | 490.0 | 130.0 | 630.0 | 370.0 |
| 1978 | 1140.0 | 520.0 | 70.0 | 30.0 | 450.0 | 140.0 | 620.0 | 350.0 |
| 1979 | 1210.0 | 520.0 | 70.0 | 40.0 | 510.0 | 120.0 | 630.0 | 360.0 |
| 1980 | 1210.0 | 460.0 | 70.0 | 30.0 | 540.0 | 110.0 | 600.0 | 320.0 |
| Percentage Change, 1973 to 1980 | (−6.9) | (−16.4) | (−30.0) | (−) | (−10.0) | (+10.0) | (0.0) | (−20.0) |

Source: Adapted from U.S. Department of Justice, National Criminal Justice Information and Statistics Service, *Criminal Victimization in the United States, 1973*, table 29, p. 82; *Criminal Victimization in the United States, 1974*, table 29, p.35; *Criminal Victimization in the United States, 1975*, table 33, p. 38; *Criminal Victimization in the United States, 1976*, table 33, p. 43; *Criminal Victimization in the United States, 1977*, table 34, p. 39; U.S. Department of Justice, Bureau of Justice Statistics, *Criminal Victimization in the United States, 1978*, table 34, p. 40; *Criminal Victimization in the United States, 1979*, table 34, p. 44; *Criminal Victimization in the United States, 1980*, table 34, p. 44.

[a]The rates are the sum for each victim-offender type across victimization categories. The sum excludes rates that are simply reported by the NCS to be below the cut-off point of 50 but for which no precise figure is given. These rates are designated "<50.0."

**Table 24.** Violent Personal Crimes: Percentage Distribution of Incidents by Place of Occurrence: United States, 1973 to 1980

| Year | Rape | | | | Personal-Sector Robbery | | | | Aggravated Assault | | | |
|---|---|---|---|---|---|---|---|---|---|---|---|---|
| | Inside or Near Own Home | Open Public Place (Street, Park, etc.) | Other[a] | Total[b] | Inside or Near Own Home | Open Public Place (Street, Park, etc.) | Other | Total | Inside or Near Own Home | Open Public Place (Street, Park, etc.) | Other | Total |
| 1973 | 33.0 | 41.0 | 25.0 | 99.0 | 19.0 | 60.0 | 20.0 | 99.0 | 20.0 | 47.0 | 33.0 | 100.0 |
| 1974 | 32.8 | 42.7 | 24.6 | 100.1 | 17.7 | 60.0 | 22.4 | 100.1 | 24.9 | 46.9 | 28.2 | 100.0 |
| 1975 | 27.4 | 54.3 | 18.2 | 99.9 | 18.8 | 59.9 | 21.4 | 100.1 | 21.8 | 48.3 | 29.9 | 100.0 |
| 1976 | 39.4 | 33.6 | 26.9 | 99.9 | 19.7 | 61.9 | 18.3 | 99.9 | 23.7 | 43.9 | 32.5 | 100.1 |
| 1977 | 31.9 | 36.0 | 32.2 | 100.1 | 21.7 | 59.8 | 18.5 | 100.0 | 22.1 | 43.4 | 21.6[c] | 87.1 |
| 1978 | 34.7 | 41.6 | 23.6 | 99.9 | 22.7 | 55.9 | 21.5 | 100.1 | 22.2 | 47.5 | 30.4 | 100.1 |
| 1979 | 35.6 | 31.4 | 33.0 | 100.0 | 21.2 | 53.1 | 25.7 | 100.0 | 24.5 | 41.4 | 34.2 | 100.1 |
| 1980 | 29.8 | 39.6 | 30.6 | 100.0 | 20.3 | 56.7 | 23.0 | 100.0 | 23.4 | 40.6 | 36.0 | 100.0 |

Source: Adapted from U.S. Department of Justice, National Criminal Justice Information and Statistics Service, *Criminal Victimization in the United States, 1973*, table 48, p. 93; *Criminal Victimization in the United States, 1974*, table 48, p. 47; *Criminal Victimization in the United States, 1975*, table 52, p. 49; *Criminal Victimization in the United States, 1976*, table 54, p. 55; *Criminal Victimization in the United States, 1977*, table 55, p. 49; U.S. Department of Justice, Bureau of Justice Statistics, *Criminal Victimization in the United States, 1978*, table 55, p. 53; *Criminal Victimization in the United States, 1979*, table 55, p. 57; *Criminal Victimization in the United States, 1980*, table 55, p. 54.

[a] Includes "Elsewhere," "Inside School," and "Inside Residential Building."

[b] Percentages may not total to 100.0 due to rounding error.

[c] This percentage is clearly discrepant from the others in the column. We suspect that it is due to a printing error. The "Other" group is a composite of three categories: "Elsewhere," "Inside School," and "Inside Residential Building." The percentage given for "Elsewhere" is far below those found in other years and accounts, we believe, for the much lower percentage for the composite "Other" category.

**Table 25.** Personal-Sector Robbery and Assault: Percentage Distribution of Victimizations in which Victims Sustained Physical Injury: United States, 1973 to 1980

| Year | Personal-Sector Robbery | | | Assault[a] | | | Personal-Sector Robbery and Assault Combined | | |
|------|--------|-----------|-------|--------|-----------|-------|--------|-----------|-------|
|      | Injury | Noninjury | Total | Injury | Noninjury | Total | Injury | Noninjury | Total |
| 1973 | 34.0   | 66.0      | 100.0 | 28.0   | 72.0      | 100.0 | 29.0   | 71.0      | 100.0 |
| 1974 | 32.6   | 67.4      | 100.0 | 27.8   | 72.2      | 100.0 | 28.8   | 71.2      | 100.0 |
| 1975 | 31.5   | 69.5      | 100.0 | 29.5   | 70.5      | 100.0 | 29.9   | 70.1      | 100.0 |
| 1976 | 32.5   | 67.5      | 100.0 | 29.5   | 70.5      | 100.0 | 30.1   | 69.9      | 100.0 |
| 1977 | 35.6   | 64.4      | 100.0 | 27.8   | 72.2      | 100.0 | 29.3   | 70.7      | 100.0 |
| 1978 | 31.8   | 68.2      | 100.0 | 28.2   | 71.8      | 100.0 | 28.8   | 71.2      | 100.0 |
| 1979 | 34.1   | 65.9      | 100.0 | 28.7   | 71.3      | 100.0 | 29.7   | 70.3      | 100.0 |
| 1980 | 34.4   | 65.6      | 100.0 | 30.3   | 69.7      | 100.0 | 31.1   | 68.9      | 100.0 |

Source: Adapted from U.S. Department of Justice, National Criminal Justice Information and Statistics Service, *Criminal Victimization in the United States, 1973,* table 57, p. 95; *Criminal Victimization in the United States, 1974,* table 61, p. 54; *Criminal Victimization in the United States, 1975,* table 65, p. 56; *Criminal Victimization in the United States, 1976,* table 68, p. 63; *Criminal Victimization in the United States, 1977,* table 67, p. 55; U.S. Department of Justice, Bureau of Justice Statistics, *Criminal Victimization in the United States, 1978,* table 68, p. 59; *Criminal Victimization in the United States, 1979,* table 68, p. 53; *Criminal Victimization in the United States, 1980,* table 68, p. 60.

[a]Includes aggravated and simple assault.

**Table 26.** Homicide Rates for Selected Countries, 1970 to 1978 (Rate per 100,000 Population)[a]

| Country | 1970 | 1971 | 1972 | 1973 | 1974 | 1975 | 1976 | 1977 | 1978 |
|---|---|---|---|---|---|---|---|---|---|
| Austria | 1.5 | 1.4 | 1.2 | 1.4 | 1.5 | 1.6 | | 1.3 | 1.4 |
| Belgium | 1.1 | 1.0 | 1.2 | 1.1 | 1.0 | .9 | .9 | | |
| Canada | 2.0 | 2.2 | 2.3 | 2.4 | 2.5 | | 2.4 | 2.6 | |
| Denmark | .7 | 1.0 | .6 | .9 | .7 | .6 | | .7 | .5 |
| Finland | .7 | 2.7 | 3.2 | 2.7 | 2.6 | | 3.3 | 2.8 | |
| France | .7 | .8 | .9 | .8 | .9 | | .9 | 1.0 | |
| Germany (F.R.) | 1.4 | 1.3 | 1.4 | 1.2 | 1.2 | 1.2 | 1.3 | 1.2 | 1.2 |
| Ireland | .4 | .5 | .7 | .4 | .7 | 1.0 | .3 | .9 | |
| Italy | .8 | 1.0 | 1.1 | 1.2 | 1.1 | | 1.4 | | |
| Netherlands | .5 | .6 | .5 | .6 | .8 | .7 | | .9 | .8 |
| Norway | .6 | .6 | .7 | .8 | .6 | .7 | | .8 | .7 |
| Sweden | .8 | .9 | 1.1 | 1.0 | 1.2 | 1.1 | | 1.2 | 1.0 |
| Switzerland | .7 | 1.0 | .9 | .7 | 1.0 | .9 | | .9 | .7 |
| United Kingdom | .8 | .9 | .9 | 1.2 | 1.0 | 1.0 | | .9 | 1.2 |
| United States | 7.7 | 9.1 | 9.4 | 9.8 | 10.2 | 10.0 | 9.1 | | 9.4 |

Source: 1970 to 1975: U.S. Department of Commerce, *Social Indicators III, 1980* (Washington, D.C.: U.S. Government Printing Office, 1980), p. 252, table 5/20; 1976 to 1979: World Health Organization, *World Health Statistics Annual, 1979 to 1981,* vol. 1, *Vital Statistics and Causes of Death* (Geneva: World Health Organization, 1979 to 1981).

[a]Homicide is here defined in accordance with the protocol adopted by the World Health Organization. The definition has two components: (1) "homicide and injury purposely inflicted by other persons," and (2) "legal intervention," which includes both homicides and injuries. The kinds of events that fall within this definition are designated by the codes E960 to E978 whose definitions can be found in World Health Organization, *Manual of International Statistical Classification of Diseases, Injuries, and Causes of Death* (Geneva: World Health Organization, 1967), 1: 355–58, 443.

**Table 27.** Mean Robbery Rates for Selected Countries, 1970 to 1975 (Rate per 100,000 Population)

| Country | Mean Robbery Rate |
|---|---|
| United States | 191.2 |
| Canada | 64.9 |
| Finland | 33.0 |
| Germany (F.R.) | 28.4 |
| Sweden | 23.7 |
| United Kingdom | 21.4 |
| Ireland | 16.7 |
| Denmark | 12.8 |
| Austria | 10.0 |
| Norway | 7.8 |
| Switzerland | 2.0 |
| France | 0.6 |
| Italy | <0.5 |

Source: Adapted from Graeme Newman, *Understanding Violence* (New York: J. B. Lippincott, 1979), table 4.1, p. 92.

# CONTRIBUTORS

*Lynn A. Curtis* is president of the Eisenhower Foundation in Washington, D.C. In the late 1970s, Dr. Curtis was urban policy advisor to the Secretary of Housing and Urban Development and executive director of the interagency committee that formulated the President's National Urban Policy. He administered the federal youth employment and crime prevention program in public housing that was part of the President's National Urban Policy and was co-director of the Task Force on Individual Violence of the National Violence Commission.

*Elliott Currie* is research associate, Center for the Study of Law and Society, University of California, Berkeley. He has just completed a book entitled *Crime in America* which will be published in 1985. He was assistant director of the Task Force on Protest and Confrontation of the National Violence Commission and has been a consultant to the National Advisory Council on Equal Opportunity of the California Task Force on Civil Rights.

*Sandra Ball-Rokeach* is professor of sociology at Washington State University, Pullman, Washington. She was co-director of the Media and Violence Task Force of the National Violence Commission. A Ph.D. from the University of Washington, she has coauthored *The Great American Values Test* and has in preparation an edited volume entitled *Sociology of the Mass Media*.

*James P. Comer* is Maurice Falk Professor of Child Psychiatry, Yale Child Study Center. He is also director of the Yale Child Study Center School Development Program. His research interests include the functioning of the black family. Dr. Comer has directed a primary prevention program in the New Haven School System over the past sixteen years. He is the author of *Beyond Black and White, School Power* and has coauthored with Alvin Poussaint *Black Child Care*. He has written monthly articles for *Parents Magazine* and a weekly column for *United Features Syndicate, Inc.*

*Alan R. Gordon* is a criminal defender with the Legal Aid Society of New

York. He is a graduate of Swarthmore College and the University of Chicago Law School. At the time the chapter was written, he was research assistant with the Center for Studies in Criminal Justice at the University of Chicago.

*Robert H. Kupperman* is executive director of the Science and Technology Committee at the Center for Strategic and International Studies, Georgetown University, Washington, D.C. He was head of the 1980–81 transition team for the Federal Emergency Management Agency. He has been Chief Scientist at the U.S. Arms Control and Disarmament Agency as well as chairman of the agency's committee on government-wide studies of U.S. counter-terrorism policies and objectives. A Ph.D. in applied mathematics from New York University, he has written many books on national security and terrorism.

*Paul J. Lavrakas* is associate professor of journalism and urban affairs at Northwestern University, Evanston, Illinois, and director of the Northwestern Survey Laboratory. During the past ten years, Dr. Lavrakas has been involved in nearly every major research and evaluation project funded by the federal government on community crime prevention. He is currently the principal investigator on the national evaluation of the Eisenhower Foundation Neighborhood Program. A Ph.D. in applied social psychology at Loyola University of Chicago, he has published widely on citizens crime prevention and fear of crime.

*Norval Morris* is Julius Kreeger Professor of Law and Criminology at the University of Chicago Law School. He has been director of the United Nations Institute for the Prevention and Treatment of Offenders in Tokyo, Japan. Professor Morris has served on councils and commissions concerned with correctional problems and practices under the sponsorship of the United Nations, federal and state governments, and other organizations. He is a fellow of the American Academy of Arts and Sciences and author of many books and articles, including *The Honest Politician's Guide to Crime Control.*

*James F. Short, Jr.,* is director of the Social Research Center and professor of sociology at Washington State University. He was co-director of research for the National Violence Commission. He has been president of the American Sociological Association, editor of the *American Sociological Review,* a fellow at the Center for Advanced Studies in the Behavioral Sciences at Stanford University, and a fellow at the Institute of Criminology of Cambridge University. He has a Ph.D. from the University of Chicago and an honorary doctorate from Dennison University.

*Neil Alan Weiner* is research associate at the Center for Studies in Criminology and Criminal Law at the University of Pennsylvania, Philadelphia, and director of the Center for the Interdisciplinary Study of Criminal Violence. Previously, Dr. Weiner was a postdoctoral fellow at the Urban Systems Institute at Carnegie-Mellon University. His work has concentrated on issues in violent crime, including offender identification and offense prediction.

*Marvin E. Wolfgang* is professor of criminology and law and director of the Center for Studies in Criminology and Criminal Law at the University of Pennsylvania, Philadelphia. He is president of the American Academy of Political and Social Science and a member of the American Philosophical Society and the American Academy of Arts and Sciences. Professor Wolfgang has served on numerous boards and commissions, including the National Violence Commission, on which he was co-director of research, the National Commission on Obscenity and Pornography, and the board of the Eisenhower Foundation.

*Franklin E. Zimring* is Karl N. Llewellyn Professor of Jurisprudence and director of the Center for Studies in Criminal Justice at the University of Chicago. He is currently serving as acting director of the Earl Warren Legal Institute at the University of California, Berkeley. He served as director of research of the Task Force on Firearms of the National Violence Commission.

# INDEX